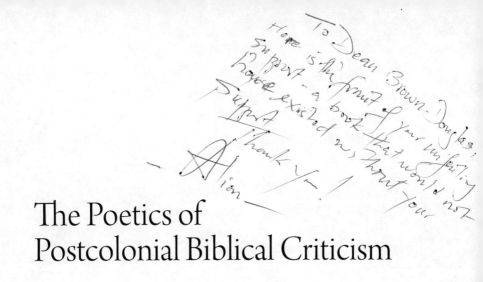

The Poetics of
Postcolonial Biblical Criticism

The Poetics of Postcolonial Biblical Criticism

God, Human-Nature Relationship, and Negritude

ALIOU CISSÉ NIANG

CASCADE *Books* · Eugene, Oregon

THE POETICS OF POSTCOLONIAL BIBLICAL CRITICISM
God, Human-Nature Relationship, and Negritude

Cascade Books
An Imprint of Wipf and Stock Publishers
199 W. 8th Ave., Suite 3
Eugene, OR 97401

www.wipfandstock.com

PAPERBACK ISBN: 978-1-5326-1729-4
HARDCOVER ISBN: 978-1-4982-4193-9
EBOOK ISBN: 978-1-4982-4192-2

Cataloging-in-Publication data:

Names: Niang, Aliou Cissé, author.

Title: The poetics of postcolonial biblical criticism : God, human-nature relationship, and negritude / Aliou Cissé Niang.

Description: Eugene, OR: Cascade Books, 2019. | Includes bibliographical references and indexes.

Identifiers: ISBN: 978-1-5326-1729-4 (paperback). | ISBN: 978-1-4982-4193-9 (hardcover). | ISBN: 978-1-4982-4192-2 (ebook).

Subjects: LCSH: Bible—Postcolonial criticism.

Classification: BS476 N53 2019 (print). | BS476 (epub).

Manufactured in the U.S.A.   DECEMBER 11, 2019

I am dedicating this book to

My Late Grandfather Abdoulaye Manga
My Late Grandmother Fayinséni Dièmé (Kamout Bassène)
My Late Mother Lucie Bassène
My Late Ante Kakaine Manga
My Step Father Édouard Diatta
My Ante Sini Bassène
My Ante Fatou Bassène (Jishēbo)
My Wife Elizabeth Renée Niang
My Son Micah Aliou Martin Niang

Contents

Figures and Tables

Preface

MY GRANDPARENTS GREW UP in Enampor and Séléki—Senegalese West African townships of Brin-Séléki and especially the Bandial Diola townships known as Mof Avvi "Royal Land."[1] Diola people of Mof Avvi were rice farmers. They cultivated their rice fields to feed their families, perform rituals, and barter. French colonial influences affected but failed to wipeout much of these Diola traditional practices. Their persistence and now gradual resurgence in post-colonial era debunk much of the conclusions reached by many sociologists and anthropologists who predicted the demise of most African tradition and religious practices influenced by foreign cultures (Western cultures) and religions (Islam and Christianity).[2] Much of their research was informed by the strictures of the British social anthropological method of the day that jettisoned local witness accounts to focus on the so-called objective observations deemed more reliable.[3]

My Diola grandparents were rice farmers. Land, for them, was life and rain life-giving under the aegis of the deity they revered, *Ala Emit*

---

1. Berghen and Manga, *Une introduction*. Berghen and Manga take a much closer look at the framing practices of the Diola of Enampor as well as a concise sociohistorical, religious, political, and economic context. Palmeri, *Living with the Diola*. Bassène, *Morphosyntaxe*, 3-6, builds on Palmeri's account on the history, life, religion and sociolinguistic setting of the Diola of *Mof Avvi*. Berghen and Manga predate Palmeri's volume but both works share much in common.

2. Horton, "African Conversion," 85-108; idem, "On the Rationality of Conversion Part II," 373-399; Humphrey, "Conversion Reconsidered," 27-40. I will also cite the French anthropologist, Louis-Vincent Thomas, *Les Diola*, 73, who reached similar conclusions.

3. Vansian, *Being Colonized*, 5, spoke of how the British model of inquiry was not always followed by some social anthropologists. He certainly parted ways with it seeing the lived experiences of local people have actionable evidence an outsider cannot possibly access.

"God." They learned to understand the language of nature, weather patterns, and performed appropriate rituals they deemed necessary to maintain their side of the covenant with their deity. The word means *visible beings*,[4] a name, I argue, reflects a Diola self-definition that is fully cognizant about their role as creatures among many visible and invisible beings, namely nonhuman creatures that populate the cosmos God created. This belief awareness anchors Diola sense of egalitarian-individualism and role in God's creation.

I recall my grandparents reflecting on and wondering why rain was becoming rarer and dry seasons longer than ever. Many of them and their priests thought what was going on with the climate was not just a natural cyclical phenomenon but was probably due to some human causes. As often was the case in the Diola world, elders and priests suspected a broken relationship between God, humans, and other creatures. In other words, humans have failed to actualize their end of the covenant between God and the deity's creature. The transatlantic slave trade and colonial occupation were often cited as being destabilizing events that did much to alter the moral structure of Diola culture. As Robert M. Baum observes, when faced with the suppressive nature of the French colonization and version of Europeanized Christianity introduced by some of the Holy Ghost Fathers missionaries, Diola priests and elders began to question the powers of their shrines in light of what they perceived to have been a massive failure of their shrines to defeat the alienating powers of French colonialism.[5]

I have lived in America since December 1990 and have been amazed at what I learned over the years. As rainfalls are flooding many parts of the world, as Artic icebergs are disappearing, as seawaters are gradually rising making the reality of global warming hard to deny and an impending irreversible environmental disaster hard to avert, many Western experts began to relexify. As far as I know Africa is statistically the least emitter of carbon compared to western industrial countries to date. It is often the case that nature is valued in so far as she benefits humans as commodity rather than a subject on her own right. As Greg Garrard says, "Nature is only valued in terms of its usefulness to us. Many environmentalists

---

4. Thomas, *Les Diola*, 73.
5. Baum, "Emergence."

argue that we need to develop a value system which takes the intrinsic or inherent value of nature as its starting point."[6]

This book offers a humble reading of Scripture in conversation with Diola Faith Traditions.

I would like to express my deepest gratitude to my dear faculty colleagues and administrators at Union, beginning with President Dr. Serene Jones, Dean Dr. Mary Boys, Vice President Fred Davie, Drs. James H. Cone, Brigitte Kahl, John McGuckin, Janet Walton, Tara (Hyun Kyung Chung), Daisy Machado, Pamela Cooper-White, Claudio Carvalhaes, John Thatamanil, Euan Cameron, and Gary Dorrien, Sam Cruz, and Troy Messenger. I extend my deepest gratitude to Dr. Barbara King Lord whose close reading of the manuscript was invaluable to its completion. The Director of the Union Center of Earth Ethics, Karenna Gore encouraged me as I was working on the project and found it insightful.

This work would not have been completed if it were not for the unfailing support of my wife, Elizabeth Renée Niang, and son, Micah Aliou Martin Niang. I wish my grandparents were alive today so I can read this book to them. I am sure they are watching my family and me, hearing the content of this book every time I am speaking about and teaching on Diola life and thought, and especially the wisdom they imparted to me.

---

6. Garrard, *Ecocriticism*, 21.

Abbreviations

b.	Babylonian Talmud (Babli)
BDAG	Bauer, Walter, Frederick W. Danker, W. F. Arndt, and F. W. Gingrich, *Greek–English Lexicon of the New Testament and Other Early Christian Literature*. 3rd ed. Chicago: University of Chicago Press, 2001
EDNT	*Exegetical Dictionary of the New Testament*. 3 vols. Edited by Horst Balz and Gerhard Schneider. Translated by James W. Thompson and John W. Medendorp. Grand Rapids: Eerdmans, 1991–93
HALOT	*Hebrew and Aramaic Lexicon of the Old Testament*. 4 vols. Ludwig Koehler, Walter Baumgartner, and J. J. Stamm. Translated and edited under the supervision of M. E. J. Richardson. Leiden: Brill, 1994–1999
KJV	King James Version (Authorized Version)
LCL	Loeb Classical Library
LEH	Lust, Johann, Erik Eynikel, and Katrin Hauspie, eds. *Greek–English Lexicon of the Septuagint*. Rev. ed. Stuttgart: Deutsche Bibelgesellschaft, 2003
LSJM	Liddell, H. G., R. Scott, H. S. Jones, R. McKenzie, *A Greek–English Lexicon*. 9th ed. with revised supplement. Oxford: Clarendon, 1996
LXX	Septuagint
m.	Mishnah
MT	Masoretic text of the Hebrew Bible
NAS	New American Standard Version of the Bible

NETS	*A New English Translation of the Septuagint*. Edited by Albert Pietersma and Benjamin G. Wright. Oxford: Oxford University Press, 2007
NIV	New International Version of the Bible
NJB	New Jerusalem Bible
NRSV	New Revised Standard Version of the Bible
OCD	*Oxford Classical Dictionary*. 4th ed. Edited by Simon Hornblower and Antony Spawforth. Oxford: Oxford University Press, 2012
OGIS	*Orientis graeci inscriptiones selectae*. 2 vols. Edited by Wilhelm Dittenberger. Leipzig: Hirzel, 1903–1905
SBEC	Studies in the Bible and Early Christianity
Tanak	Jewish Publication Society translation
TDNT	*Theological Dictionary of the New Testament*. 10 vols. Edited by Gerhard Kittel and Gerhard Friedrich. Translated by Geoffrey W. Bromiley. Grand Rapids: Eerdmans, 1964–1976

1

Introduction

> The Negro is the person of Nature who traditionally lives of and with the soil, in and by the *cosmos*. —Léopold Sédar Senghor[1]

> Most important, perhaps, is the relationship between people and nature, or how people view nature and relate to it so as to ensure their survival. The Diola feel that they are part of a totality in which they, the objects around them, the things that happen, and nature itself are elements within a single and all encompassing context. This is why the elements needed for survival, like the land and its products, the forests and animals, are not considered to be available to anyone who happens to be the first to take possession of them. Nature is not seen as an object to be exploited, but rather as a subject that meets people on equal terms. —Paolo Palmeri[2]

The Poetics of Postcolonial Biblical Criticism is a project that has germinated in the most profound sense from my roots as a son of the Diola people of Senegal, West Africa, especially the dwellers of the village of Mof Avvi,[3]

---

1. Senghor, "The Spirit of Civilization," 52: "Le Négre est l'homme de la nature. Il vit traditionnellement de la terre et avec la terre, dans et par le *cosmos*."

2. Palmeri, *Living with the Diola*, 195.

3. Geographically, I am focusing on the Diola—an ethnic group living in the southwestern region of Sénégal (Casamance), especially the milieu known as *Mof Avvi* translated to mean "Royal Land." Diola subgroups include Bliss-Karons and Fonyi, who dwell on the northern shore of the Casamance river, and those of Oussouye (Floup), Youtou/Effoc (Diamat), Diembering (Dyiwat), Kabrousse (Her/Haer), Kagnout/Mlomp (Pointe Saint-Georges), and of Brin-Séléki. See Thomas, *Les Diola*, 1.

1

now as a biblical scholar living in the global arena that is New York City, a professor at a racially and ethnically diverse theological seminary.

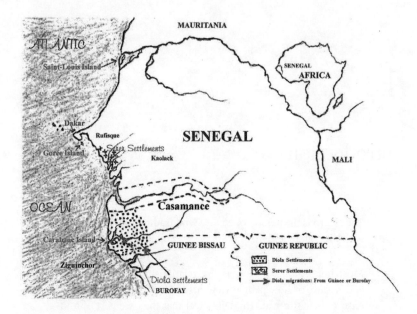

FIGURE 1

Map of Diola pattern of migration and settlements on the northern and southwest banks of the Casamance River known as *le Pays Diola* "Diola country." As a region of Sénégal, West Africa, the Casamance is the most fertile of all the regions of the country; and as a result; it is the breadbasket of the country. The Casamance River irrigates Diola rice fields and is the fishery for most Diola communities. Demographically, the region of Sénégal called the Casamance is densely settled by Diola people who number about 90% of the population in the region and 3.7% nationally. The Diola refer to this area as the Diola country. Adapted from Niang's *Faith and Freedom in Galatia and Senegal*, 71.

9–15, for more details. Also see the maps in chapter 2. The protectorate is where subjects lived in contrast to the civilized citizens of the so-called *Quatres Communes* "four towns." The French colonial policy of assimilation was carried out in these towns: Saint Louis, Gorée, Dakar, and Rufisque. Growing up, I visited my relatives in Enampor and Séléki and especially during initiation rites. The Diola migration and settlement in this area is well documented by scholars who conducted their research in the region. See the map of Diola country in chapter two.

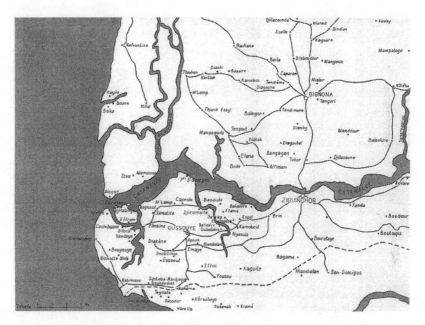

FIGURE 2

A detailed map of the area called Diola country showing all the main townships.
Some Diola people migrated to the eastern part of the region—that is east of the
city of Ziguinchor. My grandparents later moved from Mof Avvi to the village
Adéane. The map is taken from Thomas, *Les Diola*.

My academic journey in America has always been an existential endeavor
to find ways to read the Bible through my cultural lens in conversation
with others, because I believe that faith in divine revelation, as I have
come to understand it, resists any assured attempt to be its guardian. Divine revelation includes a human interpretative voice filtered through its
cultural milieu. Part of the impetus for this book has been my wondering
if there is insight to be gained by reengaging general revelation at all. If
there is something worth pursuing in that regard, then my Diola ancestors may have something to teach me and other followers of Jesus about
divine, human, and nature relationships. As far as I can tell, my ancestors
never debated the existence of God; neither did they think of the deity
as remote, unconcerned about human affairs, or annoyed by the daily
cacophonies made by the deity's creatures. My Diola ancestors believed

that humans must strive to hear, apprehend, interpret, and exercise God's pervasive speech that creation manifests.

"God created the world" is a statement often taken for granted by many children of Abraham in the faith. Some followers of Jesus Christ interpret the expression, "God so loved the world," found in John 3:16 to mean God loves only humans—a reading that sadly fails to take into account the meaning of the word κόσμος "creation, universe" (LSJM).[4] The Bible records millennia-old dynamic myths recounted in Ancient Near Eastern and Greco-Roman contexts that tell why the world was made by God and why the deity is related to her in many ways. The two creation stories told in the First Testament offer two different and yet balanced accounts. The first account depicts God as creator—making, shaping, and relating to creation through an empowering speech (Gen 1:1–3, 10–12, 26–28, NRSV).

> In the beginning when God created the heavens and the earth, the earth was a formless void and darkness covered the face of the deep, while a wind from God swept over the face of the waters. Then God said, "Let there be light"; and there was light . . . God called the dry land Earth, and the waters that were gathered together he called Seas. And God saw that it was good. Then God said, "Let the earth put forth vegetation: plants yielding seed, and fruit trees of every kind on earth that bear fruit with the seed in it." And it was so. The earth brought forth vegetation: plants yielding seed of every kind, and trees of every kind bearing fruit with the seed in it. And God saw that it was good . . . Then God said, "Let us make humankind in our image, according to our likeness; and let them have dominion over the fish of the sea, and over the birds of the air, and over the cattle, and over all the wild animals of the earth, and over every creeping thing that creeps upon the earth." So God created humankind in his image, in the image of God he created them; male and female he created them. God blessed them, and God said to them, "Be fruitful and multiply, and fill the earth and subdue it; and have dominion over the fish of the sea and over the birds of the air and over every living thing that moves upon the earth."

---

4. The word κόσμος in the LXX appears in Gen 2:1. While the NRSV translates the MT text, *wekol-ṣeba̔am* to mean "and all their multitude," the *NETS* renders the LXX Rahlf's καὶ πᾶς ὁ κόσμος αὐτῶν "and all their arrangement"—that is the arrangement of the heavens. The NAS and the KJV maintains a literal rendition of *wekol-ṣeba̔am*: "and the host of them"; and the NIV and the NJB has, "with all their array."

In contrast, the second emphasizes the deity's actions in anthropomorphic terms. God shapes dust of the ground and breathed into it the "breath of life" and transformed it into a "living being" (Gen 2:7)—a direct inspiriting[5] of "the breath of life" empowering the earth-creature to breathe, that is enlivening this being as physical addressable spiritual being.[6]

> . . . the LORD God formed man from the dust of the ground, and breathed into his nostrils the breath of life; and the man became a living being. And the LORD God planted a garden in Eden, in the east; and there he put the man whom he had formed. (Gen 2:7–8, NRSV)

Whether humans were created last and placed in a life-suited living space (Gen 1:1–28) or first in a desert-like milieu and then made to dwell in the divinely tended garden (Gen 2:7–8), it is a balanced creative act. God is the source of all forms of life created through effective words and deeds—gathering and speaking nonhuman existing matter to create the universe and everything in it. The creator God farms (Gen 2:8–9) and instructs humans to do likewise (Gen 2:15). As scripture has it, creation, humans and the land belong to the creator-deity (Exod 13:2; 19:5; 25:23; 34:19; Ezek 29:9) and Israel is a tenant (Lev. 25:12). God sends rains upon the land to ensure Israel has enough food to go around (Deut 11:10–21; 15:1–11).

In my native country, Senegalese Diola myths of my grandparents' faith traditions recount a universe made by an uncreated God called Ala Émit,[7] who is intimately involved in creation. The deity sustains creation with rain that moistens the soil to yield abundant crops, especially rice. To Diola people, rice is not just any crop, it is a sacred produce.[8] Most Diola beliefs about the role of their supreme deity in human affairs are shared by many Africans, a reality that has led some African scholars, including me, to use the umbrella nomenclature African Traditional Religion

---

5. Sarna, *Genesis*, 17. The expression *nefeš ḥayyah* ("living being") appears in Gen 1:30.

6. C. Westermann, *Genesis 1–11*, 207.

7. The Diola of Mof Avvi would refer their supreme deity as Ala Émit also pronounced Aléemit. Ata Émit/Atéemit/, Émitai/Émitey, or Émit are variants of the same divine name one can hear Diola of other subgroups use. However, the word Émit is used by most Diola groups. Henceforth, I will use Ala Émit unless I am exploring the semantic field of the word Émit.

8. Diédhiou, *Riz*; Diabone, *Les ressources foncières*.

instead of African Traditional Religions.[9] Strikingly, in both biblical and Diola faith traditions, the Earth, humans, flora, and fauna are empowered by the deity to reproduce and become participatory agents in the creative process. Seen this way, the universe, humans, earth, fauna, and flora are not objects at the mercy of human control and whimsical manipulations, but subjects. Responding to increasing contemporary climate change pressures, many biblical scholars and theologians are now scrambling for effective theological answers trying assiduously to recover descriptively or systematically.[10] In a brief but invaluable encounter with a famous theologian who joined the postcolonial conversation, I made the cardinal mistake of revealing that I read Scripture through a postcolonial lens. By "cardinal mistake" I mean that I went against what my experience taught me—that many Western scholars believe they are the sole guardians of truth, knowledge, and methodology, and surely nothing scholarly can come from black Africa, much less a postcolonial contribution to biblical

9. Magesa, *African Religion*, 4–28. The nomenclature debate has strong colonial and academic precedence, as Magesa clearly observed. The persistent refusal to recognize African Traditional Religion as a religion in its own right with many expressions instead of being reduced to a pantheon of religions in academic settings appears to have been engendered by the invectives thrown at Africans that led to the characterizations of them as primitive people. On this pertinent issue, Magesa correctly writes:

> Even though the study of African Religion engages the interest of many scholars today, its status as a world religion has not yet been comfortably accepted in some quarters of the academic and Christian religious world. The tendency of some philosophers, theologians, and students of comparative religion is still to regard African Religions as a 'primal' or 'ethnic' religion, thus robbing it of its universal character . . . This attitude also reduces the capacity of African Religion to interact with other religions and to influence and change the world and minimizes its role in conversation with other religions. It becomes a subordinate partner rather than an equal. (*African Religion*, 19)

A similar concern is taken up by P'Bitek, *Decolonizing African Religions*. Hegel's view of an Africa that is still in its infancy stage, *Philosophy of History*, 92, has certainly done much to rob African Traditional Religion of its rightful status among world religions.

10. A handful of publications calling for a rereading of the Bible, especially Gen 1:28, with creation in mind, include Barr, "Man and Nature," in Barton, *Biblical Interpretation*, 2:344–60, and others mentioned in his n1334. See also Moltmann, *God in Creation*. Earlier publications include Habel and Wurst, eds., *The Earth Story in Genesis*; Habel and Balabanski, eds., *The Earth Story in the New Testament*; Hessel and Ruether, et al., *Christianity and Ecology*; Hessel and Rasmussen, eds., *Earth Habitat*; Berry, ed, *Environment Stewardship*; Horrell, et al., *Ecological Hermeneutics*; Houston, "Justice and Violence," in *The Bible and Justice*, 93–105.

studies. I was then reminded by this theologian that postcolonial theory was born in India and not Africa. I was not that surprised.

As a Diola native, I argue that the Négritude articulated by Léopold Sédar Senghor, especially its aspect that deals with the divine–human–nature relationship, echoes many of the religious concepts that direct Diola agricultural practices, especially rice farming. This heuristic postcolonial repositioning lens, I argue, emphasizes a biblical divine–human–nature relationship—a dimension of Senghorian Négritude he expounded upon in his speech delivered in 1956 at the First International Conference of Negro Writers and Artists in Paris and published in *Présence Africaine*. The speech clearly highlights his reverence for nature and anchors his overall perspective on the divine-human-nature relationship—a reality he wanted colonizers, colonized, and diaspora people of African descent to know. In this speech Senghor firmly stated that "the Negro is a person of nature who traditionally lives of and with the soil, in and by the cosmos."[11] My questions, then, are how does this Senghorian conviction relate to Diola belief in the divine–human–nature relationship? What do Scripture and non-Christian Diola faith traditions say about human relationship to nature? Is there something in these traditions worth learning in order for humans to live symbiotically with nature and address our current climate change concerns?

Senghor believes floral and faunal life of the environment that permeates continental Africa and its climate—both warm and humid—heightens and directs Africans' unmediated sensory relationship to nature.[12] The resulting symbiotic relationship makes taming nature, as colonial agronomists did by hastily introducing European agricultural methods during the colonial period in tropical Africa, a serious mistake[13] because not only did God empower humans to understand all creatures, Senghor insists that humans "are with animals, plants, minerals, all the phenomena of nature" and that we can know other creatures "at the

---

11. Senghor, "The Spirit of Civilization," 52. Many of Senghor's critics differ on their understanding of Senghor. African critics reject his argument that "emotion is African" and "reason Greek" as insulting. Senghor's European colleague, Jean Paul Sartre, attacks Négritude as a mere "anti-racist racism," a transitory quest that will end up consuming itself and "disappear completely" (Sartre, "Orphée," xiv, xl, xli). Readers of Senghor are often confronted with a strange reality. He tends to speak in general terms when speaking about African culture.

12. Senghor, *Liberté 3*, 92; Senghor, *Liberté 1*, 266.

13. Senghor, *Liberté 1*, 305–6.

intersectionality of our shared existence and movement."[14] The universe, to Senghor, includes both individual and distinct but interdependent forces among which humans are placed in "a tight network" of binding and sustaining a "vertical and horizontal solidarity" with nature. In other words, "all the universe, visible and invisible from God to a grain of sand, through the spirits, ancestors, animals, plants, minerals, is composed of 'communicating vessels' of the solidarity of vital forces that emanate all from God."[15]

Senghor's understanding of the divine–human–nature relationship, I argue, is akin to the Diola conception of the universe. The fact that Senghor was a devout Christian who read Scripture with his African context in mind made his Négritude a repositioning trope insightful for articulating a symbiotic ecotheology. In fact, studies by anthropologists and ethnographers such as Louis-Vincent Thomas, Robert Baum, Paolo Palmeri, Constant Vanden Berghen, and Adrien Manga[16] on Diola religion echo many of Senghor's ideas. Ritualization of rice farming makes most Diola people spiritual farmers whose heightened sensibility to nature is meticulously negotiated throughout the year because, to the Diola, human life finds its best expression through its ritualized participation in the divine–human–nature relational ecosystem in which all creatures, human and nonhuman, relate mutually.

Though often missed by many of his critics, Senghor contextualized Scripture, especially biblical myths of creation (Gen 1:1—2:25; John 1:1–18; Rev 22:1-3) in many of his poems. My use of Senghorian Négritude as a method to reposition Diola farming practices displaced by French colonial occupation to re-embrace some of their farming practices sensitive to nature calls for a reading of biblical passages such as Gen 1-2; Lev 25:1-7; Deut 11:10–12; 15:1–11; Rom 8:19-23; Mark 4:26-29; Matt 13:24-30; John 1:1-18; and Rev 22:1-5. The linguistic, historical, and cultural distance between biblical and Diola faith traditions calls for a careful comparative study. Diola people are not the only ones who revere nature. Nisbert Taisekwa Taringa casts his Shona farming practices in a negative light insisting that they are based on fear and superstition rather than reverence to God, but remains committed to a Christian–Shona

---

14. Senghor, *Liberté 3*, 360.

15. Senghor, *Liberté 1*, 246.

16. Thomas, *Les Diola*; Palmeri, *Living with the Diola* = Palmeri, *Retour dans un village Diola*; Berghen and Manga, *Une introduction*; Linares, *Power, Prayer and Production*; Davidson, *Sacred Rice*.

Dialogue.[17] His stance in emphasizing fear on the Shona side was clearly precipitated by much of the counterarguments for some legitimation of Shona religious practices in African spaces contested by colonial officials, missionary Christianity, and proponents of Shona Faith Traditions.[18]

Diola people were labeled uncivilized pagans by French colonial officials because of their opposition to any form of centralized government imposed on them and determination to preserve their sociocultural, political, economic, and especially their traditional religious convictions. In Senghorian Négritude, the African lives in symbiosis with nature—a reality most Diola people exercise. Seen from this perspective, Christians can learn much from both scripture and Diola reverent negotiations of life with nature in order to cultivate a healthy relationship with God's earth and creation and perhaps avoid irreversible ecological disaster. The truth is that centuries of reception of the Bible have somewhat failed to give due attention to the agency of other creatures, especially nature. My question is: might there be other sources from which a concerned exegete can learn?

I argue that we can learn from Diola people of Senegal, West Africa, who practiced African Traditional Religion and Native Americans, just to list a few. These are people who have been negotiating life with nature since time immemorial and were aware of climate change since its onset. I understand how daunting a task it is to explore Scripture in conversation with non-textual faith traditions like Diola religion. It is risky to do so because of a long history of seeing any spiritual practice or ritual valuing a connection between nature and humanity as superstition, animism, or even Satanism. It was such an attitude that painfully helped suppress the voices of many traditional religious leaders mainly from the Two-Thirds[19] of the World—voices very much needed today. In fact, African

17. Taringa, *Towards an African-Christian*; Taringa, "How Environmental is African Traditional Religion?" 191–214.

18. Vengeyi, *Aluta Continua Biblical Hermeneutics*; Chitando, Gunda and Kügler, eds., *Prophets, Profits and the Bible*; Gunda and Kügler, eds., *The Bible and Politics in Africa*; Mwandayi, *Death and After-life Rituals*; Bishau, *Reign With Him*; Togarasei, *The Bible in Context*. Mlenga, *Dual Religiosity in Northern Malawi*, records crucial ways traditional practices are taken up by many Christians in Malawi.

19. Sauvy uses the expression *Tiers Monde*, "Third World," to refer to developing countries as opposed to the first (United States of America) and second (Soviet Union) worlds—a world he thinks is "ignored, exploited" and "despised." This designation is found to be derogatory by postcolonial critics who prefer the expression Two-Thirds of the world instead. Sauvy, "Document," 81–83. For a detailed treatment of the

Traditional Religion has been viewed that way[20] for centuries, and many missionary accounts propagated these derogatory and distorted views.[21] Peter Mark relates how these negative constructions of Africans, and especially Diola people, began.

> English and French attitudes toward Africans in the Senegambia developed and became well-defined during the late sixteenth, seventeenth, and early eighteenth century. These attitudes were influenced by three main factors: European ethno-centrism, the commercial relations which governed European-African intercourse, and the growth of the slave trade. During this period, Europeans expressed increasingly negative characterizations of Africans and their way of life. An ideology of African inferiority served, in part, to validate the Atlantic slave trade. It was easier to justify the enslavement of people who were considered less civilized or even a lower form of humanity. The formation of this ideology was facilitated by ethnocentric perceptions which led to a bias in favor of more westernized peoples. One important parameter by which Senegambians came to be judged inferior to their European counterparts was in the area of religious beliefs and practices.[22]

The good news is a conversation between Scripture and African Traditional Religion is happening[23] but not in a sustained way, especially

---

expression "Third World," see also Ashcroft, Griffiths and Tiffin, "Third World (First, Second, Fourth)," in *Post-Colonial Studies*, 212–13.

20. Magesa, *African Religion*, 18–28. For references to characterizations of Diola faith traditions or religion made by Europeans, see Mark, "Fetishers, 'Marybukes' and the Christian Norm," 95–7; Baum, "Emergence of Diola Christianity," 371–98.

21. Superstition, fetishism, and Satanism are not particular to any one nation or culture. Many missionaries sent to West Africa proved ineffective as they failed to deconstruct their essentialized Christian perspectives in spite of the resounding advice Francis Libermann gave them: "Divest yourselves of Europe, its customs and mentality. Become Negroes with the Negroes, and you will judge them as they ought to be judged. Become Negroes with the Negroes, to train them as they should be trained, not in the European fashion but retaining what is proper to them ... The people must never consider you as a political agent of the French Government, but should see in you only the priest of the Almighty," quoted in Sundkler and Steed, *A History of the Church in Africa*, 174. Religious practices other than Judaism, Christianity, and Islam pervade the pre-Christian world and helped many understand their newfound faiths. Europe was by no means immune to these practices—a point well-articulated in Jones and Pennick, *A History of Pagan Europe*; D. Westermann, *Africa and Christianity*, ably illustrates my point in his take on religious heritage.

22. Mark, "Fetishers, 'Marybuckes' and the Christian Norm," 91.

23. Holter, *Yahweh in Africa*; Getui, Holter, and Zinkuratire, eds, *Interpreting the*

in biblical studies, because of academic roadblocks. Biblical stories themselves were transmitted orally before they were written down, as the pioneering studies undertaken by Hermann Gunkel and Claus Westermann have shown.[24] Westermann not only refined and applied his study of oral traditions of the Bible to the Psalms; he also joined other scholars interested in African oral storytelling such as Ruth Finnegan and Friedemann W. Golka.[25] Louis-Vincent Thomas, Nazaire Diatta (a Diola Catholic priest), and recently Pierre Manga, published significant works on Diola proverbs, capturing for the first time in writing sayings that have been transmitted orally for centuries.[26] While Westermann's and Golka's aim is comparative, Finnegan and Diatta highlight the significance of oral storytelling in Africa as encompassing the lived experiences of the people with a didactic religious dimension.[27]

French anthropologists Jean Girard, Louis-Vincent Thomas, and Bertrand Luneau document significant prayers and songs from many African ethnic groups including those of Diola people.[28] Although these studies do offer crucial insights into the Diola world and beliefs in which the relationship between humans and nature is emphasized as an integral part of Diola religion, there are also increasing numbers of publications making substantial contributions to this area of study written by Diola experts[29] in conversation with foreign sociologists and anthropologists.[30]

Old Testament in Africa; West and Dube, eds, The Bible in Africa; Dube, Mbuvi, Mbuwayesango, eds, Postcolonial Perspectives. This Peter Lang series also includes many volumes released in the past years covering key New Testament topics that cannot all be listed here. It is important to note that some significant scholarly attempts were sponsored by the Society of Biblical Literature to start a conversation between scholars globally as shown in the following works: Räisänen et al., Reading the Bible in the Global Village; Upkong et al., Reading the Bible in the Global Village.

24. Gunkel, The Legends of Genesis; C. Westermann, Roots of Wisdom.

25. Finnegan, Oral Literature in Africa; Golka, The Leopard's Spots.

26. Thomas, Et le Lièvre; Diatta, Proverbes Jóola de Casamance; Manga, La Sœur du Bouc.

27. Diatta, Proverbes Jóola de Casamance, 15; Finnegan, Oral Literature, 167–205. Of the two, only the former deals with Diola proverbs.

28. Thomas and Luneau, Les religions d'Afrique noire; Girard, Genèse.

29. Diatta, Le Taureau symbole. Diatta, "Participation du Joola Chrétien aux rites traditionnels"; Diatta, "Femme joola à traves proverbes et rites"; Diatta, "Et si Jésus était initie?"; Diatta, "Rites funéraires joola et liturgie chrétienne"; Diatta, "La personne enter individu et communauté"; Diatta, "Le Prêtre et les députés"; Diatta, "Demain, le dialogue des religions?"; Diédhiou, Riz; Diabone, Les ressources foncières.

30. Thomas, Les Diola; Pélissier, Les paysans du Sénégal; Linares, Power, Prayer and

In this book however, I will employ cross-cultural criticism and post-colonial biblical criticism in conversation with relevant anthropological studies mentioned above to argue for the kind of repositioning I believe was central to Senghor's Négritude. Senghorian Négritude, I reiterate, re-positioned marginalized people of African descent and empowered them to reclaim their identity, culture, and faith traditions, and in the case of Diola people, their divine and human–nature relationship.

Cross-cultural studies mean many things to many people. The one biblical scholar to have made innovations from the existing ways of reading texts (especially the Bible) is Fernando Segovia. As a transna-tional person, he knew what it meant to read in his location and study alone—to use heuristic tools for interpreting texts that say little to noth-ing about his own cultural background. He traces the evolution of biblical criticism and moves from historical and literary criticisms to settle on cultural studies he thinks constitute a suitable multivalent enterprise.[31] This way of reading texts has strong affinities with postcolonial biblical criticism, especially in recognizing emergent voices from the oppressed and displaced. Thus postcolonial critics are able to speak because of new positioning—a created space where they can be heard as they rehabilitate their once distorted selves—a process "nurtured and nourished by their goals and aspirations."[32] This is the point bell hooks strongly argued when she challenged her readers to engage in reimaging their assigned margins into sites of struggle and creative "openness."[33] Margins may appear static but in many cases they are highly contested spaces always open to nego-tiation with countless possibilities.

In this introductory chapter, I am arguing that Senghorian Négri-tude is a Poetics of Postcolonial Criticism because Senghor expressed his ideas through poetry to reposition colonial Africa, as enshrined in his "Elegy of the Circumcised," which speaks to the African lived experi-ences of colonial alienation and death and the promise of new life encap-sulated in the phoenix.

> Ah! To die to childhood, let the poem die, the syntax degenerate,
>
> And all the unimportant words become spoiled . . .
>
> The poem is a snake-bird, the dawn marriage of shadow and light

---

Production; Darbon, L'administration; Journet-Diallo, Les Créances de la terre.

31. Segovia, "Cultural Studies," 3–5.

32. Sugirtharajah, "From Orientalist to Post-Colonial," 24.

33. hooks, Yearning, 145–53.

It soars like the Phoenix! It sings with its wings spread
Over the slaughter of words.[34]

He uses positionality (or repositionality) as a way of creating space within liminality—a key feature shared by postcolonial theorists Edward Said, Homi Bhabha, and Gayatri C. Spivak.

To engage Scripture from a Diola lens is not an easy task but one that can be achieved in conversation with cross-cultural analysis and postcolonial theory. Diola people are not silent readers of books. Instead they read nature and humans. In other words, humans, fauna, flora, and cosmos are all texts to be read carefully because of their interrelatedness. The famous saying, "When an elder dies, an entire library is consumed," is not taken lightly in Diola country where it is a living riddle. As a Diola follower of Jesus, I will also examine exegetically how scriptural testimonies describe God as a creator who is very much concerned about creation and especially the participatory human role in it.

Chapter 2 will deal with Diola people in general and specifically the Diola of Mof Avvi, "Royal Land," the township of my grandparents. I will highlight Diola faith traditions with particular emphasis on cosmology, agricultural practices, and economic convictions. The chapter will include maps indicating the geographical location of Diola people. My hope here is that Christians might learn from Diola people about how and why to negotiate life with nature. I will investigate the Diola socioreligious and economic realities with the backdrop of imperial France's sponsored notions of land tenure, agricultural practices, and the common good. At stake in this chapter is the situation of Diola traditional farming practice prior to and after the arrival of empire and foreign religions: Islam and Christianity.

The arrival of Islam and Christianity influenced the Diola world significantly; a reality variously described by anthropologists Paul Pélissier, Louis-Vincent Thomas, Olga Linares, and Robert M. Baum.[35] As it turns out, what altered Diola life cannot be attributed to one culprit. Complex socioreligious and geopolitical issues influenced the entire process that eventually destabilized traditional ways, as Linares argues, though she appears to downplay that dimension.[36] If religion is a source of power then

---

34. Senghor, "Elegy of the Circumcised," 142.

35. Thomas, *Les Diola*; Linares, *Power, Prayer and Production*. Works by Pélissier and Thomas are classics of Diola studies.

36. Linares, *Power, Prayer and Production*.

the new changes Diola religion underwent can be traced to the advent of Islam and colonial missionary Christianity, especially in Mof Avvi. I will draw insights from the works of Matthew Coomber on Tunisian farmers and of Baum on Diola rice farming under imperial France.[37]

The third and fourth chapters explore evidence from the Hebrew Bible and other ancient Near Eastern traditions including some Greco-Roman texts on divine and human–nature relationship. The fourth examines New Testament passages such as Rom 8:19–22; Mark 4:26–29; Matt 13:24–30; John 1:1–14; and Rev 22:1–5 in conversation with Greco-Roman literature and domestic art of the Augustan period. Questions being explored include: what might the divine concern of the God of the Hebrew Bible for land tenure teach us about God, human and nature relationship, and the divine invitation for humans to practice egalitarian economics that presupposes there is enough to go around? What might we learn from ancient Near Eastern cultures about land tenure and community in texts such as Gen 1:10–11; 2:15; Exod 12; Lev 25; Deut 11:10–12; and 15:1–11? If scholars such as Walter Brueggemann and Norman Habel have something to teach us, it is the resounding scriptural voice constantly reminding readers that the land belongs to God[38] and that land tenure, jubilee observance, freedom, and justice are integral to biblical communalism regulated under the aegis of Yahweh. Last but not least, was there any form(s) of divine–human and nonhuman relationship in the Greco-Roman literature and imperial art and how might that illuminate our reading of the New Testament informed by the mutuality of the divine and nature under empire?

The fifth chapter draws parallels from contextualized readings of selected scriptural passages and key Diola religious ideas to emphasize the centrality of religion in Mof Avvi. Though severely affected by the newly introduced economic systems, neither Diola religion nor subsistence-based economy disappeared completely. The main concern of this work is not primarily the subsistence-based economy but the destabilization of traditional farming practices that are harmless to nature and sanctioned by Diola faith traditions. In other words, I am discussing the ways Diola people negotiated life with creation. The encounter between imperial France and Diola people altered life and agricultural practices in ways that threatened the very ecosystems they once embraced symbiotically.

37. Coomber, "Prophets to Profits," 224–30; Baum, *West Africa's Women of God*.

38. Brueggemann, *The Land*; Habel, *The Land Is Mine*.

It is this relationship to nature that informs the farming techniques well-adapted to the African environment and climate that French colonists' agronomists failed to recognize when they hastily imposed their European agricultural practices.[39]

The concluding chapter draws on the case being made and offers an explanation of how Senghorian Négritude did much to reposition Diola people to celebrate their faith traditions and inculturate the biblical message. As I noted earlier, the call to reinvent liminality, which I call repositioning, is variably voiced by authors associated with postcolonial theory: Said, Bhabha, Spivak, and Sugirtharajah.[40] I will turn to their idea of space or location as a site for struggle or repositioning in postcolonial theory.

Methodological Considerations

The question of method is always an arduous one in any discipline. In this project, I will avoid the trappings of portraying my approach as being the best for an academic inquiry on *God, Human-Nature Relationship, and Negritude*. Reductionism and generalization are too great a risk especially when it comes to methodological considerations that seek to reposition and awaken the consciousness of marginalized communities with a view to liberating them to reread Scripture for themselves. Postcolonial criticism is a way of engaging texts that falls under the umbrella of reading approaches labeled ideological or existential often critiqued by biblical centrists for being too subjective.[41] A subject of many symposia, definitions of postcolonialism vary,[42] and my focus here is not to rehearse them but to argue that Négritude is a postcolonial critical lens for reading biblical texts and understanding the Diola socioreligious and theological praxis of the human-nature relationship.

Postcolonial theory owes much to critical theory and "Marxists, feminists, gender and queer theorists, structuralists, and poststructuralists

---

39. Senghor, *Liberté 1*, 255.

40. Said, *Orientalism*; Said, *The World, the Text and the Critic*; Said, *Culture of Imperialism*; Said, "Orientalism Reconsidered"; Bhabha, "Third Space"; Bhabha, "The Other Question"; Bhabha, *The Location of Culture*; Spivak, *The Post-Colonial Critic*; Spivak, "Subaltern Studies."

41. Moore and Segovia, eds., *Postcolonial Biblical Criticism*.

42. Carter, "Postcolonial Biblical Criticism," in McKenzie and Kaltner, *New Meanings for Ancient Texts*, 97–116.

all utilize critical theory to identify and locate the ways in which societies produce and preserve specific inequalities through social, cultural,
and economic systems."[43] Once "those structures that create, produce,
and reinforce mythic beliefs about natural or normal ways of being" are
detected, then follows an emancipatory process of "undoing discourses
with regulatory power that dominate and suppress subjectivity."[44] The
ultimate aim to emancipate or reposition the marginalized to interrogate
and subvert oppressive acts and restore equity and justice in society is
central to postcolonial biblical criticism. This way of reading texts, like
liberation and feminist criticism, falls under the label of ideological criticism; it often utilizes suspicion heuristically to analyze biblical texts to see
whether they legitimize colonial alienation, misogyny, or liberation. This
is clearly illustrated by Francis Watson in his exploration of Paul's reading
of Gen 1–3 by using what he calls "resistance and recovery"—reading
ways "most feminist exegetes"[45] apply to biblical texts misread by male
chauvinists. He meticulously shows how a feminist might resist Gen 1–3
as misogynistic or recover it as egalitarian. Authors of *Greening Paul* built
and expanded on and applied Watson's "recovery and resistance" reading
strategy to Paul's reception of Gen 1–3 and its potential for Pauline eco-
theological ethics.[46] This work is one of the current responses to centuries
of reading Scripture, especially Gen 1–11, devoid of serious ecological
concerns and a genuine effort to reposition biblical studies. I find repositioning operative in postcolonial theory. I will return to this idea after
substantiating how postcolonial theory is a repositioning project.

How a scholar might apply a postcolonial critical lens to any given
text is certainly a function of their context. My interest in this project is
not to summarize or rehearse all postcolonial arguments but intentionally
focus on and apply one key aspect of postcolonial theory that pertains to
my subject. In postcolonial parlance, space and language are inextricably
linked—a fact most postcolonial critics would affirm. Location and experience shape how one sees, speaks, and constructs meaning. The place

43. Mertínez-Alemán, "Critical Discourse," 8.

44. Mertínez-Alemán, "Critical Discourse," 16.

45. Watson, "Strategies of Recovery," 82. Horrell, Hunt, and Southgate, *Greening Paul*, 11–47, make fine use of Watson's argument, which I am also using in this project in conversation with Senghorian Négritude. It is my conviction that Négritude not only seeks to recover but also resists previous readings of biblical texts objectifying or lampooning African Christianity or faith traditions.

46. Horrell, Hunt, and Southgate, *Greening Paul*, 14–32.

from which one speaks is not ethereal but ponderable space—lived space deeply affected by human agencies that not only produce, negotiate or contest it but also might consider it as having a sacred dimension.

The dynamic nature of space production gave rise to current heterotopic studies stemming from the works of Jean Lefebvre and Michel Foucault,[47] to name just two. This discourse on space that began with architecture is now being applied to biblical studies as finely demonstrated by Matthew Sleeman in conversation with Edward Soja, who in turn built on Lefebvre, Foucault, and others.[48] Whether the space is experienced, perceived, or imagined, it matters. This is clearly reflected in the works of hooks, Said, Bhabha, Spivak, and Sugirtharajah as they situate postcolonial criticism in their own ways at the center of contested spaces. I argue that this task very much echoes the contributions of the founders of Négritude, in particular the works of Aimé Césaire and especially Frantz Fanon—a point I made in an earlier work.[49]

Unfortunately, much of what founders of Négritude achieved, especially Senghor, has in one way or another been reduced to a self-consuming racist or antiracist,[50] nationalist essentialist,[51] an outdated trope,[52] "a roguish regurgitation of white supremacist colonial antiblack racism by another name: 'Négritude' or 'Africanity,'"[53] or romanticized literature,[54] as if the founders were simply reacting without any inkling

47. Lefebvre, *The Production of Space*; Foucault, "Of Other Spaces."

48. Soja, *Thirdspace*; Sleeman, *Geography and the Ascension*.

49. Niang, *Faith and Freedom*, 127.

50. Sartre, "Orphée noir," in Senghor, *Anthologie*, xiv, xl, xli.

51. Mphahlele, *The African Image*, 67; Soyinka, *Myth, Literature*, 134. Said, *Culture of Imperialism*, 275–79, reduced Senghorian Négritude to nativism and fails to see his robust humanism that permeates his writings (see *Liberté 1*) and persistent call for a universal civilization (see *Liberté 3*).

52. Depestre, *Bonjour et Adieu à la Négritude*.

53. Rabaka, *Forms of Fanonism*, 178, insists Senghor "inverts Eurocentric negative descriptions and explanations of Africa and Africans, reinscribes them, and then re-presents them as Afrocentric positive evidence of an ontological difference in and for black-being-in-the-world. Senghor cannot comprehend that these descriptions are invariably situated within the contours of the Eurocentric prison house, which constantly conceptually incarcerates and (re)colonizes non-European cultures and civilizations, because European culture and civilization is always and ever the model and measure of 'true' human culture and civilization." See Rabaka, *The Negritude Movement*.

54. Uzukwu, *God, Spirit and Human Wholeness*, 27. Senghorian Négritude was also critiqued by some Senegalese intellectuals like Cheikh Anta Diop, Mamadou Dia,

for the need to create emancipatory space for both colonized and colonizer. Sartre did much to influence how Négritude, especially Senghorian Négritude, would be read onwards. In this respect, I agree with Fanon's characterization of Sartre's "Orphée Noir" as having propagated a devastating message that annihilated the Black emancipatory zeal.[55] Like many colonists before him, he tried and somewhat succeeded in tainting this hopeful trope as it was bourgeoning among black intellectuals in Africa and the diaspora. Uzukwu is right that Anglophone critics developed an aversion to Senghor. He, too, failed to read Senghor further by assuming a position, like many African thinkers, based unfairly on at least two Senghorian sentences. The first being, "emotion is African while reason is Greek,"[56] was probably part of a speech he delivered, and the second, "for I have great weakness for France" (a poem).[57] Both lines must be read in the context of his overall argument.

There are areas in Senghor's life and practice that warrant due criticism, but to tarnish his efforts to liberate and rehabilitate objectified, enslaved, and colonized peoples of African descent based on these two lines yanked out of context would be to miss the gist of his Négritude. In fact, whether conscious or not, his fierce critics find themselves taking their cues from his robust intellectual positions to bolster their arguments. Even in the same text from which Uzukwu quotes, Senghor did not write this sentence in isolation. He gave extensive explanations for this single sentence in response to his critics, but all his efforts were in vain.[58] Even Wole Soyinka, who once mocked Senghorian Négritude with his famous, oft-quoted line, "a tiger does not proclaim its tigritude," later voiced his appreciation of its contributions to the African cause. He also spoke of Senghor's humanism that extends far beyond Sénégal and Africa to other nations, especially living up to his poetics of Négritude and his understanding of reconciliation. He writes:

> what of the African continent itself, that is, quite apart from his
> gift of an immense body of poetry and his championing of black

---

and even Cheikh Hamidou Kane—all of whom participated in the Négritude movement. Césaire and Damas disagreed with Senghor's philosophical take on Négritude (Diagne, "Negritude"). Frantz Fanon repudiated it too in his *Black Skin*, 210–22.

55. Fanon, *Black Skin*, 135, 134–40.

56. Senghor, "The Spirit of Civilisation."

57. Senghor, "Prayer for Peace," 71; Senghor, "Prière de Paix," 349.

58. Senghor, "Problematic de la Négritude"; Senghor, *Liberté 1*, 23–24, 202–3, 260, 262, 264; Senghor, *Liberté 3*, 9, 13, 20, 22, 37, 270, 281.

affirmation, captured in that combative expression—*Negritude*? I can think of two areas in which Senghor can be considered an exemplar, a medium, and mediator for the future of the continent. One is his philosophy of conciliation, which, considered profound, may be regarded as the precursor of South Africa's seemingly miraculous resolution of a potentially destructive conflict . . . it was a message that was often regarded with suspicion, mostly on account of the messenger, and his insistence of a foundation of French culture as departure point for this reconciliation. Nowhere was this ambiguity provided such resonance as on the occasion of the celebration of his ninetieth birthday, in Paris, an occasion that brought together a remarkable array of scholars, politicians, and friends to pay him tribute. In a filmed address to that gathering—Senghor was too frail to be physically present—the celebrant's bequest to humanity was indeed a vision of the reconciliation of the races, but stubbornly projected through the prism of French culture and civilization! Where Senghor's bequest lacks all ambiguity, however, is his lesson in power, one that brings with it the transcendence of the humanist over the trappings of office, a lesson that one wished so desperately that other African Heads of State would heed."[59]

Founders of Négritude thought hard about location and discourse, especially assigned spaces in which they found themselves. As its main architect, Senghor is often read through Césaire, Fanon, and, to some extent, others—especially his critics.

To argue for a Senghorian Négritude as a poetics of postcolonial biblical criticism is a daunting and delicate task. I would like to begin with a concise word about three scholars mentioned earlier who are often associated with postcolonial theory/criticism. My aim is to focus on a key dimension I think connects their works to those of the founders of Négritude, particularly Senghor, which is the arduous act of repositioning the colonized.

Insights from Postcolonial Theorists

The terms post-colonial or postcolonial, as a modern construct, are contested and debates abound on what they actually mean. To me, the former marks the end of colonization and the latter the lived experience

---

59. Soyinka, "Senghor: Lessons in Power," 1–2.

of colonialism to this day.[60] The latter, however, is more extensive as it captures experiences from the onset of the colonial occupation to its aftermath. That being said, I begin with Said's *Orientalism*. In this famous work, he critiques Western hegemonic historiography as a discursive paradigm, through which the "Orient" could be filtered and understood—an ideologically binary discourse that presents itself as an epistemologically powerful, superior, and normative center and frames the margins as weak and vanquished, inferior, voiceless, and uncivilized. Conceptually, however,

> There is in addition the hegemony of European ideas about the Orient, themselves reiterating Europeans' superiority over Oriental backwardness, usually overriding the possibility that a more independent, or more skeptical, thinker might have had different views on the matter. In a quite constant way, Orientalism depends for its strategy on this flexible *positional* superiority, which puts the Westerner in a whole series of possible relationships with the Orient without ever losing him the relative upper hand.[61]

To engage this domineering geopolitical discourse and create space where creativity, imagination, and emancipation for the colonized might become a possibility,[62] the critical voice of the marginalized must be "life-enhancing and constitutively opposed to every form of tyranny, domination, and abuse; its social goals are noncoercive knowledge produced in the interests of human freedom."[63] I find in Said's take on Western imperial discourse a struggle to reposition the colonized and vanquished—a key feature of Senghorian Négritude.

Bhabha, on the other hand, insists: "I try to place myself in that position of liminality, in that productive space of the construction of culture as difference, in the spirit of alterity or otherness."[64] Here too, I find Bhabha engaged in repositioning—creating "space for a subject

---

60. Segovia, "Mapping the Postcolonial Optic," provides a detailed discussion on ways these terms have been used while highlighting his preferred nomenclature with diffidence.

61. Said, *Orientalism*, 7, 4–8, 330–31; emphasis is his.

62. Said, *Orientalism*, 329–52.

63. Said, *The World, the Text, and the Critic*, 29.

64. Bhabha, "The Third Space," 209.

peoples."[65] I also conceive of his notion of "hybridity" as a working concept that symbolizes a site for struggle and self-repositioning. He writes:

> for me the importance of hybridity is not to be able to trace two original moments from which the third emerges, rather hybridity for me is the third space which enables other possibilities to emerge. This third space displaces the histories that constitute it, and sets up new structures of authority, new political initiatives, which are inadequately understood through received wisdom . . . The process of cultural hybridity gives rise to something different, something new and unrecognizable, a new area of recognition of meaning and representation.[66]

For hybridity as repositioned space to materialize, "subject peoples" must critically "intervene in those ideological discourses of modernity that attempt to give a hegemonic 'normality' to the uneven development and the differential, often disadvantaged, histories of nations, races, communities, peoples."[67] As it is with bell hooks, Bhabha's liminal space is in the "affective experience of social marginality" where colonized peoples can be inspired to speak.[68] To me this sounds like repositioning for self-actualization—an important aspect of Senghorian Négritude.

Spivak reminds us that the subaltern, especially Indian women, are silenced and subordinated to their male counterparts—a liminal positioning that erases their history and renders them speechless.[69] This is not a hopeless situation. Using her own experience, she conceives of a viable way for a liberative speech within liminality. She opines,

> I find the demand on me to be marginal always assuming . . . I am tired of dining out on being an exile because that has been a long tradition and it is not one I want to identify myself with. But the question is a more complex one. In a certain sense, I think there is nothing that is central. The center is always constituted in terms of its own marginality. However, having said that, in terms of the hegemonic historical narrative, certain peoples have always been asked to cathect the margins so others can be defined as central. Negotiating between these two structures, sometimes I have to see myself as the marginal in the eyes of

65. Bhabha, "The Other Question," 75.
66. Bhabha, "The Third Space," 211.
67. Bhabha, *The Location of Culture*, 245–46.
68. Bhabha, *The Location of Culture*, 246.
69. Spivak, "Can the Subaltern Speak?," 24–28.

others. In that kind of situation the only strategic thing to do is to absolutely present oneself at the center. And this is theoretically incorrect. But one of the things I've said about deconstruction is that none of its examples can match its discourse. If I can't keep my hands theoretically clean anyway, why not take the center when I'm being asked to be marginal? I'm never defined as marginal in India, I can assure you.[70]

Spivak is not just countering domineering constructions of the Indian woman, her deconstruction aims at creating space within the margins—an inclusive space. To me, her argument echoes Senghorian Négritude that, as I shall soon argue, arose out of an urgent need to reposition and create space for the colonized.

Sugirtharajah compares postcolonial biblical criticism and liberation theology and finds both to be companions in the struggle. In what I consider to be one of his best works, Sugirtharajah finds postcolonial theory to have succeeded in admitting to intellectual discourse the marginalization and silencing of minoritized groups—a reality biblical studies was disinclined to address due to a debilitating aversion to the kind of changes postcolonial criticism engenders. Postcolonial criticism counters this reluctance by being

> a reactive resistance discourse of the colonized who critically interrogate dominant knowledge systems in order to recover the past from Western slander and misinformation of the colonial period, and who also continue to interrogate neo-colonializing tendencies after the declaration of independence . . . essentially a style of enquiry, and insight or perspective, a catalyst, a new way of life. As an enquiry it instigates and creates possibilities, and provides a platform for the widest possible convergence of critical forces, of multi-ethnic, multi-religious, and multicultural voices, to assert their denied rights and rattle the center.[71]

As such, postcolonial criticism enables the marginalized to critically engage centrist or geopolitical discourse with a view to creating a space from which they can position, rehabilitate and liberate themselves.[72] To me, all the theorists mentioned above have one thing in common: repositioning the colonized or marginalized—a space where conscientization and emancipation can be exercised. Although readers may find my focus

70. Spivak, "Strategy, Identity, Writing," 40–41.

71. Sugritharajah, *Postcolonial Criticism*, 13.

72. Sugirtharajah, "From Orientalist to Post-Colonial," 24.

on repositioning too limiting a category, I believe it is central to both postcolonial theory and the Senghorian poetics of Négritude to which I now turn.

Senghorian Négritude as a Poetics of Postcolonial Biblical Criticism

Senghor was born in 1906, in a Sereer village about 80 miles from Dakar, Senegal, West Africa. He was among the first generation of converts to Christianity. He attended school and was taught by Catholic missionaries in Joal, Ngasobil, and later by seminarians of Father Francis Libermann College.[73] At this early stage, Senghor began to work out a fusion between his inherited Sereer faith traditions with the missionary version of Christianity. Surprisingly, little or nothing is said about the work of Senghor in postcolonial discourse. He is often mentioned in fleeting remarks to appropriate something about Césaire or mostly Fanon, whose work he influenced, to say the least.[74] The place of Senghor's work in postcolonial discourse begins, I would argue, with his own words on Négritude. He writes:

> In what circumstances did Aimé Césaire and I launch the word negritude in the years 1933–35? Together with a few other black students, we were panic-stricken at the time. The horizon was blocked. No reform in sight and the colonizers were legitimizing our political and economic dependence by the theory of *tabula rasa*. They deemed we had invented nothing, created nothing, written, sculpted, painted and sung nothing . . . To establish an effective revolution, *our* revolution, we first had to get rid of our borrowed attire—that of assimilation-and assert our being, namely our negritude. Nevertheless, negritude, even when defined as "the total of black Africa's cultural values" could only offer us the beginning of a solution to our problem and not the solution itself. We could not go back to our former condition, to a negritude of the sources . . . To be really ourselves, we had to embody Negro African culture in twentieth-century realities. To enable our negritude to be, instead of a museum piece, the

73. As a subject in the protectorate, his education took him to metropolitan France where he excelled in the French language, and later became a poet, served as president of Senegal from 1960 to 1980, and was an inducted member of the prestigious Académie Française from 1983 to 2001.

74. Césaire, *Discourse on Colonialism*, 86, 94.

efficient instrument of liberation, it was necessary to cleanse it of its dross and include it in the united movement of the contemporary world.[75]

Négritude is a revolutionary concept born in exile and led by black intellectuals determined to reaffirm or, better, reclaim their once objectified selves. The momentous nature of Négritude and how it might be articulated to effect liberation meant that both Césaire and Senghor will end up defining it differently as they did. Césaire sees Négritude as the "recognition of the fact of being black, and the acceptance of that fact," along with that of the destiny of black people, their "history, and culture." To Senghor the concept is more than an "attitude." It enshrines "an objective reality," namely the "whole complex of civilized values—cultural, economic, social and political which characterize the black peoples, or, more precisely, the negro-African World."[76] By "exile" I mean a physical and mental displacement that gave rise to the need for acquiring French education—that is, a migration precipitated by the quest for the kind of education French colonial curriculum imposed.

The policy of assimilation was integral to French colonial geopolitical discourse that aimed at an identity construction that affected the social and cultural dimensions of the colonized. French-educated Senegalese leaders, including Senghor, embraced the assimilation policy at first but later rejected it for its failure to secure equality between the French and Senegalese people. They were confronted by its failure to actualize the equality between French and African it promised. Building on the words of Senghor, the founders of Négritude were traumatized upon realizing that their education and intellectual acumen, to most metropolitan French, failed to bring them equality.[77] In his own words, this distasteful lived experience in France engendered their need for a

---

75. Senghor, "Rapport sur la doctrine," 14. Cited in Kesteloot, *Black Writers*, 102–3, and Sylvia Bâ, *The Concept of Négritude*, 12. Although the rise of Négritude is embedded in the lived experiences of Senghor, Césaire, and Léon-Gontran Damas, their definitions of it differ as noted by Vaillant, *Black, French, and African*, 224. Whereas for Senghor, Négritude is "the manner of self-expression of the black character, the black world, the black civilization," to Césaire it is the "recognition of being black, and the acceptance of that fact, of our destiny of black, of our history and our culture."

76. Senghor, "What Is Négritude?" 54–55.

77. Senghor, "Rapport sur la doctrine," 14; Vaillant, *Black, French, and African*, 64–79, 88–92, 97–103, 108–15; Césaire, "An Interview," by René Dépestre in *Discourse on Colonialism*, 84–85, 88–94; Fanon, *Black Skin*, 38, 114, 119, 121.

space to reposition themselves—a relentless daring quest to reclaim their shattered identities.[78]

In spite of being accused of *antiracist racism*[79] and cultural essentialism, Senghorian Négritude sought to humanize the economically, politically, and culturally marginalized, directing them to embrace what French colonial lore once objectified as something good, contributive to human civilization, and worth celebrating. Senghor singlehandedly continued to recraft Négritude into a multidimensional concept designed to create a symbolic, liminal, and luminal world within and beyond imperial France and her colonies. He critically engaged his French education by delving into the classics and modern works (Henri Bergson, Leo Frobenius, Pierre Teilhard de Chardin, Lucien Lévy-Bruhl, Placide Temples, Karl Marx, Jean Paul Sartre, and Gaston Bachelard, to list just a few).[80]

Building on de Chardin and Bergson, Senghor argues that "intuitive reason alone is capable of an understanding that goes beyond appearances, of taking in total reality."[81] Reason is relational and not just analytical, it is intuitive and participatory. It is from this perspective that Senghor reformulates the Cartesian dictum, "I think therefore I am," into "I feel, I dance the other, I am" because one exists and *knows* in relation to *another*. Here Senghor recontextualizes Négritude, a diaspora concept, giving it a new dimension—an African socialism informed by the lived experiences of rural life that is religiously inspired and directed. In a village, the person's identity is contingent on the corporate participation of individuals in community. Persons learn to appreciate, enjoy, and experience the "other" since individual identity finds its ultimate expression and manifestation in the "other."[82] The African relating and knowing self and the other is the expression of the vital force integral to rhythm.[83]

78. Senghor, "Rapport sur la doctrine," 14; Césaire, "An Interview," 84, 88–92; Fanon, *Black Skin*, 35, 190–92; Fanon, *Wretched of the Earth*, 250, 311–12.

79. Sartre, "Orphée noir," in *Anthologie*, xiv.

80. Diagne, *Léopold Sédar Senghor*.

81. Senghor, *Liberté 1*, 246.

82. Senghor, *On African Socialism*, 73, 93–94. Similarly, Mbiti, *African Religions and Philosophy*, 106, agrees that the African's self-understanding hinges on the corporate personality of the group: "I am, because we are; and since we are, therefore I am."

83. Diagne, *Léopold Sédar Senghor*, 3–200, offers the best and most cogent argument on how Senghor is not only misunderstood but also may be read responsibly in context. I am indebted to much of his fine work.

> *Qu'est-ce que le rythme?* C'est l'architecture de l'être, le dyna-
> misme interne qui lui donne forme, le système d' ondes qu'il
> émet à l' adresse des *Autres,* l'expression pure de la Force vitale.
> Le rythme, c'est le choc vibratoire, la force qui, à travers les sens,
> nous saisit à la racine de l'*être.* . . De nouveau, primauté de la
> Parole. C' est le rythme qui lui donne sa plénitude efficace, qui la
> transforme en *Verbe.* C'est le verbe de Dieu, c'est-à-dire la *parole
> rythmée,* qui créa le monde.[84]

> [*What is rhythm?* It is the architecture of the being, the dyna-
> mism that gives it form, the system of waves that it emits in rela-
> tion to others, the pure expression of vital force. Rhythm is the
> vibratory shock, the force that, through the senses, seizes us at
> the root of our *being* . . . Once again, the primacy of speech. It
> is rhythm that gives it its effective fulfilment that changes it into
> the word. It is the word of God, which is rhythmed speech, that
> created the world.]

To Senghor the many interrelated forces that make up the cosmos
are manifestations of the same *vital-force* emanating from God and personified in human existence as the *life-force*—a mystical relationship
between humans, nature/cosmos and the divine. Humans dare not think
they are the only beings empowered by God to live. He writes:

> The Negro identifies being with life, or, more specifically, with
> vital force. His metaphysics is an existential ontology . . . "being
> is that which has force," or better, "being is force" . . . Being is in
> unstable equilibrium, always capable of gaining or losing force.
> In order to exist, man must realize his individual essence by the
> increase and expression of his vital force. But man is not the
> only being in the world. A vital force similar to his own ani-
> mates every object which is endowed with a sentient character,
> from God to a grain of sand.[85]

The African peasant lives of and with the soil[86]—a symbiotic life that values cosmic elements (the sun and moon), the environment, the fauna,
and the flora. This religious dimension of Senghorian Négritude explains
why he dismisses the Marxist critique of religion as irrelevant to the African lived experience while maintaining its dialectics instead.

84. Senghor, *Liberté 1,* 211–2. Emphases are his. The translation is mine.
85. Senghor, *Léopold Sédar Senghor,* 16.
86. Senghor, *Liberté 1,* 255.

The metaphysical, ontological, and mystical dimensions of rhythm helped Senghor argue for a religious symbiosis between *revealed religions*, Islam and Christianity in particular, and his African faith traditions.[87] The expression, *revealed religion*, suggests an objective reality outside the person—something that is not innate to human beings but one that can encounter them (echoing Paul's language "It is no longer I, but Christ lives in me" in Gal 2:20). This idea of revealed religion has been and still is a convenient trope some missionaries use to position their message as mediating an objective power to those they consider to be unbelievers. As a Sereer Christian, Senghor finds "mythological thought" and "intuitive reason" in biblical texts he believes are echoed in African cosmology. He writes: "biblical cosmology . . . in its form, that is of intuitive reason, of mythic thought; the gospel revealed it by rationalizing it without losing its vitality. It is in this sense that the *African Negro cosmos is close to that of the Bible*."[88] It is from this perspective that Senghor considers the voices of black priests calling for inculturation of the biblical message during Vatican II liberating for African Christianity—a postcolonial act of repositioning, recovering or reinterpreting and contextualizing the Bible for African Christians.[89]

Clearly Senghor must have had Gen 1:1-3; Gal 1:15-16; 2:11-20; and John 1:1-14 in mind.[90] In Johannine language, the biblical God becomes accessible to humans in the person of Jesus (John 1:1-14; 3:16) whose redemptive work on the cross saves those who believe (Gal 2:20; 3:1-5, 13-15, 26-29; Rom 8:1-2). So then by faith the believer has an intimate relationship with God in Christ who now lives in them (Gal 2:20)—an experience the African lives daily in a close relationship to sacred nature for "the negro is a man of nature . . . he lives of and with the soil, in and by the cosmos."[91]

Faith in Jesus Christ in no way precludes or inhibits the African sacred world; rather it encompasses it symbiotically—a relationship that

---

87. Diop, *La multivalence du sacré*, 46–56, provides a unique dimension of Senghor's thought, namely a detailed discussion of his religious perspectives.

88. Senghor, *Liberté 1*, 419. "Le cosmos de la Bible . . . dans sa forme, celui de la raison intuitive, de la pensée mythique; l'Evangile l'a mis à jour, en le *rationalisant*, sans lui enlever sa sève. C'est en ce sens que *le cosmos négro-africain est proche de celui de la Bible*." The emphases are his but the translation above is mine.

89. Senghor, *Liberté 1*, 149–50.

90. Senghor, *Liberté 3*, 61.

91. Senghor, "The Spirit of Civilisation," 52.

should not be confused with "syncretism," a term some Western missionaries often use to lampoon and abuse African Christianity and faith traditions. Senghor dissociates Jesus from institutionalized Church[92] and repositions African Christianity to symbiotize culture and traditional religion. Sereer religion that shaped Senghor's thought was labeled animism by French missionaries—a fact evident in his own writing. The same label was attached to the Diola of Mof Avvi. Diola and Sereer share much in common and were thought to have had a common ancestry that, I would argue, does not preclude fictive kinship. Most elders, including my grandparents, believe in a kinship and shared faith traditions—faith in a deity who is transcendent and imminent who communicates with them, belief in the future, burying the dead, fishing, hunting, and cattle raising.[93]

To return to my main point, although Bhabha's often quoted term "hybridity" or "third space" is a good working category, I prefer Senghorian Négritude, for it captures a lived experience articulated in Metropolitan France in 1956 that did much to actualize the independence of most African countries, especially Senegal. I heuristically employ it to ruminate boldly on Diola liminality as most colonized persons do to make sense of the overwhelming displacement in which they find themselves. Robert Baum's *Emergence of a Diola Christianity* illustrates this phenomenon. He recounts how Diola people, especially some elders and priest-kings, were overwhelmed as they realized the near ineffectiveness of their faith traditions to help them deal with the French occupation as many negotiating ways were exercised in the quest for answers.[94] Most Diola elders and priest-kings felt religiously helpless before French imperial intrusions and many resigned to the fact that the symbolic world that once sustained their culture since time immemorial was being erased. A similar experience is fictionally symbolized in the death of Samba Diallo, the hero in Cheikh Hamidou Kane's *Ambiguous Adventure*,[95] and in Ous-

---

92. Diop, *La multivalence du sacré*, 50–56.

93. Thomas, *Les Diola*, 2:489–91, has some reservations about the Diola claim of ancestry with the Sereer and thinks it is nothing more than a legend. Baum, *Shrines*, 72, makes a similar point based on linguistic differences. I will return to the Diola and Sereer kinship in the fifth chapter.

94. Baum, "Emergence of Diola Christianity," 374–75.

95. Kane, *Ambiguous Adventure*. Samba Diallo was sent to France to learn the "*art of conquering without being in the right;*" tragically, he died there and symbolically Senegal died with him.

mane Sembène's movie (*Émitay*) and novel (*The Last of Empire*).[96] They all shed light on what has become a reality for most Diola as well as other Senegalese people. This is why I conceive of Négritude as being more than "a poetics of anticolonialism."[97] To me, it is a Poetics of Postcolonial Biblical Criticism formulated then to reposition peoples of African descent from assigned liminality to emancipation by resurrecting that "life force" (of which Senghor eloquently spoke) once suppressed and nearly erased.

To Senghor, however, repositioning is a way of being with a profound religious dimension—a mystical relationship with creation in which nature is a subject, from humans to the smallest particle as Senghor reminds us. The childhood kingdom of which he spoke passionately includes a symbiosis between the fauna and the flora—a lived experience he thinks is authentically African. It is from this vantage point that Senghor emphasizes the African lived experience in relation to nature—the soil, the fauna, and the flora.[98] The African connection Senghor makes is integral to his lived experience as a Sereer. Like the Diola family, the Sereer is the first unit of society that fosters an egalitarian community among its members. The family includes living family members, ancestors who have passed (in Diola and Sereer thanatology), sacred animals, and trees. Senghor writes:

> In black Africa the family is the *clan,* and not only as in Europe, 'Father, Mother, Child.' It is not the household, but 'the totality of all persons, living and dead, who recognize a common ancestor.' And one knows that the line of Ancestors goes back even to God. It will be noted that an animal or even a tree of the native fauna and flora is often integrated into the clan. It is the famous *totemism* which is monstrous only in appearance. The in-human part of it is to isolate the man from -his milieu, to domesticate the animal and the tree. In Europe, this domestication is carried as far as destruction which breaks the equilibrium of nature and produces those catastrophes that are denounced by scientists . . .

96. Sembène, *The Last of Empire*, 134–35, a Diola himself, introduces a debate among Senegalese people over what to do now that the country is no longer the same culturally. His movie, rightly called *Émitay*, deals with the Diola refusal to surrender their rice to feed the French Empire—an imperial demand that worsened Diola resistance against colonial administrators.

97. Kelly, "Introduction: A Poetics of Anticolonialism," in *Discourse on Colonialism*, 7.

98. Senghor, "The Spirit of Civilisation," 52.

> To return to the family, its head, who is the eldest living descen-
> dant, is the link between the living and the dead, the umbilical
> cord which gives life to his world.[99]

This is not unique to Sereer people. Native Americans and Africans share similar beliefs. Senghor learned about the importance of nature from his beloved uncle, Tokô' Waly, who ensured young Senghor does not just talk about how much nature is invaluable but also maintains a relationship with her.

> Tokô' Waly, my uncle, do you remember those nights long ago
> When my head weighed upon your patient back?
> When taking me by the hand, your hand led me through storms
> And signs? The fields are blossoms of glowworms, stars lie upon
> The grass and trees. All around is silence.
> Disturbed only by the scent of the bush, hives of red bees
> Drowning out the strident vibrations of crickets
> . . .
> You, Tokô' Waly, you can hear beyond hearing,
> And you explain to me the signs spoken by the Ancestors
> In constellations as serene as the sea,
> The Bull, the Scorpion, the Leopard, the Elephant, the Fish—
> All familiar, and the milky grandeur of the Spirits
> Through the endless celestial salt flats.
> Here is the wisdom of the Moon Goddess; may the veil of shadows
> fall away.
> African night, my black night, mystical and clear,
> Dark and brilliant, you are at one with the earth;
> You are Earth and the harmonious hills . . .[100]

He, like many Diola initiates, learned a great deal about nature from his elders on how to live with the fauna and flora—that is to hear her speech, speak to, and meet her on equal term as a subject. She speaks to humans and other creatures who understand her ways. The biblical Psalter testifies to the creation speech (Ps 19:1–6). The human destructive hand and greed deafened and corrupted humanity's ability to hear the voices of nature and perceive her movements, especially with the advent of industrial revolution. Humans should relearn to speak to and hear

---

99. Senghor, "Constructive Elements," 277. In a precolonial context, a Sereer would not have used the word totem to refer to the human-nature relationship as Senghor does.

100. Senghor, "chants d'ombre," in *Œuvre Poétiques*, 38–39.

nature on equal terms. Here is how Senghor speaks about how he related to nature in his Sereer childhood kingdom.

> J'ai donc vécu en ce royaume, vu de mes yeux, de mes oreilles entendu les êtres fabuleux par-delà les choses: les Kouss dans les tamariniers, les crocodiles, gardiens des fontaines, les Lamantins qui chantaient dans les rivières, les Morts du village et les Ancêtres qui me parlaient, n'initiant aux vérités alternées de la nuit et du midi.[101]

> [So I lived in this kingdom, seen with my eyes, with my ears heard the fabulous beings beyond things: Kouss in tamarind trees, crocodiles, guardians of fountains, Manatees who sang in rivers, the Dead of the village and the Ancestors who spoke to me, initiating the alternate truths of the night and the noon.]

In these words, Senghor communicates the art of living with nature in the course of which one has to learn to hear the inaudible and see the invisible in order to actualize a genuine relationship with nature. In these words, he echoes what many African Diola spiritual leaders handed down to countless generations. In many Diola townships (such as Séléki, Enampor, Bandial), elders still speak of how God caused life to arise from the earth, a belief Diola people hold sacred so much so that farming the land becomes a means to procure food and a deep ritual path to life. To say the Negro is a person of nature suggests that Senghor is doing more than just reflecting his cosmology. He is repositioning by rereading the stories of creation in Gen 1 and John 1 as an African and fervent colonized Catholic.

To the point, Senghorian Négritude is a bifocal vision, two dimensions at once—a way to be and to live in the world embracing other cultures as a way forward, toward *la civilization de l'universel*.[102] Senghor was determined to create space for the subjugated to reclaim their values and pursue their aspirations by decolonizing missionary objectifications of African faith traditions and Christianity as syncretism into contextualized symbioses. If colonialism removes the colonized from history as well as undermines their faith traditions, Senghorian Négritude reinstates them back into history, and enables them to inculturate the biblical message and innovate on their culture. That being the case, I argue that

101. Senghor, "Postface," in *Œuvre Poétiques*, 165. My translation. The Kouss were mythological beings or Genies thought to have been the first inhabitants of Africa exterminated by the Great Negroes.

102. Senghor, *Liberté 3*.

Senghorian Négritude is relevant to current postcolonial discourses not just as a theory or movement but as a Poetics of Postcolonial Biblical Criticism. I would say with Senghor the Diola people consider themselves as persons of nature *who live of the soil and with the soil, in and by the cosmos.* This echoes what my grandparents always said during the yearly ritual of the beginning of the rice farming season: *"Children, we must ever learn to hear, understand, and interpret the delicate language of nature and see her pains and tears as ours in order to live and exercise caring mutuality with her, for her fate is ours."*[103] Preferring Senghorian Négritude as postcolonial poetics for this project, I will now turn to how it relates to Diola people.

Relevance to Diola Culture

As I argued earlier, postcolonial theory/criticism seeks to restore justice and equity—a project I consider to be an act of repositioning. To me, this is what Senghorian Négritude did for most Senegalese people to build on. In Diola cosmology, Ala Émit (God), *Mof/Etam,* (land/earth/nature) *Búgan* (humans), *synúkuren* (fauna), and *baha* (forest or floral world) are in many ways related, a symbiosis sustained by Ala Émit with the responsible participatory human agency because life, whether it be nature or animal, is delicate and requires responsible care devoid of exploitative abuse. The concern for the human role, according to the biblical myths of origins, emanates from the creative word of God and is etched in Israel's faith traditions and memory (Gen 1–2; Lev 25:1–7; Deut 11:10–11; 15:1–11).

In 1967, Lynn White issued a daring challenge asking the Western world to rethink its relationship to nature.[104] Though not the first study to address human role in creation, his point was that Christians altered antiquity's sacralization of nature and turned it into an object to dominate and exploit. Christians, he insisted, read Gen 1:27–30 anthropocentrically while ignoring the rest of the myth of creation. That being the case, he argued for an alternative way to address this pertinent issue, namely to "find a new religion, or rethink our old one."[105] About two

103. Abdoulaye Manga and Fayinséni Dièmé (Kamout Bassène). My grandfather was born in Enampor and my grandmother in Bayimbane of Séléki.

104. White, "The Historical Roots," 1205.

105. White, "The Historical Roots," 1206. He offers Saint Francis of Assisi as a

centuries ago, Joseph de Maistre (1753–1821) chillingly reminded us of the dangers human beings pose to one another and the environment. He asserted that placed above the various animals of the fauna is the human being, "whose destructive hand spares nothing that lives; he kills to nourish himself, he kills to clothe himself, he kills to adorn himself, he kills to attack, he kills to defend himself, he kills to instruct himself, he kills to amuse himself, he kills for the sake of killing: superb and terrible king, he wants everything and nothing could resist him."[106]

Most publications on the Diola people of Senegal have been the works of foreign sociologists and anthropologists. This dispels the claim for mere objectivity as these works' description of Diola people reflects very much a formulation of questions raised by their authors, with interviews from human sources implemented with their interpretations of archives. Since these sources rarely participate voluntarily, there is a sort of quid pro quo implied in the entire enterprise. This is well illustrated by the words of my late stepfather, Edward Diatta, a native of Kajional, one of the townships of Esulalu, who once said to an exchange English professor from Wisconsin who befriended my brother Jean-Paul Diatta, inquiring about Diola Palm wine tapping, "so you can write about us, right?" Foreign observers often wrongly describe Diola people's determination to safeguard their traditional practices with invectives ranging from primitive, savage, and stateless forest-dwelling anarchists to individualists who just happen to exercise egalitarian communism.[107]

This project focuses not on the lampoons and invectives colonists threw at Diola people, as I already wrote about in my earlier work on reading Galatians,[108] but on how the French imperial occupation displaced Diola people, leading many to question the effectiveness of their socioreligious traditions and farming practices. My aim, however, is to use Senghorian Négritude as a heuristic tool to unearth the Diola religious life under the aegis of Ala Émit "God," creator of the universe, to show how Diola life is guided in many ways by a keen awareness and exercise of an indissolvable bond with the land and nature—a relationship fundamental to land tenure and the act of farming rice fields in Diola country. Although my concern here is not primarily on economy, Diola

model to emulate for his belief in human–nature symbiosis. Frankfort, et als., *The Intellectual Adventure.*

106. De Maistre, *Les Soirées de Saint-Pétersbourg*, 28–29; my translation.

107. Méguelle, *Chefferie colonial et Égalitarisme Diola*, 48.

108. Niang, *Faith and Freedom*; Niang, "Seeing and Hearing," 160–82.

understanding of land tenure and symbiotic agricultural practices inevitably makes it necessary to explore that dimension of life in Mof Avvi. The question is how does this Diola cosmic symbiosis parallel that of the Bible? To that question, I now turn.

2

Human-Nature Relationship in Diola Contexts

> Oh God, Oh *Baliba*, we trust in you
> For it is thanks to you that we live on this earth.
> I thank you before my shrine
> To which you give the power to help us,
> By letting it relay our prayers to you,
> Here are our poor farmers, very happy
> To receive this very abundant water
> Which has made the earth very moist, very easy to farm.
> We hope to have ample nurseries and ample harvests.
> After our labors, everyone is so happy to bring his small harvest into
> his granary. —ALINE SITOÉ DIATTA[1]

This chapter discusses Diola myths of origins, cosmology, human and nature interrelationships, and how they inform their sustainable farming practices. Although all Diola people share a belief in symbiotic human–nature relationship, this chapter focuses on the Diola of Mof Avvi "Royal Land"—especially the Enampor and Séléki townships of my grandparents. Anthropologists tell us that identity is shaped by context in many ways. Diola people think of themselves as a large family in which individual and communal identity is inextricably linked to the entire group. It is an identity construction that expresses itself in a particular milieu—the

---

1. Poem 24 collected by Girard in his *Genèse*, 353.

land that the deity they worship, Ala Émit, gave to their ancestors, the land where they continue to farm rice—their divinely received, sacred crop in order to nourish and sustain human life. To disturb that mythical construction of individual and communal identity and space, as French colonialism did, is to erase it. This chapter delves into Diola perspectives on nature, land, and faith in God from the pre- to the postcolonial era. One way to understand how Diola people relate to the environment is through their myths of origins and cosmology.

I have argued elsewhere that there is a profound link between culture and political power, and that this link is especially sensitive for colonized persons because it prompts colonists to objectify the identity and culture of the colonized as inferior. The colonists' culture and religion—in this case, the French version of culture and Christianity—are presented as superior and normative for the colonized. The objectification drove many natives into an unbearable trauma that lingered for generations, culminating in a war for independence.[2] As I noted in my first chapter, positionality as framed by Senghorian Négritude is central to my argument in this work. It gives the colonized an opportunity to be reborn.

Diola Myths of Origins

Whether written down or transmitted orally, myths of origins are ways groups of people construct stories about their existence, cultures, and self-understanding. Every culture has stories of origins. The origin of the Diola people is still debated and ethnographic characterizations of them did little to provide a clear picture. The evidence thus far focuses on their uniqueness and determination to protect their cultural identity at all costs.[3] For this reason I argue that the quest for Diola origins has to be settled regarding who Diola people actually say they are rather than outsiders' constructions of them. I do not entirely reject foreign constructions of Diola origins, but I believe there are two reasons why they must be compared to those written by Diola historians instead of by

2. Marut, *Le conflit de la Casamance*; Manga, *La Casamance*. The war broke out in 1982 and the cease fire introduced in 2004 was often interrupted by nagging flare-ups culminating with independence advocates suing the Senegalese government in 2014. See my *Faith and Freedom* and "Seeing and Hearing" where I traced some of the objectifications I am referring to here from the Greeks to the French in Senegal, West Africa.

3. Diédhiou, *Riz*, 81.

outside informants. First, the Diola includes several groups and some of
the languages they speak are not necessarily comprehensible to all, and
therefore, should be considered languages instead of dialects.[4]

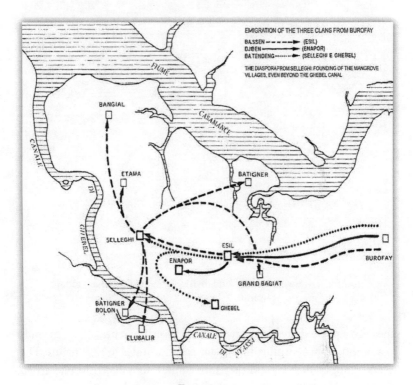

FIGURE 3

Diola migration of the three groups from Burofay to their settling in the area they
named Mof Avvi. The map is taken from Palmeri, *Living With the Diola*, 47.

4. This is the case with Diola Fony of the northern shore of the Casamance River
and the Arrameyh of the South.

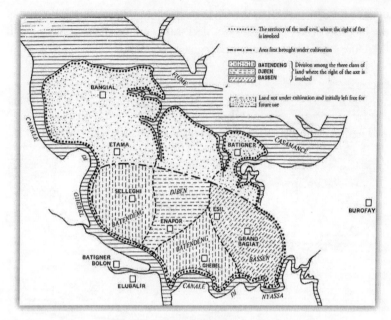

FIGURE 4

The Mof Avvi townships and land divisions among three main groups.
The map is taken from Palmeri, *Living With the Diola*, 52.

These groups do share many practices such as rites of passage from youth
to adulthood, rice farming techniques, and attitudes toward nature. Differences are contextual and therefore cannot be reduced to one group.
The linguistic difference might provide the researcher with major clues
on how Diola people conceive of their origin. Second, Diola of Mof Avvi
think of themselves as a Royal Kingdom, whereas the others do not.
This nomenclature, politically, does not mean that the land is ruled by a
monarch who exercises power over subjects in a subordinating way. On
the contrary, the king symbolizes divine mediation of shared power and
equity among Mof Avvi dwellers. That being said, who do Diola people
say they are?

Theories about Diola origin abound, but for our purpose four will
suffice. Just as it was in the cases of ancient Near Eastern, Israelite and
Judahite, and Greco-Roman myths of origins, Diola people used myths.
The difference is that Diola myths of origins remain oral and innovatively
etched in the hearts of most Diola elders. To my knowledge, the first account was written down by Thomas in his 1959 doctoral dissertation and
goes as follows:

Un père de famille de la race des Diola actuels, vint s'installer dans le Buluf en qualité de trafiquent . . . En tout cas, la prospérité de ce nouveau pays l'enchanta; il s' y installa définitivement et garda pour ses enfants le nom de Diola, déformation de Dioula. Ses descendants fondèrent par la suite, les sous-groupes Diamat, Floup, Djougout et Bayot.[5]

[An ancestor of the actual Diola ethnic lived in the area of Buluf as a trader . . . In any case, enchanted by the prosperity of this new country, he finally settled there, and kept the name Diola for his children, a distortion of Dioula. His descendants henceforth founded the subgroups of Diamat, Floup, Djougout and Bayot.]

According to this account, Diola people shared one ancestor—a trader who settled in the prosperous area called Buluf. The problem with this story is that Diola people are not known to be traders but farmers *par excellence*. The second says:

Le Diola rencontre qu'il y a de cela très longtemps, avant que l' on sache faire curie le riz, un roi habitant probablement dans la région de Kabou (Haute-Gambie) et qui avait de nombreux enfants, aimait tout particulièrement deux filles jumelles, *Agen* et *Dyambo*. Comme il ne parvenait pas à les marier dans son pays, il envoya l'une d'elle dans la région du Sine, après lui avoir remis an sarcloir (helar); c'est ainsi que *Dyambon* fut à l'origine de la tribu Sérère. Quant à *Agen*, elle fut embarquée sur une pirogue avec une bèche (kadyendo) spéciale pour la culture du riz; elle s'établit dans le Fony et devint ainsi la mère des Diola. Ses descendent à leur tour essaimèrent lentement de part et d'autre de la Casamance.[6]

[A Diola recounts that many years ago, before we learned how to cook rice, a king living probably somewhere in the kingdom of Kabou (upper Gambia), had many children, and loved particularly his twin girls, *Agen* and *Dyambo*. Since he could not have them married in his own country, he sent off one of them to the region of the Sine, after giving Dyambo a weeding hoe. That is how she became the ancestor of the Sérères' tribe. As for Agen, she boarded a canoe with a special spade (kayendo)

---

5. Thomas, *Les Diola*, 2:490; my translation; also cited by me in my *Faith and Freedom*, 68.

6. Thomas, *Les Diola*, 2:490.

for farming rice; she settled in the Fony area and became the
mother of Diola people. Her progeny, in turn, spread to each
part of the Casamance.]

This second account has a woman as the progenitor of the Diola people
but does not identify her husband. Important elements are worth noting
in this story. The myth links origin to identity, crop (that is rice), and the
special tool used to farm it—crucial clues I will discuss later. However,
the third myth states:

> Autrefois, il y a de cela un nombre incalculable d'années, un
> homme et une femme venus de l'Est décidèrent, après un long
> et pénible voyage, de s' arrêter entre deux marigots, l'un situé au
> nord, l'autre au sud, en un lieu où se trouve de nos jours Ie vil-
> lage d'Ayoun (près d'Oussouye). Ce couple ignorait jusqu'à l'art
> de construire. Mais il rencontra une très grande termitière qui
> lui servit de logement. Il s'installa dans cette région et se multi-
> plia. Et les premiers habitants de ces lieux finirent, à l'imitation
> de la termitière, par se construire de belles cases en banco. Plus
> tard, des gens qui venaient de la Gambie s›installèrent du cote du
> village actuel d'Éludia (Pointe Saint-Georges) puis essaimèrent
> dans toute la région et fondèrent le village de Diembereng (Dy-
> iwat). Ce sont eux qui apprirent ensuite aux habitants de Siganar
> (actuellement Ayoun) à cultiver le riz. Enfin, les terres devenant
> insuffisantes, des sujets de Diembereng et d'Ayoun s'installèrent
> dans l'autel pays diamat (région de Youtou et d'Effoc).[7]

> [Once upon a time, a man and a woman coming from the east
> decided, after a long distressing journey, to stop between two
> rivers, one in the north and the other south, where the current
> village of Ayoun is located (near Oussouye). This couple did not
> know how to build a shelter. But they found a large termite nest
> as shelter. They settled in the region and multiplied. Dwellers of
> this region ended up, by imitating the termite nest, building nice
> mud houses. Later, people from the Gambia also settled near the
> actual village of Eludia (Point Saint-Georges) and then spread all
> over the region and founded the village of Diembereng (Dyie-
> wat). They are the ones who taught the inhabitants of Siganar
> (now Ayoun) to farm rice. Then, due to scarcity of land, some
> Diembereng and Ayoun resettled in the actual Diamat country
> (region of Youtou and Effoc).]

7. Thomas, *Les Diola*, 2:490–91.

A fourth story builds on migratory patterns that Paul Pélissier thought best explain the possible origin of Diola people. Based on "linguistic, religious and cultural similarities," this view has the Diola and the Floup, who were once among the people of Guinea-Bissau, migrating and settling northward in the lower region of the Casamance, now known as Diamat. According to this perspective, Diola people emerged after the demise of the Baïnounks who were once occupied by the mighty *Kassa Mansa* king, "decimated by the Balanta, enslaved by the Mandinka, repulsed by the Diola and to some extent assimilated by the Portuguese."[8] The rationale for this is that kinship lies in the fact that Diola people spoke of the Guinea-Bissau area as being their heaven—an eschatological place to which they will one day return after death.[9]

It is unfortunate that Thomas discredited most of the three myths he himself recorded because of his subjective take and pursuit of scientific facts in myths. Despite characterizing them as merely legendary, he does see some value in them. One thing remains irrefutable: the Diola settled in lower Casamance before the colonial era, in a milieu in which they constitute the majority ethnic group (about 90% of the population) that included about ten subgroups. These Diola subgroups include those of Mof Avvi who have their own myths of origins. The question is: who are they?

To answer this, I am building on evidence from the fine work of Paolo Palmeri conjoined with mine, of course. In Palmeri's estimation, there were many legendary-like stories and true myths that, at first, appeared contradictory. He soon realized the current Mof Avvi dwellers provide myths as well as facts about their origin. The story goes like this. As it was the case in antiquity and still is today for many human relocations, a famine forced Diola families to leave Burofay [located in south of Ziguinchor and north of Guinée Bissau] for the territory they ended up settling called Mof Avvi. It was the new and fertile land, the new Promised Land, found by the three Diola hunters initially sent by the elders to find inhabitable rich lands. As the three families set out from Burofay to the Promised Land, so to speak, one of them "stopped at Esil, and subsequently became the Bassen clan. The Djben family continued on, and stopped in what is now Enampor, and the Batendeng family, the largest

---

8. Pélissier, *Les paysans du Sénégal*, 659–65. See also Thomas, *Les Diola* 2:492.

9. Baum, *Shrines of the Slave Trade*, 72–73.

group, occupied the lands of Selleghì and Ghèbèl."[10] Common to how humans negotiate space, family feuds in Selleghì led to the creation of new villages located in the outskirts of Mof Avvi near a dense mangrove forest. They include "Bangial, Etama, Batigner, Batignet Bolon, Great Bagiat and Elubalir"[11] (see maps 1–4).

Of the myths discussed above, the last two offer actionable information for our purpose. They do not aim at providing modern queries into the fabric of the Diola universe, rather they deal with the formation of a group of people and how they came to view and distinguish themselves from other Diola subgroups. This brings to mind biblical stories about the Abrahamic migratory journey to Canaanite land (Gen 11–22), Hebrews in Egypt and later Israelites in the Promised Land—a parallel I will discuss in the next chapter. In Israel's memory, the Promised Land is a space where individual and corporate identity is lived in relation to the deity and the land. The myths discussed above, though complex, tell how Diola people arose from an ancestor(s) and expanded into groups of people who migrated and settled in an area where they began to relate to the land by reverently farming rice in a unique manner—a crop inextricably linked to their identity and deity, Ala Émit. As I noted earlier, my focus in this project is on the Diola of Mof Avvi "Royal Land," my grandparents' homeland. I now move from the myths of origins to the cosmological dimension. To my knowledge, all the Diola subgroups share the same conviction—they are all made by Ala Émit who is the creator of the cosmos.

Ala Émit in the Making of Diola Cosmology

Diola believe Ala Émit (God) created the world, and governs and sustains all the dimensions of life. Diola mythology has various features that echo the biblical accounts of creation in Genesis 1 and 2 and echoes Ancient Near Eastern and Greco-Roman cosmologies. As in the Bible, divine speech creates and sustains life.[12] Human activity and material posses-

---

10. Palmeri, *Living with the Diola*, 45, 81–83. Myths of Diola origins are variegated but as a Diola myself raised in this region, I would say we are related to other ethnic groups, especially the Baïnunk (see map)—an absorption wrought by inter-group negotiation of space from skirmishes to peaceful interaction. I am changing Palmeri's spelling of the Diola townships from Selleghì and Ghèbèl to Séléki and Kameubeu.

11. Palmeri, *Living with the Diola*, 46.

12. Thomas and Luneau, *Religions d'Afrique Noire*; Thomas, *Les sages dépossédés*.

sions are believed to be always under the watchful eyes of Ala Émit. The deity is all-powerful and creator of all things from water, air, wind, fire, earth/land, the fauna and flora, celestial bodies and earthly beings including humans. Ala Émit is the source of all life and of the cosmos, who orders creation and most important for Diola people, commands rain as well as directs the existence of other creatures.[13] This picture suggests that the Diola is far from being a deist,[14] animist, or worshiper of animals but one who recognizes the pervasive divine presence in nature. Diédhiou appears to have misread Baum, thinking that the latter agrees with Peter Mark's characterization of the Diola deity as distant from humans, as in deism. To the contrary, Baum was debunking Mark's deist take on Diola belief. In fact, after quoting Mark's assertion, Baum says that "a very different view of Émitai emerges when informants are asked directly about the importance of a supreme being; the history of the various spirit shrines, and Diola concepts of life and death. It becomes clear that Émitai was active in the microcosm of Esulalu both as a provider of the necessities of life and as a source of aid in times of troubles."[15]

The Diola believes in divine transcendence and immanence. To Baum's point, such dynamic divine involvement in Diola affairs is firmly asserted. Diola concepts of the divine cannot be fully understood outside of Diola language and thought forms—a mode of communication that is foreign to most Western commentators on Diola religion. One feature of Diola theology is that the deity is creator of humanity, the fauna, flora, and the entire cosmos and everything is anchored in the name of this deity. A Mof Avvi dweller, like most Diola, understands Ala Émit to mean "heaven or the one who owns heaven, owner of heaven." The root word "Émit" means year and is also used to speak of a person's age or delineate timelines and major events such as yearly rite of passage (Bouhout[16]), feasts, and festivals. A Diola also associates Émit or Ala Émit with rain. To say "it rains" in English does not carry all the meanings intended by a Diola speaker. Émit or Ala Émit is the one who rains or commands rain to water the rice fields, grass, plants, and trees and provides drinking water for humans and animals as well. I will now focus on divine and

13. Palmeri, *Retour dans un village Diola*, 60–1; Diédhiou, *Riz*, 172. See also Diabone, *Les ressources foncières*, 46.

14. Thomas, *Les Diola*; Mark, *Cultural, Economic, and Religious*, 84–85.

15. Baum, *Shrines of the Slave Trade*, 38.

16. The word *Bouhout* should be spelled *Bukut*.

human agencies, communal relationships, and how the Diola views the land, rice farming, and animals.

Divine and Human Agency

To the Diola, divine agency works in many ways. Ala Émit created addressable beings who participate in divine governance by supervising and regulating aquatic and land life. These beings are often referred to by outsiders as genies. The word "genie" is often translated poorly and thus corrupts how one might understand the role and status of this being in Diola sacred universe. For a Diola, these creatures are divine agents created to administer divine justice where human agency fails. The ānmāhl /amāhl, (ān "human being" of māhl "water") is a mysterious and multivalent amphibian who might live in water, forest trees, termite mounds,[17] and appear at central shrines where inquiring worshipers may be advised on matters ranging from "healing, war, farming, and other important and socially useful activities."[18]

Most Diola people, especially those of the Séléki and Énampor townships believe in the good nature of the ānmāhl/amāhl as protector of children from inimical persons (sorcerers) and spirits as well as aquatic animals from human abuse like improper hunting, fishing and forest clearing. Besides the ānmāhl/amāhl is the complementary function of the akus/ẹkus or akouche. Many Diola people believe this being protects the fauna and the flora from the human destructive hand and helps healers find the appropriate medicinal plants and trees they may need for their patients.[19] The belief in the existence of the ānmāhl and akus/ẹkus or

17. Thomas, Les Diola, 2.615, believes the ānmāhl/amāhl is not created by God for a definite end or a specific action. It is the soul of someone who has passed. What Thomas failed to understand is that to a Diola the ānmāhl/amāhl as soul of a dead person does not preclude that person from being a creature of the Diola deity—Émitai, Ala Émit or Émit. See also, Baum, Shrines of the Slave Trade, 45–46, 94.

18. Baum, Shrines of the Slave Trade, 45–6, 94, rightly emphasizes the role of ānmāhl/amāhl in inspiring wise council for worshipers or individuals to make wise decisions. This recalls the role of Apollo at Delphi as adviser of individual Greek worshipers on various matters such as when to wage war. The oracle sponsored Greek colonial efforts by sending colonists to colonize foreign lands (see Graham, Colony and Mother city; Dougherty, Poetics of Colonization).

19. Thomas, Les Diola, 2:616, "akus/ẹkus" reflects the linguistic particularities of the various Diola subgroups living in the region in contrast to Diabone, Les ressources foncières, 46–48, 52–55, who spells the name of this being akouche as his Diola

akouche has a didactic dimension in the Diola world. It inspires a healthy behavior toward nonhuman creatures, encourages the practice of appropriate rituals associated with well-being, and regulating agriculture, hunting, fishing, and medicine. Ritual practices direct everything most Diola should observe and pass on to younger generations.[20] This is true for both the Diola of Houlouf and those of Mof Avvi.

From a Christian perspective, we often hear believers passionately relate miraculous acts of sparing life by beings referred to as "guardian angels." These wonderful testimonies are often reduced to humans and seldom to other beings.[21] I will return to this idea when dealing with how the Diola relates to nature. In the meantime, how then do the Diola, especially those of Mof Avvi, communicate with Ala Émit? The manifestation of divine agency varies and the Diola is keenly aware of this reality and commits to playing a responsible relational participatory role at all costs. By means of shrines, inspired elders such as priests and prophets mediate the necessary rituals. The dichotomization of space, sacred and profane, is foreign to the Diola because the deity pervades everything. This is not pantheism as such but panentheism, a sort of perichoresis of which the apostle Paul and the Johannine author have written (1 Cor 15:28; John 1:1–18; 1 John 4:16).

As a Mof Avvi priest would have it, *gaccimen* "sacrifice" at gaccine "a spirit-shrine," not a fetish, is one way in which the divine will is mediated by human agents (priests) to community members who would then officiate appropriate rituals that make divine immanence tangible. They also interpret dreams and visions, perform healing rituals, investigate and settle disputes, and administer oaths; all done to ensure that divine justice, as it relates to human interrelationship, is carried out responsibly. Spirit-shrines, dating back to the time of the first ancestors,[22] function as sociocultural, religious, and healing centers. In addition to human priestly agency is the prophetic agency.

Prophets often emerge in traumatic times to communicate divine awareness of the pressing conditions like the overwhelming pressures

---

subgroup of Houlouf would instead of Thomas' *akus/ekus*.

20. Diédhiou, *Riz*; Diabone, *Les ressources foncières*, 46–53. Malevolent beings are also in God's creation.

21. We may accept the wisdom of dogs to detect hidden drugs or diagnose some illnesses. We may agree that many wild animals can detect and move away from dangers such as natural disasters, a capacity that appears to evade modern human ingenuity.

22. Girard, *Genèse*, 44; Roche, *Histoire*, 37–8; see also Diédhiou, *Riz*, 174–79.

wrought by French colonial occupation or to simply remind elders about a need to perform rituals. They receive divine messages through dreams, trances, "mystical visions," or "words from beyond the grave."[23] Similar prophetic calls are recounted by Diola prophets Aline Sitoé Diatta and Sibeth. Aline Sitoé Diatta is the most famous and revered prophetic figure of the colonial period for her radical stance against the French imperial occupation.[24] Oneirically called to minister as prophet and priest, Aline Sitoé Diatta reframed faith traditions about extant spirit-shrines but Sibeth remained somewhat conservative. Like la Grande Royale of Kane's *Ambiguous Adventure*, Sibeth advised submission to the French imperial occupations which led most of her people to revolt against her as she was suspected of caving under imperial demands. Aline Sitoé Diatta, on the other hand, had devotees and pilgrims visiting her shrine from around the country. She proclaimed freedom from French imperial occupation and human equality under the aegis of her spirit-shrine. French colonial officials found this too threatening and took swift action to stop and silence her ministry forever by exiling her to Timbuktu.

The relationship between divine and human agencies does not preclude the presence of or inhibit the participatory role of ancestors. Here Diabone insightfully notes the fact that since the Diola believes death is a transition to an afterlife with Ala Émit—a world invisible to the living where ancestors intercede before the deity on behalf of the living as a way of protecting them when faced with danger,[25] a similar function ascribed to both the ānmāhl and *akus/ẹkus/ akouche*. At no point do Diola people confuse such a role with an actual worship of ancestors or ānmāhl and *akus/ẹkus/ akouche* as deities.

Communal Relationships in Mof Avvi

Against conclusions drawn by some anthropologists and ethnographers, Diola people conceive of a world in which divine presence pervades all facets of human life. This is not just true for dwellers of Mof Avvi but most Diola subgroups as well. Many studies have explored Diola beliefs

23. Diédhiou, *Riz*, 173; Girard, *Genèse*, 217–67; Roche, *Histoire*, 40, 284–86; Samb, *L'Interprétation des rêves*, 143–49.

24. Girard, *Genèse*, 217–67; Roche, *Histoire*, 40, 284–86; Samb, *L'Interprétation des rêves*, 143–9.

25. Diabone, *Les ressources foncières*, 49–52. One can read the parable of Lazarus and the rich man from this perspective.

in general but to my knowledge only the works of Palmeri, Berghen, and Manga are devoted to Mof Avvi.[26] As a Diola Christian, my present work introduces a conversation with selected biblical texts, exploiting key parallels and in the process illuminating biblical exegesis at the intersection of the phenomenology of religion, culture, and political identity, especially in the wake of traumatic experiences of colonialism. Most of the sources I am using in this work are written by outsiders as I said before who relied on evidence drawn from their observations of Diola people, Diola informants, the conclusions made by many colonial administrators, anthropologists, geographers, and ethnographers often shaped by their pre-understanding. Even those of us born Diola and trained in the West hardly escape the danger of becoming what Anthony K. Appiah has chillingly termed

> Comprador intelligentsia: a relatively small Western-styled, Western trained, group of writers and thinkers who mediate the trade in cultural commodities of world capitalism at the periphery. In the West they are known through the Africa they offer; their compatriots know them both through the West they present to Africa and through an Africa they have invented for the world, for each other and for Africa.[27]

To that end, I now return to the question of Diola religious system. Priests, prophets, shrines, and drums mediate the sacred in Diola country. Embedded in this process is the role of tradition and rituals. Here space as such is not created but recognized under the aegis of Ala Émit.

A shared language among Mof Avvi dwellers enabled them to construct a society that fostered a diverse unity between its members. In this society, the reigning king is nothing more than a symbol and does not assume a leading role as the people negotiate life with no preset hierarchy, "centralized political structures," slavery, and patronage. As in most Diola groups, elders decide and appoint a temporary spokesperson for the community whose function is that of reporter/speaker.[28]

---

26. Berghen and Manga, *Une introduction*; Palmeri, *Living with the Diola*. Most of the works I consulted do mention Diola of Mof Avvi in some ways as they focus on specific Diola subgroups. That is certainly the case of Baum, *Shrines of the Slave Trade*; Diabone, *Les ressources foncières*; Diédhiou, *Riz*; Francoise Ki-Zerbo, *Les Sources*.

27. Appiah, *In My Father's House*, 149.

28. Berghen and Manga, *Une introduction*, 18–21.

Tout le monde s'y trouve sur un pied d'égalité, du 'roi' jusqu'au plus pauvre des paysans, les femmes come les hommes. It n'y a pas de castes dont les membres, par hérédité, occupant une position soit dirigeante, soit subordonnée ou, encore, ont l'obligation d'exercer une activité bien déterminée, celle de guer-rier, de forgeron ou de pottier, par exemple.[29]

[Everyone is on the same equal footing, from the king to the poorest of the peasants, women and men. There are no castes whose members, by inheritance, occupy a leading position, ei-ther subordinate or even obliged to exercise a given activity, that of warrior, silversmith or for example a porter.]

In Mof Avvi, the basic community unit is the family. Individual families are always spiritually, socially, and economically connected to the larger community. From this arises a socialism similar to the one Senghor described in his *African Socialism*.[30] It is a diverse unity of people marked by what may appear to an onlooker as a patriarchal society where there are male and female associations. That picture is hardly accurate. The problem foreign anthropologists face is this: they are describing a society using Western constructions of reality, namely language, concepts, and behavior they clearly understand in a Western context that mean little or nothing to the people being described. In Diola country all members of a community are equal and elders ensure that each individual exercises equity. In precolonial times, each spouse of a household owned his or her own land; even today some Diola people still observe this practice[31] in spite of the overwhelming influence of French culture. Diola sense of equality is something I have yet to observe in other cultures. Mindfulness and empathy guide their relationship with one another and nature—a belief that manifests itself as *practical-egalitarian-hope* in divine, human and nonhuman mutuality. Berghen and Manga describe this unique re-lationship as "viscerally, individualistic and egalitarian."[32] One should be cautious not to confuse individualism engendered by industrialized ur-ban life with Diola individualism.

A Diola is first a community member whose individuality is de-fined and valued as a person who belongs to a group. The Hebrew Bible,

29. Berghen and Manga, *Une introduction*, 165; my translation.

30. Senghor, *On African Socialism*.

31. Berghen and Manga, *Une introduction*, 163; Palmeri, *Living with the Diola*.

32. Berghen and Manga, *Une introduction*, 21. See also, Thomas, *Les Diola*.

especially Yahwist voices, reflects a similar self-definition of persons in community. Beyond what I have come to term a diverse unity or communal individuation, is how those sociocultural organizations are anchored, moved, and directed by the Diola deity, Ala Émit. The resulting faith in the deity should infuse all socioreligious, cultural, and economic practices, a reality echoed in biblical admonitions such as Deut 15:1–11.

As it is in many societies, family units make up the Diola community. Unlike many societies, however, the Diola community hinges on a firm associational solidarity of men and women tempered with a deep sense of individuality and directed by the practice of communalism and observance of common faith traditions. The individual cohesion of Mof Avvi dwellers based on the shared belief in a common ancestry in no way precludes the existence of individual families—such as the Tendeng, Bassène, Manga, Diatta, Sambou and Diédhiou.[33] Equity among Mof Avvi dwellers transcends gender, economic status, and age. Wealth is measured by how many rice fields and bovines one has; these are Diola banks, so to speak. Although husband and wife have separate rice fields, they farm them together. It is a collaborative work devoid of any competition in the modern Western sense.

Diola solidarity is clearly exercised throughout the year. Those who cannot farm their land such as the elderly, widowed, and ill are assisted by male and female associations to farm and harvest their fields. In other words, the Diola ensures that each community member is not in need—a concern that echoes Deut 15:1–11.

> Every seventh year you shall grant a remission of debts. And this is the manner of the remission: every creditor shall remit the claim that is held against a neighbor, not exacting it of a neighbor who is a member of the community, because the LORD's remission has been proclaimed . . . There will, however, be no one in need among you, because the LORD is sure to bless you in the land that the LORD your God is giving you as a possession to occupy, if only you will obey the LORD your God by diligently observing this entire commandment that I command you today . . . If there is among you anyone in need, a member of your community in any of your towns within the land that the LORD your God is giving you, do not be hard-hearted or tight-fisted toward your needy neighbor. You should rather open your hand, willingly lending enough to meet the need, whatever it may be. Be careful that you do not entertain a mean thought, thinking,

33. Berghen and Manga, *Une Introduction*, 163.

"The seventh year, the year of remission, is near," and therefore view your needy neighbor with hostility and give nothing; your neighbor might cry to the LORD against you, and you would incur guilt. Give liberally and be ungrudging when you do so, for on this account the LORD your God will bless you in all your work and in all that you undertake. Since there will never cease to be some in need on the earth, I therefore command you, "Open your hand to the poor and needy neighbor in your land."

This biblical admonition clearly expresses the divine concern for community solidarity and an implicit invitation for human participatory agency. Mutuality translates into networking to assist the sick and differently able during the arduous season of rice farming and harvest. This *imaginaire* sustains the belief that there is enough to go around and is etched in the Diola conscience and faith traditions, and rooted in the basic conviction that the human responsible participatory agency summoned by Ala Émit will somehow follow through.

Diola and Nature: The Importance of Land and Rice

Again, Ala Émit as the first creator is central to understanding how Diola people relate to the earth and the land they farm. Anthropologists have documented this dimension of the peoples of Mof Avvi as well as other Diola subgroups. If the earth is sacred and endowed with productive capacity, so is the land one farms. The relentless resistance the Diola mounted against French colonial occupation was inspired by a strong determination to preserve their freedom, faith traditions, and subsistence-based economy that is inextricably linked to their farming practices. The land, whether inherited or allocated by "usufructuary lease," belongs to Ala Émit "God" who made earth and heaven a "coherent natural order of which humans are an integral part."[34] Humans and nature share the earth and it is "the quality of the relations that people maintain with nature that determines whether they will escape illness, hunger and scarcity."[35]

To Palmeri, this conviction gives rise to "human-land relationship" in which the farmers "pledge to cultivate the land, and the land in return is obliged to feed them."[36] The Diola of *Mof Avvi* might prefer to describe

34. Palmeri, *Living with the Diola*, 82, 81–83.
35. Palmeri, *Living with the Diola*, 82.
36. Palmeri, *Living with the Diola*, 82.

their view of the land's role as its "natural productive power" over Palmeri's use of the word "obliged" to describe their expectation of the land's role. The human-nature relationship that Mof Avvi Diola call *shil* is, I would argue, the exercise of mutuality, (not "obligation" as Palmeri maintains) to farm the land. In fact, a Diola sees not a routine obligation or task to agonize over but a human response to the divine-human and nature relationship. Again this Diola perspective echoes Gen 2:15 where God commands humanity to relate to the land in a similar fashion—an idea I will address in chapters three and four.

The deity-people-land-fauna-flora relationship is highly ritualized in Diola country. I once asked my grandparents to explain the rationale for such a meticulous observance and their response can only be understood in ecological terms. My grandmother once said to me, "You have to understand the connectivity of everything that lives, from the invisible to the visible creatures Ala Émit made. Ala Émit rains to empower the land to incubate and birth abundant produce for humans, animal and vegetal creatures to live on." I suspect this is the reality Palmeri captured during his research in Mof Avvi when he posits that in Diola cosmology,

> land, rain and fertility are inseparably linked to the idea of God. *Ata* Émit (the god that guarantees the rains) is unique in his ability to influence nature to dispense its favors, or in other words see to it that the land produces rice so that human beings can live. One of the essential institutions in Diola life is the rain priest (*evvi gie* Émit) who performs rituals before his *ufulungs* that allow him to intercede with *Ata* Émit and to ensure that the rains will come and the earth will be fertile, in effect guaranteeing the general welfare of the people.[37]

What appears in Diola cosmology is a symbolic and sacred universe in which everything is balanced—a world Peter L. Berger characterized decades ago as a sacred canopy which humans assiduously seek to maintain through a process he terms externalization, objectivation, and internalization.[38] Taking my cues from Berger, I see this task as a process that reflects a human dimension rarely acknowledged in most institutionalized and textual religions—the participatory interplay between the divine and human agencies. Humans create a world in which they can live and respond once it becomes an objective entity acting back on them as a

37. Palmeri, *Living with the Diola*, 97.
38. Berger, *Sacred Canopy*, 4; see also 1–51.

subjective reality indispensable for "an ordering of experience," a sort of "nomos" that meaningfully shapes the lives of its producers.[39] He rightly sees this process of world construction as strikingly fundamental to how religion shapes a two-dimensional sacred universe that manifests itself as a powerfully transcendent and yet immanent reality that regulates human life.[40]

Building on Berger's theory, Diola sacred cosmology is a reality many Diola people firmly believed in such a way that:

> sanctity pervades every aspect of the agricultural cycle, and this is apparent everywhere. There is a ceremony that confers a blessing on each phase of the process of cultivation, involving either the priest-king and his *ufulungs* or priests and *ufulungs* of each individual patrilineage. Thus, for example, it is the rain priest who inaugurates the work in the rice fields with his blessings, and each succeeding phase of the cycle is preceded by propitiatory celebrations involving the *ufulungs* of each patrilineage. The end of the work is once again presided over by the priest-king, who offers the appropriate libations to his *ufulungs*. Finally, it is significant that the *ufulungs* and the rites to pacify the god are connected only with the cultivation of rice, which, for this reason, acquires a deeply sacred quality.[41]

Once again, the role of the priest is clear in mediating divine will. Among the spirit-shrines mentioned earlier were those associated with rainmaking, as one might expect in an agrarian context, that would be consulted in case of serious droughts. One of the main roles of the deity is not only to command rain but also to do so at the request of human agents such as priests and prophets. This is not far from what Christians do when they pray for rain in drought-stricken regions. This is one of the main roles Aline Sitoé Diatta and Sibeth played during the French occupation. For example, Aline Sitoé Diatta offered the following prayers/songs:

> "Oh my shrine of charity, charity, charity,
> By the power of the Creator God,
> I ask you to please grant me the water of rain.
> Like all the villagers, I raise my hand

---

39. Berger, *Sacred Canopy*, 19, 18–25.

40. Berger, *Sacred Canopy*, 25–28. Here *nomos* means law.

41. Palmeri, *Living with the Diola*, 97. *Ufulungs* mean "the spirit of the family's ancestor." In the next chapter I will draw from the Greco-Roman understanding of the cosmos and how it affects humans in the Ps.-Aristotelian, *On the Cosmos* 1–7.

To ask you for rain.
We salute you with our devotion,
Grant us our request by the power granted you, God."
"Oh God!
Even our ancestors recognized that without you
There would be no human beings in this world.
It is thanks to you that they managed to have these sacred devotions
From where they called upon you in prayer when they were suffering
     from illness or drought.
Oh God!
Oh God, we are here to believe in your power from the bottom of our
     hearts
And to thank you for all the gifts you have given us
To us, your children
To you for the power you have given our devotions,
You make us confident
In all our thoughts
To the end of the earth."[42]

Although Sibeth was suspected to have sided with the French empire against her people, she noted that she received a third message during her divine call in which the deity said: "if you live always in harmony, you will never lack water."[43] It is conceivable to argue that implied lack of harmony among the Diola of which she spoke might have been caused by French colonial administrative divide and rule policy. Her words echo those spoken to Israel in Lev 25:1–2; Deut 11:10–12; 15:1–11: obedience on the part of Israel is a non-negotiable condition to live in God's land and future. In fact, they might also have lent credence to her opponents' charges that she was collaborating with French colonial officials.

The Fauna and Flora

Where then do the fauna and the flora fit in this sacred world of Mof Avvi? What difference does it make if the forest were to be cleared and animals subjected to sport hunting? Does Ala Émit care at all? To address these questions it is important to return to the Diola sacred universe described earlier. Life is not just limited to humans. The animal world

42. Aline Sitoé Diatta, "Song 10 and 22," in *Genèse*, 359 by Girard; my translation. See also Niang, "Space and Human Agency," 887–88.

43. Girard, *Genèse*, 209, "Si vous vivez toujours dans l'entente, vous ne manquerait pas d'eau"; my translation.

and non-animal world teem with life. It is striking that works in biblical studies and theologies written to this day say little to nothing at all about this crucial dimension. I will first start with farm animals, those Diola consider sacred, namely goats and cattle (black bulls). Diola people are somewhat zookeepers whose households often include animals ranging from chickens, ducks, pigs, and goats to bovines. Ducks or chickens, especially roosters, are not only raised for occasional consumption usually during particular feasts or festivals, they are often used to honor and hospitably entertain relatives, strangers, and friends. Black bulls in particular are reserved for important events such as funerals, initiation rites, and rainmaking ritual ceremonies.[44]

Humans and animals are created by Ala Émit. Animals are considered sacred and some are set apart for sacrifice during specific rituals. Wild animals are carefully treated and hunting for sustenance is ritually regulated due to the sacred dimension animal life shares with humans. In spite of his troubling and derogatory language, Thomas' work among Diola people provides good insights on the ritual dimension that paves the way for hunting excursions. Here, context matters. The so-called mandingized[45] Diola hunting, agricultural, and economic practices are heavily influenced by assimilated Islamic values.

A mandingized Fogny Diola hunter might wear gris-gris/amulets for their assumed powers to ward off inimical forces, or perform variegated auspicious rituals before hunting expeditions. The rituals range from a meticulous reading of pieces of wood thrown into water contained in a vase to determine the outcomes of the planned hunting trip or lying down on the eve of the hunt to mimic the dying prey as a way of propitiating for the would-be hunted animal.[46] Though one hunts for sustenance, it remains a dangerous undertaking because of the human-animal kinship and the protective role of the *Akouche*. A "sea pig" or "whale-pig," manatee, or hyena, may never be hunted. In spite of raising cattle and other domestic animals as Thomas, Berghen, and Manga noted, the Diola is a peasant who attaches more importance to their rice farms.

---

44. Thomas, *Les Diola*, 93–99; Berghen and Manga, *Une Introduction*, 105.

45. Mandingized Diola are those who were converted to Islam spread by the Mandinka.

46. Thomas, *Les Diola*, 65–74. The Diola of Floup do engage in some of the pre-hunting rituals Thomas labels as "process of divination" because spilling blood is involved which could unleash "vengeance" between the killed animal and the hunter (Thomas, *Les Diola*, 69).

Sustainable Farming Techniques and Nature

To deal with ways Diola people farm rice, I will reframe and adapt Senghor's dictum. To that end, I would say the Diola is a person of nature *who* *"lives of and with the soil, in and by the cosmos."* Diola farmers developed a unique and ingenious farming technique with which to negotiate life with the land and nature as Odile Journet-Diallo rightly opines.

> Les géographes s'accordent sur l'originalité de ces techniques de mise en valeur du terroir, qui n'ont guère d'équivalent dans d'autres régions africaines ni même dans d'autres régions du monde: conquête et aménagèrent des parcelles sur terre salée, lessivage des sols, maitrise des entrées et sorties d'eau salée ou saumâtre par un système de buses qui permet de contrôler à la fois acidité et salinité des sols, efficacité du billonnage pratique avec cet outil remarquable qu'est le *kajendu* joola (identique au *kop baga* ou *kebinde* balant), repiquage et parfaite adaptation d'innombrables variétés de riz, d'origine africaine et asiatique, ont suscité l'admiration de tous les observateurs.[47]

> [Geographers agree on the originality of the techniques to work the land that have no equivalent in other African regions or even in other regions of the world: conquer and management of lots on salty soil, restructuring the soils, mastering entrances and exits of salty water or briny by a system of channels that allows control at the same time of the acidity and saltiness of the soils, the efficacy of the practical ridging with this remarkable farming tool, the Diola called the *kajendu* (identical to the Balanta's *kop baga* or *kebinde*), sowing and perfect adaptation of countless varieties of rice, of African and Asiatic origin, have given rise to the admiration of all observers.]

These techniques for rice farming stood the test of modern agricultural innovations and apply mainly to fields bordering the salty Casamance River banks. Rice farming is arduous and requires resourcefulness—a task most Diola people believe is honorable and worthy of children of Ala Émit. Fields, farming tools, and methods of fertilizing the soil are sensitive to the divine human–nature relationship.

Belief in Ala Émit inspires a labor-intensive ethic and ingenuity all marshaled to work the uneven surface of the land of Mof Avvi. Diola

---

47. Journet-Diallo, *Les Créances de la terre*, 24, cites Pélissier, *Les paysans du Sénégal*; my translation.

people learned to work the land effectively not so much for high yield but for sufficient family sustenance and community support. The land is meticulously worked with a *gajandu*,[48] an ingeniously crafted, well-suited tool for farming rice. As Pélissier, Palmeri, and Journet-Diallo aver, this tool is so-crafted that it has no modern equivalent.[49]

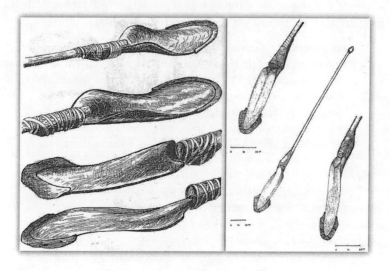

FIGURE 5

The *Gajandu*. Plate 5 is taken from Thomas, *Les Diola*.
See also Pélissier, *Les Paysans du Sénégal*, 661.

Thomas is correct in describing the Diola as people who practice "sylviculture, horticulture, and agriculture."[50] These are not randomly practiced but are very much embedded in Diola understanding of the inextricably linked human–deity–land–animal relationship, a sort of symbiosis that maintains a delicate balance between human/animal species and non-animal creatures. Enough to go around is not just for human needs but for nature as well—a reality integral to Diola belief.[51]

48. Mof Avvi Diola people would refer to this instrument as *gajandu*. Anthropologists and ethnographers use various spellings that range from *gajandu, gajendu* to *gadiandou*. This word will henceforth be spelled as *gajandu*.

49. Pélissier, *Les paysans du Sénégal*, 710; Palmeri, *Retour dans un village*, 157; Journet-Diallo, *Les Créances de la terre*, 24.

50. Thomas, *Les Diola*, 99.

51. Thomas, *Les Diola*, 103.

What measures do the Diola take to avoid violating the inner workings of nature? How do they exercise and maintain a delicate symbiosis with nature? First, rice farming is a laborious process faithfully devoted to growing traditional rice—the *Oryza glaberrima*. Rice is integral to Diola culture, as I noted earlier. It is a precious produce used for various kinds of ceremonies and rituals. Hosts use it to feed strangers who often bring their own to avoid freeloading. I recall when I was growing up there were Diola people from Kadjinol (one of the Essulau Villages) who stayed with us in Adéane to tap palm wine.

In the village of Fanda where my mother and stepfather lived they hosted a wine tapper from Kadinol with whom I had many conversations concerning his role in his village. Each time wine tappers came during the dry season they brought their share of rice along. This practice should not be confused with individualism but independence from the would-be hosts—a Diola ideal. The beginning of Diola rice farming dates to between 1800 to 1500 BCE.[52] Foreign or Asian rice was introduced in West Africa by Portuguese traders in the 15th century, then spread to Diola country, especially Mof Avvi by Mandinka merchants in about 1850.[53] I will return to the role of foreign rice in the last chapter.

Diola farmers depend on rainfall and before the rainy season, fields are meticulously fertilized, traditionally with green or organic fertilizers. Green fertilizer is obtained from the grass that grew during the first rainfalls and grows about knee high. Farmers use the *gajandu* to ridge and bury the green grass underneath a thin layer of soil left to decompose and become fertilizer for the rice. As Diola live in symbiosis with nature, they learned that rice nursed for later planting in about knee-deep flooded fields would grow rapidly under Acacia Albida trees as the roots of these special trees dispense nitrate fertilizers because of symbiotic bacterial interactions with their roots. The leaves, fruits, and wood of this special tree dispense nitrogen, potassium, magnesium, calcium, and phosphorus.[54]

52. Diédhiou, *Riz*, 99. Sources either attribute the introduction of Arabs from the Mediterranean area into the African context between the fifteenth and eighteenth centuries or spread from ancient Sudan in 1500 BCE.

53. Berghen and Manga, *Introduction*, 55.

54. Diédhiou, *Riz*, 108.

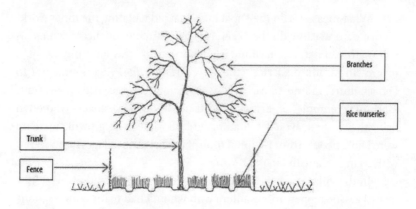

FIGURE 6

This drawing of a *Faidherbia* or Acacia Albida tree is adapted from Berghen's *La végétation des plaines alluviales*, 141. The tree sheds its leaves during the rainy season. The leaves decompose and fertilize the soil on which rice nurseries are planted. The decomposed leaves provide additional nutrients for the rice nurseries planted around it. Berghen's drawing is inspired by Diola rice farming practices in Enampor. The fence protects the rice seedlings from grazing cattle and other animals.

The Acacia Albida is an invaluable tree not just for Diola rice farmers. Many traditional West African peasants from Senegal to Mali covet its presence in their field due to the wealth of nutrients it dispenses to fertilize the soil.[55] Diola people particularly found the Acacia Albida's natural fertilizing capacity actionable for their rice nurseries which they cultivate under. Nurseries are often healthy and grow up to a height suitable for later planting in knee-deep flooded fields. The statistics in the table below illustrate the mutual sustainability rice farmers of my grandparent's village of Enampor foster with the land, flora, and fauna.

55. Berghen, *La végétation des plaines alluviales*, 141.

186 kg of nitrogen	48 % from leaves 38 % from fruits 14 % from the wood
76.5 kg of potassium	70 % from fruits 23 % from leaves 7 % from the wood
38.8 kg of magnesium	60 % from leaves 15 % from fruits 25 % from the wood
222 kg of calcium	44 % from leaves 10 % from fruits 46 % from the wood
3.89 kg of phosphorus	49 % from the leaves 31 % from fruits 20 % from the wood

Table 1. Nutrients from the Acacia Albida tree; adapted from Diédhiou, *Riz*, 109, who inadvertently mislabeled 70% of potassium to have come from leaves instead of fruits as documented by Koné, *L'acacia Albida Del*, 32.

The scientific evidence confirms what Diola people knew all along about the nutritious elements within the Acacia Albida trees. They dispense up to 40% of their fertilizing capacity to rice planted in their vicinities.[56] Since this tree is not ubiquitous, Diola people, especially those of Mof Avvi, resorted to other effective and meticulous ways of extracting organic and natural fertilizers.

Other sources of natural fertilizer are made from ashes of cleared and burned shrubs which are spread over the fields then left fallow for one to two seasons. Scripture commands leaving the land fallow (Exod 23:10–12; Lev 25:1–7). The land rejuvenates as a result of these crucial practices. Fertilizers are also acquired from waste placed in an intentionally dug hole near the household. This includes animal to floral wastes later burned and ashes spread on the fields prior to, or sometimes during, the first rainfalls. Animal waste is often used to neutralize weeds, a fact confirmed by Berghen and Manga.[57] In cases when the weeds overtake the planted rice, they are simply removed by hand and then placed or buried between the ridges and left to decompose.

56. Koné, *L'acacia Albida Del*, 32.

57. Berghen and Manga, *Introduction*, 77, also note that at times, "mud from termite summit nests is spread on the field to improve the texture of the soil."

FIGURE 7

Diola farmers overturning dead grass into dikes on which rice will be planted. The
buried grass will decompose into organic fertilizer. Plates 43 (left) and 45 (right)
are taken from Pélissier, *Les Paysans du Senegal*, 660 and 709. The top right shows
freshly created dikes and an irrigational canal filled with water.

This is also another way of fertilizing the soil. There are instances when
Diola farmers would extract lime from burned oyster shells known to
contain about 57 % of silicon, a mineral that helps the growing rice ward
off parasites.[58] Flooding planted fields with rainfall is an ingenious way
of negotiating with nature. The rice being planted is often taller than the
weed and the water regulated by flooding also slows down the growth of
the weeds.[59]

58. Diédhiou, *Riz*, 109–11.
59. Berghen and Manga, *Introduction*, 93–94.

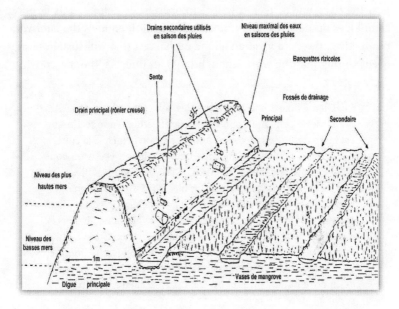

Diagram of the meticulous irrigation system; taken from Diédhiou, *Riz*, 104.

Rice affected by some natural diseases is carefully treated with ashes from bark, roots, and leaves of special trees. Being a descendent of Mof Avvi natives, I learned these fertilizing techniques and practiced them in our rice fields. Since religious devotion pervades Diola life, there is also a religious dimension to the process of farming the land that includes prayers and religious rituals[60] during which the deity is invoked to protect the planted fields. Diola farmers carefully work the land to ensure equilibrium is maintained between humans and nature. Harvested rice is stored in granaries where smoke from carefully burned tree leaves, bark, and roots wards off rodents and insects.[61]

To conclude this section it is essential to note that Diola people, without the kind of technology used by industrial nations, clearly know something crucial about human and nature relationship that can help us address our modern ecological crisis in many ways. The Diola is not just any peasant; they farm rice—a sacred crop whose farming is labor intensive. Diola traditional rice is well adapted to the region and is cultivated

60. Diédhiou, *Riz*, 110–11.

61. Berghen and Manga, *Introduction*, 94–95.

near the river, under trees as well as in open fields as long as its farming techniques do not violate divine intent. Ala Émit endows the land with productive powers to yield an abundant harvest that will sustain family needs throughout the year—enough to go around. As Thomas convincingly notes,

> Le Dieu Diola . . . opère par les lois générales auxquelles l'homme se contente d'obéir et la signification d'une technique est inséparable de sa réussite. Mais, dans son principe, la culture est religion. Tout d'abord parce que la religion est avant tout ce qui assure la cohésion du groupe dans the temps et l'espace; elle est ce par quoi la société visible et invisible se représente la manière dont elle vit. Vu sous cet angle, c'est le geste qui se fait rite et non l'inverse. Ensuite, parce que l'homme vit sous la dépendance de Dieu: il faut donc remercier Dieu d'une culture enrichissante et bienfaisante; et, puisque le riz nourrit l'homme, lame du riz ne peut manquer de nourrir le fétiche et l'âme du défunt. Ce qui est un don de Dieu par excellence doit pouvoir servir au culte de Dieu.[62]

> [The God of the Diola . . . operates with general laws in which humanity is pleased to obey and the meaning of a technique is inseparable for his success. But, in its principle, culture is religion. First of all, because religion is after all what ensures the cohesion of the group in time and space; that is why society is often visible and invisible presenting itself as alive. Seen from this angle, it is the gesture that makes up the rite and not the universe. Because the human lives under the divine dependence, one has to thank God for an enriching culture and salutary culture; and because rice nourishes humans, the soul of the rice does not miss to nourish the shrine and the soul of the deceased. What is a divine gift *par excellence* can serve the divine cult].

To the Diola of precolonial Senegambia, rice farming is not only suitable to the environment, it is the way the deity provides sustenance to humans. In fact,

> it is the most positive of the Diola farming techniques because it is the most indispensable for biological equilibrium. But the person could not live without rice, and the farming of this plant depends not on human power but on the power of God to bring

---

62. Thomas, *Les Diola*, 119–20; my translation. To compare Diola traditional belief with Dante's demons is outrageously abusive. It is a collapse of diametrically opposed constructions of reality. A person of his intellectual caliber should have known better.

rain; consequently, no other agricultural technique has either efficiency or religious significance than rice growing.[63]

Rice in Diola country is a divine gift for sustenance treated with reverence—the same applies to the land.[64] Much of what Thomas is saying here about Diola belief can also be teased out of the Hebrew Bible as I noted in my introductory section. Unfortunately, Diola religion was viewed as not only primitive or savage but also dangerous and evil as I have written elsewhere.[65] This negative attitude toward Diola people is unfortunate and must be abandoned. To speak about Diola beliefs it is important to ask about the Diola concept of community and the resulting relationships of its members. To that dimension of Diola life, I now turn.

Negotiating Foreign Religions: Encounters between Diola Religion, Christianity, and Islam

Thomas thinks the "God of the Diola, like all the African gods, remains after all . . . *deus incertus et deus remotus*, always surrounded by a halo of vagueness."[66] Robin Horton followed suit, reducing African religious belief in a supreme deity to no more than a pantheon of lesser spirits, whom he thinks immanently and microcosmically affect people's lives.[67] Framed differently, Peter Mark insists that the Diola have faith in a "remote being, and even today, when *Émitai* is frequently identified with a personalized God resembling the supreme being of Christian belief, prayers are offered through the intermediaries of the *sínáátí*."[68] These conclusions seriously miss the complexity of Diola belief that Ala Émit is very much involved in the lives of the people; transcendence and immanence are maintained in Diola religion with Diola, not Christian, syntax. To me, that is the

---

63. Thomas, *Les Diola*, 120; my translation.

64. Palmeri, *Living with the Diola*, 97–101; Palmeri, *Retour dans un village*, 151–62; Diabone, *Les ressources foncières*, 70–71.

65. Niang, *Faith and Freedom*, 77; Niang, "Seeing and Hearing Jesus," 172.

66. Thomas, *Les Diola*, 2:584, 587. Thomas seriously undermines his initial argument since he further maintains that Diola people do believe in a "supreme," "indivisible," "non-representable," "immortal," "spiritual," "all powerful," "omniscient," and "omnipresent," being who "spoke the world into existence" but explained away these beliefs (Thomas, *Les Diola*, 2:588). On the remoteness of God in African religions, see Thomas et René Luneau, *La terre africaine et ses religions*, 141–48.

67. Horton, "African Conversion," 100; Horton, "On the Rationality of African Conversion," 219–20.

68. Mark, *Wild Bull*, 25.

mistake many ethnographers make, despite their emphasis on how much they depend on Diola informant translational accounts.

Mark is aware that the "Jola conceive of the existence of a high god, whom they call *Émitay.*" As I noted earlier, Émitay also means year, or simply rain. The term is also associated with the sky, in its all-encompassing, transcendent vastness. Émitay is associated with the annual cycle of agriculture, as well as with the life-giving rain without which rice—and ultimately humans—cannot live. To say this Diola view was influenced by Christian monotheism is to underestimate the fact that the divine presence of Ala Émit predates Diola encounters with Muslim and Christian faiths, especially the Diola of Mof Avvi and Esulalu as we will see later.[69] To describe the deity as a mere *deus incertus* "uncertain God," *deus remotus* "remote God," or *deus otiosus* "idle God" is a serious mischaracterization of Diola socioreligious convictions, given the fact that Ala Émit is believed to heal, inspire human understanding, establish a moral order in Diola communities, see their deeds, command rain and secure good harvests for human sustenance. That being the case, what was the Diola encounter with Islam and Christianity like?

Islam

As historians have it, the initial introduction of Islam by Mandinka marabouts to Diola people was a violent event that, in some ways, can be characterized as holy war. Jihad, for the branch of Muslim invaders, has little to do with its ontological meaning, an internal struggle for spiritual maturity or spiritual growth, but much to do with the eschatological preeminence of the soul over the body which is nothing but material.[70] As is clear in this misinterpretation of Jihad, Platonism was instrumental in persuading new adherents to mystify the destruction of the body and take up the sword, if necessary, to spread Islam among Diola people. In spite of his militancy and failure to subdue the Pular[71] to conversion in the nineteenth century, Fodé Kaba, the main cleric leading this invasion, turned his attention to the Diola whose religious practices both Muslims and Christians scorned as paganism and lampooned as evil and uncivilized.

69. Baum, *Shrines of the Slave Trade,* 39.
70. Diédhiou, *Riz,* 152.
71. The *Pular* is one of the major ethnic groups of Senegal.

The Diola of the northern bank of the Casamance River got the brute force of his proselytization campaign as this area was Islamized long before the Diola of Mof Avvi. Kaba's nonnegotiable attitude can be summarized as follows: accept his version of Islam or be compelled to proselytize with the sword. This position is not that different from the one advocated by some French colonial enthusiasts such as Jules Michelet, who strongly believed in the divine legitimation of France's colonial efforts to convert nations to French culture with the "sword in hand" if necessary.[72]

Kaba soon met his fate as his proselytizing campaign ran counter to imperial interest and was a menace to the Diola and Pulars. Put differently by Diédhiou,

> provocateur pour les Peulhs, agresseur aux yeux des Diola, ennemi des Français dont il défiait consternent l'autorité, et enfin, honni des Anglais qui cherchaient à contenir ses ambitions expansionnistes vers la Gambie où il commençait à faire des émules, Fodé Kaba ne put résister plus longtemps aux oppositions tous azimuts.[73]

> [provocateur to the Pulars, aggressor in the eyes of the Diola, enemy of the French whose authority he constantly defied, and finally, spurned by the British who sought to contain their expansionist ambitions toward the Gambia where they started to make rivals, Fodé Kaba could not resist for long to the oppositions from all sides.]

Kaba's enemies breathed a sigh of relief upon his death at the hands of the British and French but Islam survived in the areas between the Gambia and the northern bank of the Casamance River due to a convergence of many factors: urbanization, expansion of the newly introduced trade economy based on peanuts that supplanted rice farming, tolerance for polygamy and divorce, prohibition of alcoholic beverages, and especially supernatural powers vested on amulets to fight colonial occupations.[74]

72. Michelet, *Autobiographie*, 221.

73. Diédhiou, *Riz*, 152–53. Méguelle, *Chefferie colonial*, 203–51, offers many details on the meandrous interactions between the French, Diola elders, and the so-called Mandinka Muslim.

74. Diédhiou, *Riz*, 157. Muslim leaders in the northern areas of the Casamance preached against both the trans-Saharan and transatlantic slave trades. On the belief of the amulet powers, see also Niang, "Seeing and Hearing," 176; Baum, "Shrines, Medicine," 283.

Although most Diola people believed converting to Islam would liberate them from French colonial occupation, it led to a significant stratification of Diola society where there was none before the introduction of Islam in the area. The resulting hierarchy does not mean that Diola people abandoned their traditional customs; rather, most of them assimilated Islamic elements while remaining true to their ancestral traditions—an inculturated Islam.[75]

Islam reached Mof Avvi in 1959, by way of Diola converts who migrated in search of work in the already Islamized northern areas of the Casamance River. One of these converts is said to have been a descendent of Affilédio, king of Mof Avvi—my distant relative. This new religion disrupted long held beliefs and according to Berghen and Manga, it might have led to the disappearance of traditional kingship.[76] Diola Muslims became the main agents for spreading Islam and the introduction of peanut and other non-traditional crops that initiated new agricultural and economic practices in Diola country.

Christianity

It is important to note that Christianity was introduced to Esulalu as early as 1880 by French missionaries. In his fine article, "Emergence of a Diola Christianity," Baum relates the dawn and growth of Christianity in Esulalu and the concomitant rise of a contextual Diola Christianity. Diola Christianity, as Baum calls it, meant that indispensable elements of Diola culture have been preserved. He sees this taking shape, not under the Holy Ghost Fathers' tutelage, rather,

> with a cadre of Diola Catholic priests and cross-culturally aware missionaries, new possibilities for the growth of Diola Christianity became possible. Clergy and laymen alike became aware of the need to root the Christianity of the Diola in the concerns and needs of Diola communities. With members of the Diola community in positions of authority and with access to the entire Scriptures, this process could begin. The new Christian leaders sought to develop the points of contact between Christian and Diola traditions and to build their religious edifice on a

75. Diédhiou, *Riz*, 160–61. This is also true in other areas of Senegal, especially central, northern, and eastern Senegal. This is one of the main reasons why Senegalese Islam is uniquely complex.

76. Berghen and Manga, *"Introduction,"* 207.

shared foundation. This implied a reaffirmation of Diola cultural vitality that would distinguish them from other Christians and an involvement of Christian beliefs and practices in the daily lives of Diola Christians. Still, whilst the "mission" Christian acceptance of an unassimilated Christianity appears to be losing its power, the return of Diola Christians to the awasena path, through reconversion, continues to be a major force in Diola-Esulalu religious life.[77]

Whereas the encounters between Diola people and Christian missionaries were meandrous at best, France's persistent attempt to pacify Esulalu's neighbors of Mof Avvi was a nagging and tumultuous experience that lasted until 1920 when they somewhat accommodated to imperial demands. As Palmeri rightly notes, this was not surrender by any means, for the Diola never abandoned their sense of autonomy or gave in totally to any form of power, even the one independent Senegal inherited from France.[78] To be true to my concern in this project, I am refraining from further elaborations on colonial conflicts as that is another project by itself. It suffices to note that the Diola response to foreign occupation and Christian missionaries has something to do with their belief in Ala Émit and how such a conviction guided their way as they related to one another and land/nature. Anything that destabilizes such a worldview is bound to be met with a fierce antagonism. That is not savagery or hostility but a sense of freedom and autonomy under the aegis of Ala Émit.

As Christianity made its way from Esulalu to Mof Avvi areas, it did so by introducing foreign religious, agricultural and economic practices. Here I am building on insights drawn from Palmeri, Berghen and Manga and my own ideas as a Diola whose grandparents call Mof Avvi home. The Island of Carabane was an entry point for both French Christian missionaries and colonial officials (see figure 2). Efforts to spread Christianity from 1880 onward, as I mentioned earlier, were marred with difficulties and it was not until 1926 that some missionaries reached Mof Avvi and churches were built in Enampor, Séléki, Badiate, Esil, and Bandial. Intriguingly, most of the converts managed to contextualize their newfound Christian faith by exercising some aspects of their Diola religion.[79] In fact, this was not a new development. This is how the Diola negotiated

77. Baum, "Emergence," 394–95.

78. Palmeri, *Living with the Diola*, 78–79; Berghen and Manga, *Introduction*, 204–5.

79. Berghen and Manga, *Introduction*, 204–5.

life amidst colonial occupation. The encounters between the Holy Ghost Fathers' presentations of the Christian message to the Esulalu Diola engendered various responses as noted by Baum. He observes five crucial patterns in the process of what might be termed conversion.

> First, there is the sudden and far-reaching conversion in which one embraces a new faith fully. In this case old ways appear to have given way in a radical shift of one's life orientation. This is exceedingly rare and is difficult to analyse. In the second pattern, there is a decisive shift of religious authority, but one in which the paradigms of Christian thought are only partially incorporated . . . In the third method, that of indigenisation, the convert attempts to resolve the tension between religious systems by bringing to his new religion the spiritual and moral questions of the old . . . In the fourth pattern, a syncretic mode, the new Christian maintains a dual allegiance by recognising two sources of religious authority. He develops a sense of each faith having its own areas of knowledge and expertise as well as its own areas of ignorance or error. Finally, there is the alternative of reconversion, a return to the traditional faith and a rejection of Christianity. In this mode the tension between two systems of thought becomes too intense and the convert resolves the conflict by abandoning the newer tradition and embracing his former religion. This fifth mode has been the most frequently used and has been a means for the introduction of Christian ideas into Diola religion.[80]

One should be reminded that the Christianity being spread at the time included some aspects of France's civilizing mission through education. The work of Fathers Picardia in the Casamance (1876–83), Dodds (1947), the Holy Heart Sisters (1950–53), and the Holy Ghost Fathers and Sisters of Saint Joseph-de Cluny (1911) in the Casamance won converts to Catholicism. As in the Islamic case, most Diola converts assimilated the missionary version of Christianity with Diola extant faith traditions.[81] As it were, in addition to their own religion, Diola people were exposed to two cultures (European and Arabic) with their religions and thought forms. They negotiated both through their traditional lens of Ala Émit with devastating consequences—displaced subsistence-based economy, and as noted earlier, gendered and hierarchical society.

---

80. Baum, "Emergence," 375–76.
81. Diédhiou, *Riz*, 162–63.

To conclude, Diola people in pre-colonial Casamance believe in a deity called Ala Émit—a nomenclature variation found among the subgroups. Put differently, these spelling variations are a function of the various groups that make up the larger group generally known as Diola people of the Casamance. Diola people are by nature rice farmers who depend on the rainy season. For most of them, the deity created a balanced cosmos with inextricable relationships between creatures and the earth/land. In this sphere of existence, humans must diligently negotiate with nature, namely the land/earth as the deity has already caused her to produce by responsibly relating to her as a subject. This human-nature relationship is in turn human-nature and deity relationship. The nature of this relationship as far as humans are concerned is what I have come to call the delicate *mutual participatory human agency,* a relationship I believe is echoed by scripture in Gen 1:1–3, 10–12, 26–31; 2:7–10, 18–23; Lev 25:1–2; Deut 11:10–12; 15:1–11. Senghorian poetics of Négritude and the contextualization of "school curriculum"[82] did much to reposition Senegalese people to embrace their culture. In his reading of the Bible, Senghor also repositioned Diola people to reclaim some aspects of their farming practices suitable to the environment—a lesson ecologically mindful scholars and persons of faith can learn. I will now turn to reading scripture in conversation with Diola human-nature relationship.

82. Baum, "Emergence," 391.

3

The Divine–Human–Nature Relationship in Israel and Her Neighbors

> The land shall not be sold in perpetuity, for the land is mine;
> with me you are but aliens and tenants. Throughout the land
> that you hold, you shall provide for the redemption of the land.
> —Lev 25:23–24 (NRSV)

> The wolf shall live with the lamb,
> the leopard shall lie down with the kid,
> the calf and the lion and the fatling together,
> and a little child shall lead them.
> The cow and the bear shall graze,
> their young shall lie down together;
> and the lion shall eat straw like the ox. —Isa 11:6–7 (NRSV)

> We know that the whole creation has been groaning in labor
> pains until now; and not only the creation, but we ourselves,
> who have the first fruits of the Spirit, groan inwardly while we
> wait for adoption, the redemption of our bodies. —Rom 8:22–23

> May Mother Earth, who is fertile in crops and livestock, present
> Ceres with a crown of corn; may Jove's wholesome showers and
> breezes nourish all that she brings forth. —Horace, *Carm.* 30

This chapter discusses and compares the divine, human-nature relationship in the Bible and some Ancient Near Eastern faith traditions to the

Diola sustainable farming practices and the roles of empires in the making. It shows how some Greco-Roman literary traditions affirm similar concerns. As I noted in the previous chapter, the chilling awareness of impending ecological crises should we fail to devise and exercise effective ways to slow down, counter or even stop global warming, pervades our media outlets. Biblical scholarship is increasingly mindful of this reality and is revisiting scripture in an assiduous quest to provide an adequate and lasting response to this dilemma. This noble vision is being impeded by unresolved debates marred by profit. I mean good and actionable solutions being tested by scientists and seasoned farmers are often impeded by an unwavering capitalistic mindset that shrewdly succeeds in convincing many Westerners that exploitation of nature and insatiable acquisition of nature's resources in the name of technological advancement and economic opulence is a divine mandate. Blame it on the haunting interpretation of Gen 1:28, right? We can do better!

My question is whether scripture and other ancient texts offer some clues to understanding symbiotic human-nature relationship in biblical and Greco-Roman antiquity. About forty years ago, W. D. Davies lamented over the scant attention biblical studies paid to the pervasive importance of the Land and Jerusalem as geographical center of the world in scripture, Talmudic, and pseudepigraphic texts. This is inconceivable, according to Davies, since the birth of Israel, the significance of Jerusalem, and the Temple are inextricably linked to the Land once promised to Israel's ancestors as testified by the Torah, the prophets, wisdom literature, Josephus, and some Jewish authors.

The following biblical passages bespeak the connectivity between creatures and the land, and human participatory agency to care for God's land and creation as a whole is emphasized by many Torah (Gen 1:10–12; 1:26–2:24; Lev 25:1–2; Exod 20:8–11; Deut 5:12–15; 11:10–12; 15:1–11), prophetic (Jer 12; 23:10, 23–24; Amos 8:4–6; 9:14–15; Hos 4:1–3) and wisdom (Ps 8; 19; 104; 148; Job 38–41) voices. Scholarly attempts to distinguish Israel's concept of how the divine relates to her land from that of her neighbors led to a near-Platonism that haunts biblical studies to this day. Except for a handful of voices noted earlier and remarkable Catholic thinkers, especially ecofeminists,[1] for centuries scholarship focused more on the reconstruction of the history and religious traditions of the Hebrews, Israelites, Jews and systematization of selective Rabbinic and

---

1. Davies, *The Gospel and the Land*, 4–5. Ragaz, *Die Bibel Eine Deutung Erster Band*, 29, insists that humans dare not usurp the role of the creator in creation.

Christian theological themes.[2] Some concerned theologians maintained that divine care for nature can be found among non-biblical traditions[3]— an argument I am making in this book. In a crucial article, James H. Cone made profound remarks in which he called both ecologically minded "white middle class" and activists for black liberation to reposition their well-intentioned and yet compartmentalized causes to deal with race relations and environment justice. In other words, to stand solely for environmental justices without dismantling racism or advocating freedom for blacks only and other marginalized peoples is pointless. He writes:

> Ecology touches every sphere of human existence. It is not just an elitist or a white middle class issue. A clean safe environment is a human and civil rights issue that impacts the lives of poor blacks and other marginal groups. We therefore must not let the fear of distracting from racism blind us to the urgency of the ecological crisis. What good is it to eliminate racism if we are not around to enjoy a racist free environment? The survival of the earth, therefore, is a moral issue for everybody. If we do not save the earth from destructive human behavior, no one will survive. That fact alone ought to be enough to inspire people of all colors to join hands in the fight for a just and sustainable planet.[4]

Senghor and my Mof Avvi Diola compatriots would have agreed with Cone. It is important to reiterate that the Senghorian perspective on divine transcendence and immanence is shaped by his Sereer faith traditions and Chardenian thought. That being said, to explore the divine-human-nature relationship in scripture, an analysis of some ancient myths of creation is expedient. I will look at Mesopotamian, biblical and Greco-Roman myths for actionable clues.

Creation Myths, Nonhuman, and Human Creatures

Most scholars have long maintained that biblical creation stories share much in common with those found in Mesopotamia. These accounts of creation come from periods in which people were used to expressing

2. Albertz, *A History of Israelite Religion*.

3. Keel and Schroer, *Creation*, 4–15.

4. Cone, "Whose Earth Is It Anyways? 41–42; 36–46. He also cites key Womanist theologians who have been doing much to ensure that freedom for people of African descent and the alienated does not preclude environment justice.

their ideas and beliefs in stories called myths. It is unfortunate that the word "myth" is commonly used today to refer to something that is not true. A myth may be defined as a story full of symbolism that delves deeper than scientific or historic facts to express basic truths about life which are difficult to express in any other way. Myths therefore express the common view of life held by a whole group of people, rather than that of an isolated individual. They are told and transmitted from one generation to the next in order to pass on their insights and values. To me this is what creation stories mentioned above meant to convey as they are more concerned with why the cosmos was made, its meaning and the status of its creatures, than with how and when it was made.

Most introductory courses to the Hebrew Bible read these stories with variegated emphases comparing Gen 1:1–2:4a and 2:4b–24 with two famous Babylonian creation accounts: the *Enuma Elish* and *Atrahasis*.[5] Resulting comparisons often end up pinning the Babylonian creation story against the Genesis accounts with the latter being more progressive and therefore theologically sounder. I am not ignoring or downplaying the differences among these stories. My question however is what might these texts inform us about the relationship between the deity, humans, and nature? In other words, what is the role of divine and human agencies in nature? Does nature play any significant role in human life? Do animals and vegetation matter at all? I will briefly discuss the *Enuma Elish*, Gen 1–2, and some Greek stories, especially some texts from Hesiod's *Theogony*.

The *Enuma Elish*, written between 1700 and 1200 BCE, predates our Genesis account and tells of the creation of the cosmos, everything in it and how *Marduk* became the supreme deity;[6] thus according to Rosemary Radford Ruether, we have both a cosmogony and theogony.[7] *Apsu* and *Tiamat* were the primal formless deities from whose watery mixture birthed a generation of deities, the earth, and the heavens.[8] The creation

5. Pritchard, ed., *Ancient Near Eastern Texts*, 3–11; 60–101. For more creation stories, see Beyerlin, ed., *Near Eastern Religious Texts*, 3–12; 68–99. Almost every culture has its creation myths written or told from its cultural construction of meaning (see *Oxford Handbook of African Myths*).

6. Tiamat is the god of salty waters and Apsu the god of fresh waters. The creation of humans in both the *Enuma Elish* and *Atrahasis* resolves the conflict among the younger and older gods and in relieving them from work, humans become servants of the gods.

7. Ruether, *Gaia & God*, 15–22.

8. Trible, *God and the Rhetoric of Sexuality*, 18.

of the skies, land and horizon is linked to the Tigris and Euphrates Rivers. *Apsu* proposed a theocide—that is the extermination of the younger gods because of their irritating noise—a decision *Tiamat* vehemently opposed. Upon learning *Apsu's* plan, the younger gods decided to kill him just to have *Tiamat* take them on. As a plan is being hashed out to face *Tiamat*, *Marduk* introduced a *quid pro quo* that he be made supreme god once he kills *Tiamat*. As the story goes, he defeats and dismembers *Tiamat*, creates the universe, and then kills Kingu whose blood he mixes with mud to make humans as slaves for the gods.[9] As Brigitte Kahl observes, not only were humans reduced to a servile status to work the earth, the earth itself was enslaved.[10] One of the many names *Marduk* received during his enthronement was "lord of the lands," that is to say one who governs nature. Put differently, *Marduk* was the source of all life in heaven and earth and directed nature. An intriguing biblical reference has the God of Israel giving lands and wild animals to the king of Babylon, Nebuchadnezzar.

> It is I who by my great power and my outstretched arm have made the earth, with the people and animals that are on the earth, and I give it to whomever I please. Now I have given all these lands into the hand of King Nebuchadnezzar of Babylon, my servant, and I have given him even the wild animals of the field to serve him. (Jer 27:5–6; cf. 28:14)

The relationship among God, humans, animals, and the environment is evident in Gen 1–2 and 6:1–9:31. Other than Gen 2:15 that focuses on working the land/earth, scholars attribute the remaining passages to the priestly (P) author(s) whose concern for creation and her relationship to God is explicit and unwavering. In the world of biblical studies, one can hardly speak of any unanimity among scholars on how one should interpret Gen 1–3. Contestations gravitate around the syntax of Gen 1:1–3—a reality that should be expected in biblical interpretation since modern exegetes are by no means disinterested readers as evident in the following translations of the Hebrew text.

> In the beginning when God created the heavens and the earth, the earth was a formless void and darkness covered the face of the deep, while a wind from God swept over the face of the

---

9. In the myth of *Atrahasis*, younger deities grew weary of working for their seniors and went on a strike. The conflict was resolved as their leader was killed and his blood mixed with clay to create humans to be slaves for the gods.

10. Kahl, "Fratricide and Ecocide," 55.

waters. Then God said, "Let there be light"; and there was light. (Gen 1:1–3, NRSV)

When God began to create heaven and earth—the earth being unformed and void, with darkness over the surface of the deep and a wind from God sweeping over the water—God said, "Let there be light"; and there was light. (Gen 1:1–3, Tanak)

The question is what in reality does Gen 1:1–3 mean to convey? In the current stage of the debates some interpreters render Gen: 1:1a "In the beginning God created . . ." while others insist on "When God began to create . . ." as the most appropriate interpretation.[11] The first reading presupposes a creation out of nothing and the latter argues for a divinely ordered creation from extant materials. This work builds on the latter reading maintained by Sarna, Westermann, and Brueggemann,[12] just to name a few.

Brueggemann observes that the Hebrew Bible embeds "Israel's practice of testimony," a two-dimensional conversation that is a divine address to Israel and to which Israel responds. Put differently, the text itself "is *Israel's testimony* that God has spoken so."[13] This conversation, to me, is a lens to unlocking the divine and human-nature relationship experienced by Israel. Seen that way, Israel speaks from her lived experience of divine creativity, faithfulness, deliverance, love, and sustenance of which Brueggemann eloquently writes. Israel's speech, "is ordered by strong, transformative verbs with Yahweh, the active agent, as subject, acting on a variety of direct objects, whose shape and destiny are completely in the

---

11. I will not rehearse these debates but would point to Wenham, *Genesis 1–15*, 11–15, who discusses the traditional reading and its counterpart. For detailed discussions on ways of reading Gen 1:1–3, see G. F. Hasel and M. G. Hasel, "The Unique Cosmology of Genesis 1," who highlight the interpretive trends on Gen 1:1–3 while arguing for the former with a clear emphasis on distancing the Genesis account from the *Enuma Elish*. While there are crucial distinctions between the two accounts, both stories share much in common. I do not think, however, that seeing the Genesis accounts as more progressive and authentic helps. My point is that both stories say something crucial about human origins and their relationship to the respective deity: Marduk (who is not creator) in the *Enuma Elish* or God (creator who orders) in the Hebrew Bible.

12. Brueggemann, *Theology of the Old Testament*, 153; Nahum, *Genesis*, 3; C. Westermann, *Genesis 1–11*, 93–112. Of the three, Westermann has the most extensive discussion of the readings of Gen 1:1–3.

13. Brueggemann, *Theology of the Old Testament*, 117.

hands of the subject of the verbs."[14] Israel bears witness to the acts of the God who creates, shapes, directs by ordering extant matter (Gen 1:2–10), and endows it with productive powers [earth, the fauna, the flora, and humans (Gen 1:11–12, 26)]. This is clearly conveyed by the Hebrew text itself in the syntax of Gen 1:11–12—the imperfect 3rd person feminine hiphil "to cause to sprout" from דשׁא/daša' (LXX βλαστάνω, "to grow," "to sprout" or to "blossom") with the earth as its subject (Gen 1:11). The earth is caused to produce by the speaker who, in this case, is God the creator.

> Then God said, "Let the earth put forth vegetation (דשׁא): plants yielding seed, and fruit trees of every kind on earth that bear fruit with the seed in it." And it was so. The earth brought forth vegetation: plants yielding seed of every kind, and trees of every kind bearing fruit with the seed in it. And God saw that it was good. (Gen. 1:11–12 NRSV)

> And God said, "Let the earth sprout vegetation (יצא): seed-bearing plants, fruit trees of every kind on earth that bear fruit with the seed in it." And it was so. The earth brought forth vegetation: seed-bearing plants of every kind, and trees of every kind bearing fruit with the seed in it. And God saw that this was good. (Gen. 1:11–12 Tanak)

This same hiphil force continues with reference to the productive role of the earth יצא in v. 12a (LXX ἐκφέρω, "to bear, to bring forth").[15] Although the imperatival command is noted by the LXX, all the verbs are in the aorist active indicative with the earth as subject: "Earth becomes God's agent. Nature carries responsibilities on behalf of God."[16]

The words דשׁא/daša' in v. 11 and יצא/yaṣa' in v. 12 convey an intriguing mutual-relational role as the earth responds by producing vegetation at the divine command—distinct and yet interconnected creatures: plants, grass, and trees. The divine jussive and cohortative syntaxes in divine speech signal the mutual participatory divine intention—the former is consultative, the latter responsive; as Terence Fretheim convincingly evinces "'let there be' leaves room for creaturely response (vv. 11, 24); the cohortative 'let us make' (v. 26) leaves room for consultation (v. 26);

14. Brueggemann, *Theology of the Old Testament*, 135.

15. *HALOT*, "דשׁא," 2175; *HALOT*, "יצ," 3886; *LEH*, "βλαστάνω," and "ἐκφέρω." See discussion in Sarna, *Genesis*, 9; C. Westermann, *Genesis 1–11*, 124.

16. Trible, "The Dilemma of Dominion," 29; Trible, *God and the Rhetoric*, 25.

'let them have dominion' (v. 26) entails a sharing of power."[17] Nonhuman and human creatures have a relational role to exercise consistent with the divine creative intention. Genesis 1:24–31, as one unit, offers keen insights into the divine consultative tone and intention. The plural "us," whether taken to mean divine court, council, or a mere divine self-intentional reflection, underscores a relational intentionality presented as a non-negotiable divine ownership and vision that invites a mutual response from creatures. In other words, divine speech:

> often involves a speaking with whatever is already created (vv. 11, 20, 22, 24, 28) in such a way the receptor of the word helps shape the result. While God's work creates the potential for this creaturely response, it is creation from within the creation, not from without. Both the human and nonhuman creatures are called to participate in the creative activity made possible by God . . . Verses 11–13 witness to a shift in God's way of creating; the earth itself participates in the creative process . . . the description of the plants and trees with their capacity to reproduce by themselves gives evidence for probing interest in what we would call science . . . Israel has not yet related plant growth to the sun, ascribing it entirely to the powers of the earth.[18]

As preposterous as these notions may sound to skeptics, the idea that nonhumans are interlocutors responding to God pervades Scripture (Gen 1:11–13; Exod 7:1–12:51; Num 22; 1 Kgs 17:6; Mark 1:13, just to list a few). The creation of landed, creeping, other living, and human creatures on the sixth day (Gen 1:24–31) emphasizes their common origin as earth creatures—a connection humans should learn to embrace. In fact, the Diola prophet Aline Sitoé Diatta instituted the sixth day as a Diola day of rest—that is a Diola Sabbath,[19] so to speak. I will return to the Diola Day of Rest later. The language describing the relationship among creatures has been vigorously debated. As I noted above, humans are created by God, set apart but also summoned to exercise a crucial relational role in line with God's plan. Humans are commanded to be "fruitful and multiply," and "fill the earth and subdue it;" and "have dominion over land and sea creatures" (Gen 1:28, NRSV). Ecologically minded scholars call for a rereading of this passage due to the strong verbs such as

17. Fretheim, "The Book of Genesis," 343.

18. Fretheim, "The Book of Genesis," 343–44. To me, both the earth and sun play their unique and yet symbiotic roles in creation.

19. Girard, Genèse, 218. See also Baum, " Innovation," 270.

multiply (Gen 1:28), cultivate, and keep/care (Gen 2:15) that emphasize how humans might relate to God's creation. Has God outsourced divine governance to humans or do the words "subdue" and "govern" beg for alternative interpretations?

As he looks at much of Christian history and its reception of Gen 1:26–28, White writes:

> While many of the world's mythologies provide stories of creation, Greco-Roman mythology was singularly incoherent in this respect . . . In sharp contrast, Christianity inherited from Judaism not only a concept of time as nonrepetitive and linear but also a striking story of creation. By gradual stages a loving and all-powerful God had created light and darkness, the heavenly bodies, the earth and all its plants, animals, birds, and fishes. Finally, God had created Adam and, as an afterthought, Eve to keep man from being lonely. Man named all the animals, thus establishing his dominance over them. God planned all of this explicitly for man's benefit and rule: no item in the physical creation had any purpose save to serve man's purposes. And, although man's body is made of clay, he is not simply part of nature: he is made in God's image. Especially in its Western form, Christianity is the most anthropocentric religion the world has seen.[20]

Upholding Saint Francis of Assisi as a model, White warns that the "ecological crisis" will continue to deteriorate "until we reject the Christian axiom that nature has no reason for existence save to serve man."[21]

In her insightful essay entitled "Fratricide and Ecocide," Kahl insists that God's creation in Gen 1–2 is one based on a mutual relationship anchored and sustained by *'ădāmâ*—the primal mother-like matter.[22] To me, this mutuality of which Kahl spoke should force the Bible-reading world to relinquish the idea that God created nature just for humans to exploit servilely[23] and embrace a symbiotic relationship instead. Terms like *kābaš* "subdue/subjugate" and *rādā* "domininate" in Gen 1:28a call for an alternative interpretation. James Barr thinks these verbs would have made sense only after the flood when humans were authorized to

20. White, "Historical Roots," 1205.

21. White, "Historical Roots," 1207.

22. Kahl, " Fratricide and Ecocide," 54–55.

23. Kahl, "Fratricide and Ecocide," 55, sees the kind of service the earth needs which humans are created to exercise—that is an "earth slavery" but not "slave labor in the ordinary social sense."

consume meat. The initial command to eat fruits and vegetables (Gen 1:29–30; 2:9–10 compared with Gen 2:17; 3:1–22, 9:4) had more to do with the human role—a caring and responsible "leadership."[24] Trible understands these verbs to describe a "hierarchy of harmony"[25]—one that is responsible but not domineering, and Kahl uses "mutuality."[26] Harmonious hierarchy and mutualism are very much part of how Diola people understand life and how it should be negotiated with other creatures—human and non-human alike. Senghor also sees this relationship permeating the cosmos.[27]

The readings of Gen 1–2 offered by Trible and Kahl are quite fascinating and my Diola elders would have welcomed them wholeheartedly. The connotations of "subdue" and "rule," as domineering as they may sound, embed a symbiotic relationship, especially when one considers Gen 1:1–3, 10–28 and Gen 2:7–10, 15. When these verses are read in isolation, however, one cannot help but hear incongruent and terrifying words from creator God who, for reasons that defy human explanation, confuses the very creation the deity describes as "good" with something to objectify, dominate, occupy, and exploit. According to Brueggemann, the Hebrew slave—now liberated Israel—is a human agent summoned by God to be a participatory human agent. Although God is the causative force empowering the earth to carry out her productive function, a participatory function of the earth as agent is implicitly conveyed. Israel is invited to relate to the land on its own terms as subject and not object. Just as God empowered the earth to produce, the sky is empowered to rain at God's command to water the land (Deut 11:10–13).

> For the land . . . is not like the land of Egypt, from which you have come, where you sow your seed and irrigate by foot like a vegetable garden. But the land that you are crossing over to occupy is a land of hills and valleys, watered by rain from the sky, a land that the LORD your God looks after. The eyes of the LORD your God are always on it, from the beginning of the year to the end of the year. If you will only heed his every commandment that I am commanding you today—loving the LORD your God, and serving him with all your heart and with all your soul—then he will give the rain for your land in its season, the early rain and

24. Barr, "Man and Nature," 31, see 19–32.

25. Trible, "Dilemma of Dominion," 29.

26. Kahl, "Fratricide and Ecocide," 54–55.

27. Senghor, *Liberté 3*, 311.

the later rain, and you will gather in your grain, your wine, and
your oil; and he will give grass in your fields for your livestock,
and you will eat your fill (Deut. 11:10–15, NRSV).

Liberated and obedient Israel will no longer depend on the Nile River to
irrigate her farms as she once did as slaves in Egypt.

Many but certainly not all biblical experts failed to see the divine
concern for the fauna and flora. God sustaining the life of nature and
human beings is central to Israel's veneration of the deity as rhythmed by
the festivals Israel was summoned to observe. Animals are just as much
subjects as human beings were in the sight of God. Frank Crüsemann
observes:

> The exclusive veneration of the God of Israel took the form of
> a praxis that from the very beginning included what we call
> nature. . . The seasonal rhythm of the annual festivals and the
> completely independent week participate in this, as well as the
> offering of the firstborn of animals (Deut 15:19ff.) and firstfruits
> . . . or the relations to animals in customs of sacrifice and food
> . . . An animal is not a thing for the Mishpahtim but a subject
> of law, for whom the death penalty applies as it does to guilty
> people . . . which as we know has been practiced in the west until
> modern times.[28]

Clearly Baal owns and affects the land by raining and making the land
fertile for human sustenance—a role Israel "transferred to Yahweh,"[29] as
Davies insists, with some innovations. In Israel's memory, God causes
rain to make the land produce for the deity's people (Deut 11:10–12, 14–
15, 17). God is the landlord and Israel a tenant who is sternly summoned
to offer the land's firstling back to God (Lev 18:24; Deut 14:22; 26:9–15,
21), farm it wisely by making room for gleanings (Lev, 19:9; 23:22; Deut
26:21) and ensure she observes her Sabbath (Lev 25:2–4).[30] Doing otherwise would undermine the agency of the land (Gen 1:10–11). Israel
is to faithfully respond to God and God's land through its ordering of
its times, seasons, and festivals as spiritual service.[31] Davies thinks ex-

28. Crüsemann, *The Torah*, 261, cites Exod 21:18 and Gen 9:5 to highlight the
kind of administration of justice Israel is called to actualize based on what I call the
human–nature relationship except that in this case one has the human–fauna relation
before God.

29. Davies, *Gospel and the Land*, 12.

30. Milgrom, *Leviticus*, 298–316; Davies, *Gospel and the Land*, 28–29. See also
Brueggemann, *The Land*, 59–62.

31. Brueggemann, *The Land*, 1–83; Harrelson, *From Fertility Cult*, 1–18.

ile and colonial displacement during the Maccabean period might have been due to the violation of the personified significance of the land of which God warned Israelites to ensure they observe. The interrelationships among God, the land and Israel were rooted in Divine justice to God's creation. Israel as an addressable agent is called to replicate divine justice to humans, land and the created order. The divine ordering of time spearheaded by God's rest is paradigmatic for an agrarian people as we will see in the language of the Sabbath and Jubilee to which I now turn.

Creation, Sabbath, and Jubilee:
A Biblical Agrarian Vision of Sustainable Life

This subtitle offers some clues into how some biblical voices understood God's invitation of Israel to heed divine imperatives and serve as co-creator primarily in the role of tenancy. James Muilenburg writes that the Hebrew:

> knew that he had been addressed, that he had been told what was required of him; and he knew perfectly well when and where he had been told, what the demands were which were incumbent upon him, and Who it was Who had exacted of him such demands. He knew perfectly well that he had not been confronted with ethical abstractions, but rather had been addressed by One who had spoken to him in the events of the great tradition of which he was a part, to which he inwardly belonged, and which described him as a person. What is good is what God requires; what is evil is what God forbids. Yet this is not the manner of the divine speaking; rather, God confronts his people with the basic imperative of all biblical speech: *"Hear my voice!"*[32]

One non-negotiable aspect of this divine voice of which Muilenburg speaks, I would argue, is that Israel must never forget the land belongs to God (Lev 25:23). Creation and divine–nonhuman–human rest are inextricably linked and they both embed an agrarian vision for a sustainable subsistence economy and farming practices. As I already argued in chapter one, creation, as participatory agent in the co-creative process, was empowered by God according to the divine command (Gen 10–12; 28). The initial creative (Gen 1:1–9) and resulting co-creative (Gen 1:10) processes were marked by divine rest (שׁבת/*šabbat*, Gen 2:2–3). It is an integral dimension that anchors the divine–nature human relationship.

32. Muilenburg, *Way of Israel*, 15.

The initial divine creative act (ברא/*bara'* marked by the strong verb and the participatory responses of earth, land, and vegetation to God's invitation/call co-creative acts are framed by the same verb ברא/*bara'* "created/creates" (Gen 1:1; 2:2–3)—the seventh day. Although the Sabbath is thought to have been invented by Israel and its religious significance lively debated,[33] the socioeconomic, ethical, and theological motif echoes the divine concerns for nonhuman and human mutuality mentioned elsewhere in the Hebrew Bible in the intertextual context of Gen 2:2–3; Exod 20:10; 23:12 and Deut 5:14. David M. Gordis saw this rationale and posited that:

> Through narrative, poetry, law, and prayer, the Bible conditions its readers to feel reverence for nature, enjoins restraint in the exploitation of natural resources for human needs, elicits awe in response to the diversity and complexity of creation, and articulates the principle of human responsibility for faithful trusteeship over the natural world. Beginning with the Creation narrative in Genesis, every component of the Hebrew Bible is a strand in the fabric that defines the biblical approach to issues of ecology. Human beings are commanded: "Be fertile and increase, fill the earth and master it; and rule the fish of the sea, the birds of the sky, and all the living things that creep on the earth" (Gen 1:28) . . . The commandment to be fertile and master the earth is understood as directed primarily to the obligation to procreate, not to dominate or to exploit.[34]

Divine rest (Sabbath) and its ecological significance rests on how one reads Gen 2:2–3 in relation to other passages such as the one noted above. The aorist, κατέπαυσεν [Gen 2:2–3 (LXX)] means both God "rested" or "left off"[35] and was the subject behind all that existed, namely an orderly good space for life. The causative meaning of the verb κατέπαύω hints at the idea that God caused the already empowered participatory agencies to rest.[36] This might have been the reason for Philo's interesting argument. In spite of his assertion that God caused created participatory agents to rest while (δραστήριος) energizing them (Philo, *De Cher.* 87,

---

33. Harrelson, *From Fertility Cult*, 21.

34. Gordis, "Ecology," 1369.

35. Hiebert, *Genesis*, 7.

36. LEH, "κατέπαύω," 322. *EDNT* agrees with BDAG in rendering the primary meaning of κατέπαύω "to cause to cease, stop, bring to an end" or "to cause to rest, rest."

86–90; *Leg. All.* 1.5–6), Philo admits that the deity rested; especially τὰ θνητὰ γένη παύεται πλάττων "from forming the species of mortal creatures" (Philo, *Leg. All.* 1:16). Philo's perspective on divine rest of Gen 2:3 is not unique; some Rabbinic voices held a similar view according to R. Alan Culpepper.[37]

For our purpose, it suffices to note that since human participatory agency as co-creator with God was integral to the divine creative process (Gen 1:26–28; 2:15), God's rest served to order Israelite agrarian life, especially for an exilic and postexilic community, caution against greed, and the temptation to engage in self-serving labor, and summon Sabbath observance. As Brueggemann has it, the celebration of God's day of rest is "an assertion that life does not depend upon feverish activity of self-securing, but there can be a pause in which life is given to us simply as a gift."[38] Creation is good and "can be improved upon by no human work" because she is the source of abundant life, satisfaction,[39] mystical experience, and health.[40] The didactic aspect of Sabbath observance in the life of Israel found its clearest illustration in the Exodus story. Israel liberated from the harsh servitude to Pharaoh must learn that the divine rest introduced in Gen 2:2–3 does not preclude or inhibit God's work of sustenance in her most vulnerable moments (Exod 15:22–27 and 17:1–7). The wilderness' *mana-menu* Israel ate was a nonnegotiable

> alternative to the oppressive Egyptian economy (Exod 16:6). 'Bread rain from heaven' symbolizes fertility as Divine gift, a process that begins with rain and ends with bread . . . The manna is thus a 'test' to see if Israel will follow instructions on how to 'gather' this gift . . . The people's first lesson outside of Egypt, then, is an economic one. I believe it represents a parable about the primal value of the most basic human competence - hunting/gathering and local horticulture—the cooperative, egalitarian lifeway that sustained human beings for tens of thousands of years prior to the rise of concentrated agriculture, cities and eventually imperial economies based on slavery.[41]

37. Culpepper, "Children of God," 27, citing Dodd, *The Interpretation*, 320–23.

38. Brueggemann, *Genesis*, 35.

39. Myers, *The Biblical Vision*, 10. I believe creation is "mystical" (rather than "magical" as Myers has it) to avoid the kind of misinterpretation associated with magic.

40. See Gen 2:9; 3:22, 24; Prov 3:18; 11:30; 13:12; 15:4; Rev 2:7; 22:2, 14, 19; 4 Ezra 2:12; 8:52; 18:16.

41. Myers, *Biblical Vision*, 11.

The alternative vision God was etching in the memory of liberated Israel was the inextricability of life and creation, life and land, life and sustainable economy[42]—a reality Israel must not only understand but also practice through life-ordering events: the festivals. The land God gave to Israel precludes any modern idea of gift. The land is a relational subject and source of life humans share with other creatures—an exhaustible gift when shared mutually. In spite of persistent setbacks, this divine vision was meant to be actualized by Israel in her observance of the Divine Rest that rhythms all the other festivals and life. Biblical authors made this clear when they have Divine Rest preset "the appointed feasts (Lev 23:3)" and "community work-stoppages define each of the main observances: Passover (23:6f); *Shavuot* (23:21); Feast of Atonement (23:24, 31); and Booths (23:35f)."[43]

Scholars have long argued that the Jubilee was not fully observed as prescribed in the Bible. Humans, as illustrated in the life of liberated Israel, often failed to hear and observe the Sabbath but also appropriately gather the manna. There is no evidence that these violations of the divine vision ever ceased. Some biblical voices suggest that there were some in ancient Israel who heeded and observed not just the Sabbath but also strove to keep the Jubilee and other festivals.[44]

Israel as a result must be vigilant as she exercised the Mosaic egalitarian version of community enshrined in the Covenant, Holiness and Deuteronomic Codes (Exod 20:22–23:33; Lev 17–26; and Deut 12–26). The leadership of Israel must heed this divine voice and shun, at all cost, corrupt, and self-serving leadership. Unfortunately, divine attempts to stymie Israel's desire for the kind of leadership that might lead to human exploitation was echoed in its costly and disastrous outcome for the people—a divine warning rejected by the elders of Israel and thereby invited upon themselves an existential suicide (1 Sam 8:1–22). Just as an unnamed new Egyptian king shrewdly obliterated any memory of Joseph and probably his God as a pretext to enslave and wipe out the Hebrews, so did an Israelite monarchy that managed to do away with the delicate

---

42. Brueggemann, *Land*; Habel, *Land is Mine*; Myers, *Biblical Vision*; Russell, *Space, Land, Territory*.

43. Myers, *Biblical Vision*, rightly sees how land as God's gift to Israel should be shared to avoid its exploitation as well as that of community members. This divine vision is actualized by Israel in her observance of divine rest that rhythmed all the other festivals.

44. Weinfeld, *Social Justice in Ancient Israel*, 152–78.

Mosaic egalitarian vision. Samuel's ire against such a move was met with divine reluctance followed by stern divine warnings about the ways of kingship. King David was the first to part with the Mosaic egalitarian vision.[45] According to Brueggemann it was particularly Solomon who actualized a "self-serving" and "self-securing of the king and dynasty"—a program that gave rise to two social strata—wealthy and poor, namely economic opulence, social marginalization, and tamed religion.[46]

It is important to highlight the fact that the economic practices that threatened divinely instituted festivals meant to order Israelite agrarian practices and ensure equity predated the Roman occupation of Palestine. The rise of kingship in ancient Israel threatened the Mosaic egalitarian vision of agrarian life—a fact traceable back to the reign of Kings David and especially Solomon[47] whose exploitation of his compatriots was mimicked by many Israelite kings. Two texts offer a good illustration of the divine reluctance to sponsor the rise of the monarchy and subsequent monarchical abuses in ancient Israel.

> Samuel reported all the words of the LORD to the people who were asking him for a king. He said, "These will be the ways of the king who will reign over you: he will take your sons and appoint them to his chariots and to be his horsemen, and to run before his chariots; and he will appoint for himself commanders of thousands and commanders of fifties, and some to plow his ground and to reap his harvest, and to make his implements of war and the equipment of his chariots. He will take your daughters to be perfumers and cooks and bakers. He will take the best of your fields and vineyards and olive orchards and give them to his courtiers. He will take one-tenth of your grain and of your vineyards and give it to his officers and his courtiers. He will take your male and female slaves, and the best of your cattle and donkeys, and put them to his work. He will take one-tenth of your flocks, and you shall be his slaves. And in that day you will cry out because of your king, whom you have chosen for yourselves; but the LORD will not answer you in that day." (1 Sam 8:10–18)

45. Fager, *Land Tenure*, 85.

46. Brueggemann, *Prophetic Imagination*, 23. See also Grimsrud, "Healing Justice," 69–70.

47. Brueggemann, *Prophetic Imagination*, 21–37; Brueggemann, *The Land*, 74–83; Fager, *Land Tenure*, 86.

The rise of kingship was problematic and by the time of Rehoboam it became clearer to most Israelites that kinship was indeed oppressive. The ways of the king proved too burdensome as some Israelite elders thought future protective successors of Solomon should know. The following account captures their deepest concerns.

> "Your father made our yoke heavy. Now therefore lighten the hard service of your father and his heavy yoke that he placed on us, and we will serve you" . . . The king answered the people harshly. He disregarded the advice that the older men had given him and spoke to them according to the advice of the young men, "My father made your yoke heavy, but I will add to your yoke; my father disciplined you with whips, but I will discipline you with scorpions." (1 Kgs 12:4, 13–14, NRSV)

As the saying goes, the king has spoken so let it be done. As one might expect, kingship failed to serve as a caring and liberative mediator between God and many Israelites, especially most non-elites and farmers. Abuse of power (1 Kgs 11), Naboth's vineyard (1 Kgs 21 and 2 Kgs 9:21–26), Amos' ire against southern and northern priestly and elitist greed (Amos 2:4–16) all testify to the failure of kingship. The intertestamental period was not immune to exploitation of land and peasants by elites. Victor Tcherikover's comments on the role of tax farmers such as Joseph the To-biad[48] offer good insights into how elites related to peasantry during the Hellenistic period in Palestine. I will return to this reality in the Herodian period—Palestine in the time of Jesus.

The God of the Fauna and Flora

If the earth is God's according to the traditions explored thus far, then it goes without saying that the same can be said of every creature. The *Enuma Elish*'s portrayal of animals as monstrous and dreadful does not tell the whole story of how animals are viewed in antiquity. Material culture that predates or is contemporary to both *Enuma Elish* and *Atrahasis* provides alternative perspectives on divine and human-nature. Scripture, too, offers a mixed picture but insists that humans became a danger to the fauna after the flood (Gen 9:2). White's argument is well taken but did not go far enough in his historical analysis of the ecological crisis we face today. Although much of his take on Christianity as a culprit

---

48. Tcherikover, *Hellenistic Civilization and the Jews*, 126–62.

in worsening the ecological crises is well-taken, the human conquest of nature appears to have begun millennia ago. I am not trying to rationalize, excuse, or ignore the danger we pose to the environment. I concur with Keel and Schroer that sometime during "the Neolithic Revolution, around 10,000 BCE, humanity gradually shifted from purely consuming to partially producing its means of subsistence. With animal husbandry and farming, humans began in some aspect to be creator themselves."[49] This subtle change, I argue, would not have affected the climate globally as our industrialized world has to date. That being said, the shift has a profound effect because it was not limited just to agriculture.

In antiquity, the sacred was gradually affected in such a way that the "Divine Gamekeeper can no longer have served as the leading notion of the deity."[50] Images portraying the divine-nature relationship remained visually etched on some Mesopotamian stamp seals, sculptures, marble reliefs, and ivory carvings,[51] just to name a few. One particular aspect I would like to highlight is that of the divine and animal symbiotic relationship captured in visual representation of different species of animals playing and dancing as they are being entertained by their protector and lord. Of the Mesopotamian goddess Ninhursanga, Lang writes:

> As the Mother of Wildlife, she gives birth, she gives form to the unborn animal, and helps their mothers to give birth. After birth, she continues to love her animal children and laments their loss, whether they are killed by hunters or captured and tamed. While her original sphere of influence is wildlife, she can also be considered the tender mother of domesticated herd animals. Moreover, she can be said to preside over the birth of humans, and especially the birth of important individuals such as kings and lords.[52]

The picture of God in the Hebrew Bible as creator of nature and everything therein is clearly stated in Gen 1–2 and especially in Gen 1:22; 2:7–10, 15–20 as I have discussed above. This deity creates and sustains God's creatures (Gen 1–2; Job 38:39–41; 39:1–6; Ps 104:10–18, 24–28; Matt 6:26). Keel and Schroer rightly caution about essentialist views of human–nature relations. They insist that such a relationship "must have

49. Keel and Schroer, *Creation*, 23; Lang, *The Hebrew God*, 77–78.

50. Lang, *The Hebrew God*, 78.

51. Lang, *The Hebrew God*, 78–89; see also Keel and Schroer, *Creation*, 24–31; Keel and Uehlinger, *Gods, Goddesses*, 182–98.

52. Lang, *The Hebrew God*, 79–80.

been ambivalent from the very beginning. Anyone who gathered plants or even hunted wild animals knew themselves to be in a relationship of dependency and responsibility with Earth the Mother of Plants, the goddess of flocks, or the 'lord of the animals.'"[53]

In Scripture the flora and especially fauna were not the culprits for driving a wedge between God and humanity. A reading of Gen 3:1–7 raises troubling questions about how one might interpret the mysterious presence, character, and role of the נחש/naḥāš "serpent", especially as one of God's creatures. Since both the Priestly and the Yahwist authors concur that creation is good but never describe it as perfect, does this serpent symbolize that not-yet dimension of God's creation that requires the participatory role of the human agent? This is not the place to discuss all the views on the identity and role of this enigmatic creature. What is obvious in the story is that something happened in Eden that significantly disturbed God's creation—a plight the deity is determined to redeem (Gen 1–11). Textually, the serpent is described as one of the creatures God made and conceivably one among the many creatures the deity described as being good. It is also clear that only humans are given prohibitions. When Gen 1 is read with Gen 2–3, an intriguing picture emerges on how one might reread Gen 1:28 and 2:15. The syntax of Gen 3:1–17 offers a curious pun, as many exegetes point out, expressed by the words "shrewd" (ערום/'ārûm) and "naked" (ערומים/'arûmmîm) in Gen 3:2.[54] Nahum on the other hand thinks Gen 3:1–7 demythologizes the agency of the serpent from an entity "endowed with divine or semidivine qualities" to an "extraordinarily shrewd" creature of God who simply stirs up human desire.[55] Whether this is a pun or demythologization, David Carr convincingly argues that Gen 2–3 was redacted as a subversive story inspired by the futility of human wisdom as some exilic returnees saw their hopes for a new start dashed.[56] At any rate, the role of the serpent appears to be a symbolic function of the failed human participatory agency— much like Job's prosecuting attorney (Job 1:6–8, 12; 2:1–4, 6–7; cf. Zech 3:2) the creature in Eden raises a profound question about divine and human-nature relationship. In other words, how should humans exercise the divine command to rādâ "have dominion," kābaš, "rule, subdue, or

53. Keel and Schroer, Creation, 23.

54. Wenham, Genesis, 72; Fretheim, "Genesis," 359.

55. Sarna, Genesis, 24.

56. Carr, "Politics of Textual Subversion," 577–95.

subjugate" (Gen 1:28) *ʿābad* "cultivate or serve," *šāmar* "watch or care for" (Gen 2:15), and obey God's prohibition not to *ʾākal* "eat" (Gen 2:17) from the "tree of the knowledge of good and evil."

> "Let the earth bring forth living creatures of every kind: cattle and creeping things and wild animals of the earth of every kind." (Gen 1:24 NRSV)

> "Let us make humankind in our image . . ." (Gen 1:26 NRSV)

> ". . . the LORD God formed man from the dust of the ground, and breathed into his nostrils the breath of life; and the man became a living being." (Gen 2:7 NRSV)

> ". . . out of the ground the LORD God formed every animal of the field and every bird of the air . . ." (Gen 2:19 NRSV)

This is not the place to annotate all the conclusions reached by scholars on the content and message of Gen 1–3. For reasons that might have risen from exilic experiences, the priestly author(s) counters the Yahwist's vision of human-nature relationship as imitation of divine care—a divine-like human care of God's creation. The resulting unresolved tension between Gen 1:28 and Gen 2:15 leaves two competing voices at once—*ʿābad* "cultivate/serve," and *šāmar* "care for/watch" versus *kābaš* "subjugate/subdue" and *rādâ* "rule/dominate" (Gen 1:28–29). Could this unresolved textual tension have been introduced by biblical authors as a form of an earlier biblical check and balance on human participatory agency? The relationship between humans and animals changed drastically in the postdiluvian age. If the language of service and care were meant to balance out that of subjugation and domination, the postdiluvian world problematizes as well as repositions it on chilling divine assertions to Noah and his family and descendants. "The fear and dread of you shall rest on every animal of the earth, and on every bird of the air, on everything that creeps on the ground, and on all the fish of the sea; into your hand they are delivered" (Gen 9:2).

Though the divine attribution, namely giving (*nātan* "give") non-human land, birds, and sea creatures to humans, raises a chilling question if the oldest account of creation (J—Gen 2:4b–31) is read alongside the later (P—Gen 1:24–31). Human participation in the divine creative process should be guided by reverent restraint (Gen 2:9, 15–17) and divine wisdom (Gen 3:1, 3). It is not surprising that postdiluvian Noah, said to be "a man of the ground/soil" (MT)/ "farmer" (LXX), exercised humanity's initial participatory vocation in God's new beginning by planting a vineyard (Gen 9:20 NRSV). The relationship between humans and the fauna and, I might add the flora, changed in the postdiluvian age according to scripture—introducing an unresolved tension between human and nonhuman creatures (Gen 9:2). The biblical story does not preclude the challenges animals pose to humans, especially when one considers some of the biblical disasters. In the previous chapter, I made mention of the human-animal relationship from domesticated and wild animals. I am not providing a comprehensive discussion of this relationship in this book; instead I am concisely focusing on a specific dimension of the human-fauna relationship in antiquity. Animals were hunted and domesticated for food, labor, and profit—a relationship dangerously tilted towards insatiable exploitation with animals at the losing end.[57] In many religions of antiquity, and especially the religions of the First and Second Testaments, divinely selected animals[58] were sacrificed—rituals that communicate or maintain the mysteriously intertwined divine-animal-human and nonhuman relationship. I will return to the specific prohibition against eating pork in the next chapter.

A restored human-nature relationship is a function of a deep human transformation from a domineering creature to one that relates to nature symbiotically and justly. That might have been the promissory vision the prophet Isaiah anticipated when he wrote:

> The wolf shall live with the lamb, the leopard shall lie down with the kid, the calf and the lion and the fatling together, and a little child shall lead them. The cow and the bear shall graze, their young shall lie down together; and the lion shall eat straw like the ox. The nursing child shall play over the hole of the asp, and the weaned child shall put its hand on the adder's den. They will not hurt or destroy on all my holy mountain; for the earth will be full of the knowledge of the LORD as the waters cover the sea. (Isa 11:6-9)

This biblical vision transcends monarchical abuse and imagines a responsible leadership in line with God's initial intent for creation—an antediluvian vision perhaps (Gen 1-2). The rationale behind the idea of sacred animals, trees and plants can be conceived of as a constant

---

57. Firmage, "Zoology (Fauna)."

58. Firmage, "Zoology (Fauna)," 1124, "The sacrificeable species, cattle, sheep, and goats, thus became the paradigm against which the 'cleanness' of all other animals could be measured."

reminder to humans that they belong to God. It could also be an earlier recognition of and need to limit human dominion over them—a human limitation that calls for the supervisory role of the *Annmal* and *Akouche* in the Diola universe. As Lang observes, hunting and gathering must be negotiated with and sanctioned by the guardian deity—interdependency between human and nonhuman creatures is ritualized in such a way as to make the deity "an intrinsic part of the economic life of the hunters and gatherers."[59]

Human–Earth–Water Relationship

As I noted earlier, to say God created the world means God made everything humans have come to know, such as the skies, the firmament, celestial bodies, earth/land, waters, trees/plants and species of grass. I am limiting my discussion to the human-earth-water dimension. Israel and her neighbors understood the importance of earth/land and water as indispensable for life and caring for both as living wisdom. The ancient belief about deities who protect the fauna, flora, earth, and water evolved over time. In postexilic times Israel moved forward with some of these beliefs and transferred them to YHWH who governs creation. This is the precise case of the Syrian earth and flora goddess whose functions are transferred to the God of Israel as echoed in Hosea 2:8, 23; Isa 45:8; Exod 23:10–12; Lev 25:1–7; Job 28.[60] This human-nature negotiation is regulated by conditions enforced by God who threatens to withhold rain and reclaim the land should the terms be violated.[61] This is not just limited to land but to humans' failure to maintain a symbiotic life (Lev 25 and Deut 15). On account of this, Ellen F. Davis writes: "Overall, from a biblical perspective, the sustained fertility and habitability of the earth, or more particularly of the land of Israel, is the best index of the health of the covenant relationship. When humanity, or the people of Israel, is disobedient, thorns and briars abound (Gen 3:17–19); rain is withheld (Deut 11:11–17; 28:24); the land languishes and mourns (Isa 16:8; 33:9; Hosea 4:3)."[62] Cultivating and caring for the Garden (Gen 2:15) is very much the role of a tenant obedient to God's command.

59. Lang, *The Hebrew God*, 89–90.

60. Keel and Schroer, *Creation*, 36–37. See also Lang, *The Hebrew God*, 99–108.

61. Brueggemann, *Land*, 1–13.

62. Davis, *Scripture, Culture, and Agriculture*, 8.

The message of Lev 25:1–7, 18–19 is very much consonant with that of Deut 11:10–21—obedience to YHWH, the owner of the land. The God who owns heaven will provide rain to ensure farming leads to a good harvest. Many scholars have noted the fact that the temple symbolized a miniaturized legitimation of God's creation. As Keel and Schroer observe,

> the Temple is the visible symbol of the world order created by the divinity and thus a confirmation of the existence of this order. The so-called basic Priestly writing sees the presence of YHWH in the sanctuary as the continuation of the divine act of creation. Blessings go out from the Temple to the entire land and especially to pilgrims: the water of the Temple spring fertilizes the entire land; rain (Ps 84), thriving of animals and plants (Ps 65:10–14), and the blessing of children (Ps 128) come from the sanctuary. Even after the exile, the circles of the prophets [Haggai (Hag 1:2–11, 2:15–19) and Zechariah (Zech 8:9–12)] were certain that the Temple building and Temple worship were essential for the fertility and welfare of the land.[63]

In this universe anything that affects God's creatures would also affect human life. To a Diola of Mof Avvi, Ala Émit owns everything that is created, both visible and invisible, and orders the universe, in such a way that interdependence of creatures is sustained by the deity. Every creature, human and nonhuman, is moved by the presence of the divinity manifested as a vital force that makes symbiotic life possible and organically negotiable.

Greco-Roman Myths of Origins, Nonhuman, and Human Creatures

According to John Van Seters, Greek myths of origins:

> focus more on the origins of particular states, tribes, and peoples than on mankind in general. They are in the nature of 'charter myths' that legitimate custom, institutions, and territorial claims. These states and tribes it traces back to heroes and eponymous ancestors, many of whom are the offspring of a deity. Subgroups within a larger political or ethnic entity may be represented as descendants or branches in a segmented

---

63. Keel and Schroer, *Creation*, 67.

genealogy. The first ancestors were also regarded as the first rulers of the peoples they represent.[64]

Hesiod

Besides Homer, Hesiod is considered one of the main references for Greek
myths of the origins of the cosmos and humanity. There appear to have
been many myths of origins but for our purpose a concise statement on
Hesiod and Erechtheus will suffice. While he was tending sheep, Hesiod
claimed to have been encountered by Zeus and divinely inspired by the
daughters of Zeus, who gave him a rod and laurel sprig to sing to the gods
and humans (Hesiod, *Theog.* 25–32). The theophany-like experience gave
rise to his crucial works: *Theogony* and *Works and Days*. In his *Theogony*,
the sky, humans and even the gods owe their existence to Gai/a or "earth"
(Hesiod, *Theog.* 104–147). The fertile arable land and underworld as
earth, she is the underlying principle of life that birthed gigantomachic
inimical beings to her spouse, heaven (Hesiod, *Theog.* 45–52).[65] In *Works
and Days*, we learn that the gods created golden, silver, bronze metal, and
iron races of people. The latter are today's humans whose life is marked
by toil and grief (Hesiod, *Op.* 109–174)—an idea that recalls God's words
to Adam in Gen 3:17–19. Hesiod went on to inform his readers that
farming is inextricably linked to god(s)—a divinely ordered seasonal task
(Hesiod, *Op.* 383–398).

Seeing no reason to mention the word "nature," Hesiod simply emphasized the inextricable symbiosis he conceived of between humans and
nature. The divine permeates nature, especially since the sacred earth/
land is πάντων μήτηρ "mother of everything," and makes farming sacred
and humans natural farmers[66]—a reality he hoped his dear brother Perses
would embrace (Hesiod, *Op.* 35–39; 416–419; 563).

Everything comes from Zeus. He orders time and yearly seasons,
especially the timing of rains which farmers need.[67] Farming is just and

64. Van Seters, *The Prologue to History*, 79–80.

65. Hesiod, *Theog.* 154, suggests at times that both earth and sky birth—ὅσσοι γὰρ
Γαία τε καὶ Οὐρανοῦ ἐξεγένοντο δεινότατοι παίδων, "for these who came from Earth
and Sky as the most terrible children."

66. Nelson, *God and Land*, 107–9; Edward, *Hesiod's Ascra*, offers a fascinating discussion on Hesiod's preference of farm life. The city appears to have been a human
invention that counters Zeus' plan for life.

67. Nelson, *God and Land*, 110.

honorable even if one earns just enough for basic sustenance. Hesiod contrasts agricultural with urban life he thinks is riddled with injustices (committed by ruling classes). Justice involves modes of farming that are sensitive to the land that include hoeing and leaving land fallow to produce enough to live on in contrast to mass production that urban life demands.[68] This seeming aversion to urban life appears to have been engendered by the plight of Perses and the ruinous prodigal-like life he led (Hesiod, *Op.* 274–388). In spite of the cultural and linguistic distance between the Diola of Mof Avvi and Hesiod's farming community, there are striking similarities on the importance of the farming life that are not only just but also in line with Zeus's ordering of the cosmos. The question is what did Hesiod mean by cosmos? I will return to this question after the following concise discussion of the myth of Erechtheus.

Erechtheus

Fifth and fourth century BCE Athenians trace their chthonic origin to Attica where their ancestor was believed to have lived since time immemorial. Echoing Gen 2:7, their common ancestor, Erechtheus, was birthed by the ἄρουρα "arable land" or earth (Homer, *Iliad* 2.547–8).[69] Respected Greek authors such as Isocrates, Plato, and Aristotle ensured that this construction of identity, whether disputed or not, lives on. Athenians are Hellenes who not only αὐτόχθονος "sprung up from the earth itself" (Isocrates, *Panath.* 12.124; Isocrates, *De Pace*, 8.49; Plato, *Menex*, 237–239a; Aristotle, *Rhet.* 1.5.5 = 1360b31–2) she, the earth, "nurtured" them. This claim is known to Josephus who refers to Ἀρηναίοις "Athenians" as ὃυς αὐτόχθονος εἶναι λέγουσιν, "the ones who pretend to be birthed by the earth" (Josephus, *Apion* 1.21). In Hesiod and Homer, ancestral origin begins with one mother—the earth. This self-understanding developed into a sense of superiority that did much to shape an Athenian attitude toward others coupled with environmental determinism that eventually helped legitimize Greek imperialism. What does this have to do with human-nature relationship? Hesiod's Golden race is said to have ". . . good things: the grain-giving arable land bore crops of its own accord (αὐτομάτη) . . ."

68. Edward, *Hesiod's Ascra*, 127–40.

69. See Kearns, "Erechtheus," *OCD*, 554–55, who quotes Homer on the myth of Erechtheus and offers more details on its making. Greek sources use different terms such as ἄρουρα, αὐτόχθονος, or γηγενής to speak about their chthonic origins. The divine involvement we read of in Gen 2:7 is missing from the Greek myth.

(Hesiod, *Op.* 118). Diodorus of Sicily who used the same word to describe the land of Islanders south of Ethiopia in the Indian Ocean, said: "These islanders . . . spend their time in the meadows, the land supplying them with many things for sustenance; for by reason of the fertility of the island and the mildness of the climate, food-stuffs are αὐτομάτους 'produced of themselves' in greater quantity than is sufficient for their needs" (Diodorus 2.57.1).[70] The texts explored so far show that the earth is not only the source of life; she sustains it with her productive powers.

De Mundo: Classical Thinkers on the Cosmos

Creation and her destruction were much debated from the Presocratic, Hellenistic to the Christian era. Many thinkers in antiquity conceived of an ordered creation out of existing but less organized matter that made up the entire universe that is beautifully and morally good. I concur with Andrew D. Gregory that creation is cosmos as ordered features and universe is the entirety of unorganized matter. He writes:

> I will use "universe" for all that there is and "*cosmos*" for a well ordered world within the "universe." In general, cosmos consisted of earth, sun, moon, five planets, and some surrounding stars. In some views, one *cosmos* exhausted the universe, in others there were many *cosmoi* (plural of *cosmos*) within a universe, with variations on earth, sun, moon, and five planets. In some views there was one *cosmos* eternal once generated; in others, *cosmoi* were subject to destruction and replacement.[71]

Most Greek thinkers did not necessarily see creation as being the work of a deity. Egyptians, Babylonians, Israelites, and many Africans used myths in which creation as ordered place was ascribed to deities. Hesiod, son

---

70. As utopian as this description of the islanders and their land is, lessons can be learned. Diodorus, 2.59.1, further comments that in spite of the fact that "all the inhabitants enjoy an abundant provision of everything from what αὐτοφυεῖς 'grows of itself', in these lands, yet they do not indulge in the enjoyment of this abundance without restrain, but they practice simplicity and take for their food only what suffices for their needs." The attitude it offers toward abundance and social life—as in collecting enough to live on and exercising an egalitarian communal life - echo Diola attitude toward wealth and equity, especially those of Mof Avvi.

71. Gregory, "The Creation and the Destruction," in *A Companion to Science*, 13. For a detailed discussion of creation and cosmos in antiquity, see 13–28.

of an ancient Near Eastern shepherd migrant who settled in Boeotia,[72] connected creation and cosmogony, and his *Theogony* provides an account of creation and deities.[73] What this existing matter that gave rise to the cosmos was depends on which Presocratic or Hellenistic philosopher one reads. The cosmos originated from a single matter ἀρχή/*archē*, as Aristotle understood his predecessors to have concluded—a principle he thinks is the source of the basic elements earth, water, air, and fire[74] which Empedocles called "elemental roots of things"[75] of the physical world. It is the interaction of these στοιχεῖα "elements" that sustains the cosmos. Pertinent about the word nature φύσις/*physis* is its iridescence in the Greco-Roman literature, especially with reference to creation. Whereas Aristotle and Paul spoke about human *physis* (*Metaph.* 980.1; Gal 2:15), the meanings of the word nature range from the power to become, grow, change, personified "'Goddess Nature'/'Mother Earth'" to things such as stars, trees, birds, and humans.[76]

An important work titled *De Mundo* or Ps.-Aristotle, a pseudonymous peripatetic Aristotelian, offers yet another intriguing take on the cosmos, its elements' composition and the divine role. Ps.-Aristotle reflects a sophisticated view by an author(s) well-versed in the variegated Greco-Roman literary traditions on the cosmos, especially on its making in relation to its creator from the archaic to the Roman period—that is divine transcendence and immanence (with the cosmos as earth, heaven, and nature). The work's self-description as theological or discourse on divine matters led Johan C. Thom to describe it rightly as a "cosmotheology."[77] The relevance of this work lies in its novel contribution. It synthetizes the best of centuries-old debates on cosmos that ancient thinkers thought was threatened to be ripped apart by its pairs of opposites. *De Mundo* (Ps.-Aristotle) insists on a harmonious relationship between the opposite elements anchored by a divine immanence that

---

72. Mazon, "Introduction," *Hésiode*, vii.

73. Gregory, "Creation and the Destruction," 15.

74. Graham, "Matter," in *A Companion to Science*, 29.

75. Jaeger, *The Theology*, 138.

76. Slaveva-Griffin, "Nature and the Divine," in *A Companion to Science*.

77. Thom, "The Cosmotheology of *De Mundo*," in *Cosmic Order and Divine Power*, 109. Thom's nomenclature is based on the theological language inherent in the text itself but also an intertextual reading of *De Mundo*, Plato, *Resp.* 397b 3–5; Aristotle, *Mete.* 353a 35; *Metaph.* 983b 29. See also Burri, "The Geography of De Mundo," in *Cosmic Order and Divine Power*, 95.

does not abrogate the transcendence of the deity. Behind the conflicting interactions among the elements, namely pairs of opposites—air, water, fire, and earth—the author thinks is a dynamic force that sustains the cosmos. According to Thom, the author portrays

> harmony (ἁρμονία) . . . not as a product of something else (e.g. the constitution of nature or some action) but as an active force that has arranged (διεκόσμησεν) the composition of the universe by means of the mixture of the opposites principles. It is described as power (δύναμις) pervading all things, a power that set everything in order. It has created (δημιουργήσασα) the whole cosmos from diverse elements and compelled them into agreement. The agreement (ὁμολογία) or concord (ὁμόνοια) between the opposing elements results from the equality or equilibrium enforced by cosmic power, which thus ensures preservation (σωτηρία) for the whole.[78]

I once noted Louis Martyn's complete overlook of Ps.-Aristotle, *Cosmos*, 392a28–396b9, especially 396b5, in his discussion of Gal 4:3–9 focusing instead on Aristotle, *Metaph.* 986, Wisd, Philo and others.[79] Thematically, Ps.-Aristotle appears to have been widely read in antiquity. The author shows great skills in synthetizing philosophical debates on the making of the cosmos among Pre-Socratic thinkers to third century CE. stoicism but also Jewish and Christian authors as well.[80] Paul's language of τὰ στοιχεῖα τοῦ κόσμου "the elemental spirits of the world," appears to have been his way of joining the debate on cosmic elements (Gal 4:3, 9). As I also noted elsewhere, Ps-Aristotle synthesizes Platonic with Aristotelian ideas to portray his deity as both creator and preserver of the cosmos—a thought that echoes divine providence.

> The notion that there is a divine force holding the world together and thus preserving it from chaos was already present in the time of Plato and Aristotle, but the phrase συνεκτικὴ αἴτιον seems to be a direct reaction to Stoic doctrine, because it is a variant of the formula συνεκτικὸν αἴτιον coined by the Stoics. The transcendent Aristotelian god is thus put in place of the

78. Thom, "Cosmotheology of *De Mundo*," 111.

79. Niang, *Faith and Freedom*, 106, 106n50, 114n88; see Martyn, *Galatians*, 395–418, for an extensive discussion of the elements and Galatian ordering of time.

80. Smith "The Reception of On the Cosmos," in *Cosmic Order and Divine Power*, 121–31; Tzuetkova-Glaser, "The Concepts of *Ousia* and *Dunamis* in *De Mundo*," in Thom, *Cosmic Order and Divine Power*, 123–52.

immanent Stoic *pneuma* as cohesive cause of the cosmos. The author refers to 'an ancient account' (397b13–20) with which he apparently agrees, according to which everything owes its existence and continued preservation to god; all things have come to be "from god and because of god" (ἐκ θεοῦ πάντα καὶ διὰ θεόν). Nothing is self-sufficient (αὐτάρκης), i.e. can exist in and of itself, if deprived of god's preservation.[81]

That everything owes its existence to god as noted by Ps.-Aristotle does not preclude humans. Ps-Aristotle thinks nature works with opposites from which she creates harmony; and similarly τὸ ἄρρεν συνήγαγε πρὸς τὸ θηλυ "she has joined the male to the female"[82]—an interesting echo of "male" and "female" in Gen 2:28 and Gal 3:28. What is significant in this work is the interconnectedness of elements that make up the universe and the divine power that preserves such a relationship. Senghor would have understood divine power to be the life force that permeates all life.

Roman Imperial Cosmology

Like their Greek predecessors, Roman authors appealed to the founding ancestry motif, divine legitimation, and the environmental theory. Aeneas, a divinely sent Asiatic refugee is the founding ancestor of Latium-Rome (Virgil, *Aen.* 7.135–60). He is simultaneously the displaced Trojan and *Romanized Odysseus* with his family and army heading home (Dio, *Ant. Rom.* 1.31.1–52)—the promised land under the guidance of Jupiter (Virgil, *Aen.* 1.225–236a). As this myth unfolds, Aeneas becomes the father (Dio, *Ant. Rom.* 1.72) or grandfather (Dio, *Ant. Rom.* 1.77.1–2) of the twin brothers, Romulus and Remus, whose ancestry is traced back to divine Mars and human Ilia/Rhea.[83] Romulus began to reign over Rome in about 754 BCE, which "would be governed by a legendary sequence of kings, some of decidedly foreign origin" showing that Roman myths of origins are "strikingly porous to outsiders from the very beginning."[84] Pliny credits divine providence for favorably shaping the Mediterranean milieu, especially Italy, and turning Italians into a superior people apt to

81. Thom, "Cosmotheology of *De Mundo*," 113.

82. Ps-Aristotle, *On the Cosmos*, 392a28–396b9, especially 396b5.

83. Compare with Livy, *Hist.* 1.3.10–4.3 and Ovid, *Fast.* 3.31–40. See Niang, "Seeing and Hearing."

84. McCoskey, *Race*, 69.

rule others (Pliny, *Nat.* 2.189–90). Fundamental to his argument is the role of the gods in shaping Italy into a "land that is at once the nursling and mother of all lands" (Pliny, *Nat.* 3.5.39–40) and "single fatherland of all people" (Pliny, *Nat.* 3.5.39–42). Hellenism might have influenced Romans to believe their conquest of the world or civilizing mission was divinely legitimated[85]—Rome is "divinely sanctioned with the mission to civilize barbarians."[86]

Rome's divine mandate to rule and civilize others (the uncivilized) is assumed by some of her rulers beginning with Aeneas and his successors—Romulus and later Augustus Caesar who claimed to have been divinely sent to pacify, propagate his imperial good news,[87] and thus fulfill Jupiter's promises of a Roman limitless empire as intimated in Virgil, *Aeneid* 1.278–82, 1.231–6.278–83; 6.791–807, 851–3.[88] He was the "son of god" in Rome's imperial theology, who claimed to have liberated and brought peace to the state (*Res Gestae* 1.1), ended civil wars on land (*Res Gestae* 34.1) and liberated the sea from piracy (*Res Gestae* 25.1), and whose birth was the inception of good news to the Romans.[89]

Nonhuman–Human Relationship

Wild animals struck dread to the Greco-Roman agrarian world as arch competitors for the same commodity—food. Citing Plato, *Prot.* 322b and Livy, *N.H.* 8.104, Johannes Nollé argues that farmers in Asia Minor feared animals that threatened their lives and crops.[90] Although wild animals posed great danger to humans, some were hunted to near extinction for

---

85. Woolf, *Becoming Roman*, 48.

86. Woolf, "Beyond Romans and Natives," 339–50; Woolf, *Becoming Roman*, 48–76.

87. Price, "Rituals and Power," in Horsley, *Paul and Empire*, 47–71; Price, *Rituals and Power*.

88. See *Res Gestae Divi Augusti*, a document that I think elements of our US State of the Union echoes, especially when Augustus emphasizes his achievements as ruler of Rome.

89. *OGIS* 458 (ca. 9 BCE): ἤρεξεν δὲ τῷ κόσμῳ τῶν δι αὐτὸν εὐαγγελίων ἠγενέθλιος ἡμέρα τοῦ θεοῦ ("and the birthday of the god Augustus was the beginning of the good tidings for the world that came by reason of him"). See a discussion of this inscription in relation to the gospel of Mark in Craig Evans, "Mark's Incipit and the Priene Calendar Inscription."

90. Nollé, "Boars, Bears, and Bugs."

either their meat or simply captured for sale or entertainment.[91] Roman raiding of the fauna for imperial purposes[92] echoes the words of Joseph de Maistre I mentioned previously: no living being escapes the destructive human hand for "he kills to nourish," "adorn," "attack," "defend," "instruct," "amuse himself . . . he kills for the sake of killing: superb and terrible king," who "wants everything and nothing could resist him."[93] The Roman case documented by Toynbee clearly depicts the horrifying killings of wildlife for entertaining the empire. The brutality carried out to expand the Roman Empire was enacted at home to entertain the public— that is, colonial violence abroad was brought home as a ritual atoning for annihilated and vanquished lives. As evidenced in Roman colonial and imperial praxis backed by Pax Romana, the danger humans posed did not preclude human life. That being said, the Roman imperial treatment of animals in no way precluded images of symbiotic life between human and nature. Voices of Virgil and Horace offer an eschatological paradisiacal picture of this symbiosis enshrined in the Augustan Golden Age[94]—a constructed imperial gospel for Romans and her conquered nations. I will return to this topic later in relation to Rom 8:19–23 and Rev 22:1–5.

Whether humans should live symbiotically with nature is debated in antiquity. Hesiod's option for an agrarian lifestyle as honorable is not the norm in antiquity as his ire against his brother, who chose a different path, clearly shows. Debates on the divine-human-nature relationship, like that of cosmic elements, remained unresolved and voices on either side strongly defended. Some Greek authors embraced a divine and human-nature relationship but others did not. This is clearly exemplified in Matthew P. J. Dillon's fine observations—the Empedoclean, Pythagorean, and Platonic advocacy of human and nonhuman symbiosis contrasted with the Sophoclean and Aristotlean emphasis on human exploitation of

91. Toner, *Roman Disasters*, 22–23, 135–36. The Roman empire was not only brutal to those she occupied, she captured animals from Africa and other parts of the empire to entertain metropolitan dwellers. War atrocities were brought home, staged, and sanitized to entertain the empire.

92. Toynbee, *Animals in Roman Life*, 21–23. Romans relate to the fauna in many ways. Animals are used for transportation, food, clothing, adornment, farming, entertainment, and war. They are also hunted for meat, sports, or domesticated as pets (15–21).

93. De Maistre, *Les Soirées de Saint-Pétersbourg*, 28–29; my translation.

94. Toynbee, *Animals in Roman Life*, 283–99, quoting Virgil, *Ecl.* 4:22 and Horace, *Epod.* 16.33.

nature.[95] The Neopythagoreans and some of the Platonists resolutely took up the cause of animals because of their belief in the transmigration of the soul—a conviction that Augustine refuted and thus "influenced" much of Christendom.[96] Sacred groves were protected from being chopped down and any violations of this prohibition were often met with fines depending on the status of the culprit. Divine and human-nature relationship also involves protecting the earth and water. The ancient Celts appear to have been unique in maintaining a relationship with animals and nature. Miranda Green offers insightful thoughts to that effect noting that her:

> brief exploration of the realm of modern and early modern attitudes to animals serves to highlight the contrast between the so-called 'civilized' world and that of the pagan Celts, who shared with the American Indians the regard for a maintenance of harmony and balance with the natural world and its creatures. The belief that beasts and humans are close and essential associates, joint owners of the earth, does not preclude exploitation or meat-eating, which occurred widely in the Celtic world, as previous chapters have shown . . . The world of the Celts was less anthropocentric than either that of modern peoples or of classical societies. This meant that animals were regarded as occupants of the landscape in their own right and were not there simply for the use of man. The strong ritual element in so many aspects of Celtic life involved with animals implies that beasts were valued and belonged to the gods. Activities such as hunting were only permissible if certain criteria were met, which included sacrifice and other ritual activities.[97]

Divine, human, and nature relationship, as I have shown thus far, is not so much about its ambivalent nature in the biblical and the Greco-Roman worlds as it is how humans constructed and exercised their function in nature—a relationship I term vocation. I now turn to key New Testament texts.

95. Dillon, "The Ecology of the Greek Sanctuary," 11.
96. Kearns, "Animals, Attitudes," 87.
97. Green, *Animals in Celtic Life and Myth*, 241.

4

Nonhuman-Human Relationship
in the New Testament

God, Land, and God's People under Empire

As I have already argued, the Mosaic egalitarian vision in ancient Israel
was threatened from its inception to the New Testament era. The divine-
human-nature relationship was also affected as Israel moved from tribal
confederacy to monarchy.[1] In recent years, social sciences shed much
light into the dynamic nature of economic relationships between elites
and peasants in Roman Palestine.[2] The land was important to both elites
and peasants. She was life and how one regards and thinks about her "will
to a great extent determine how one uses" her "both of himself and of his
fellow."[3] Although she belongs to God and is a subject with productive
powers in her own right, the land is a coveted, contested, and controlled
commodity by imperial and collaborating national elites.

The scholarly view that Imperial Rome might have adopted and
heavily applied Ptolemaic and Seleucid or Hasmonean tax systems on
the Jewish population is now contested by recent publications. Roman

1. Gottwald, *The Tribes of Yahweh*, 642–63. See also Boer, *Tracking the Tribes of
Yahweh*, on the significance of Gottwald's approach for understanding ancient Israel.

2. Oakman, *Jesus and the Economic*; Fiensy, *The Social History*; Horsley, *Covenant
Economics*.

3. Fiensy, *The Social History*, 1.

exploitation of the Jews, Fabian E. Udoh observes, took on the form of exactions rather than officially sustained tax levy—"Rome . . . derived no direct taxes from Herod's kingdom, or portions of it, while the territory was governed by Herod and his descendants."[4] Udoh's assertion that taxes levied on the Jews by the Herodian rulers may not have been as harsh as once thought, is not convincing. Archeological evidence from Galilee, Oakman observes, shows that wealthy elites not only controlled and shrewdly manipulated markets for gain, but also owned the largest granaries leaving the non-elites to scramble for subsistence. Herodian policies caused the kingdom to prosper, especially the Herodians and landed elites.[5] This is not of course to suggest that Judean and Galilean peasants were not exploited in Roman-Herodian Palestine. Roman extraction should not be reduced to a state of imperial *lasses-faire* either since Herodians were not entirely freed from Roman scrutiny. In fact, their tenure depended much on how well they supported Roman interest in the region.

Rome had much to gain from taxes levied by the Herodians. Many farmers, whether they were in frequent or limited contact with urbanite elites and large estate owners, would have been economically affected. The Galilean land has many features that pervade eastern Mediterranea for centuries such as climate and soil composition. Dendroarchaeological studies found Galilean vegetation to be stable for most of the biblical period. "Plant materials recovered in Tel Beer Sheba, Arad, and Tel Ta'anach were analyzed, the earliest samples dating to the tenth century BCE and the latest to the seventh to eighth centuries CE. In each case it was found that the flora of the region had remained stable from ancient times to the present, for the plant species represented in the ancient plant material corresponded to the plant species of the present."[6]

Josephus eulogized the land of Galilee as naturally rich for farming for which it was coveted, contested, and defended. He writes that the Galileans,

---

4. Udoh, *To Caesar What Is Caesar's*, 180; Udoh, "Taxation and Other Sources," 371–84.

5. Oakman, "Elite Control of Food Production." For a broader discussion of the economy, see also Hanson and Oakman, *Palestine in the Time of Jesus*, 57–120.

6. Choi, "Never the Two Shall Meet?" 298, citing Reed, *Archaeology and the Galilean Jesus*, 13; Freyne, "Urban-Rural Relations in First-Century Galilee: Some Suggestions," 75–91; Freyne, "Urban–Rural Relations."

surrounded with so many nations of foreigners, have been always able to make a strong resistance on all occasions of war; for the Galileans are inured to war from their infancy, and have been always very numerous; nor has the country been ever destitute of men of courage, or wanted a numerous set of them; for their soil is universally rich and fruitful, and full of the plantations of trees of all sorts, insomuch that it invites the most slothful to take pains in its cultivation, by its fruitfulness; accordingly, it is all cultivated by its inhabitants, and no part of it lies idle. Moreover, the cities lie here very thick; and the very many villages there are here, are everywhere so full of people, by the richness of their soil, that the very least of them contain more than fifteen thousand inhabitants. (Josephus, *J.W.* 3.42b–43, trans. Thackeray, LCL)

Rainfall satisfied the farming of "wheat, grapes, olives, and fruit trees. . . stepped terraces allowed exploitation of the rich slopes for grains, olives, fruits, nuts, and likely vegetables . . . rainfall was plentiful and still varies between 50 and 80 cm (20 to 32 in) annually."[7] In spite of the fertility of the soil and good climate, Galilee was not immune from natural and human challenges. Besides Herodian taxation and land confiscations and control of fisheries,[8] farmers had to negotiate climate fluctuations, crop diseases, pests, rodents, fowl, and weeds[9] as most of the farming world had, especially subsistence level peasantry. Douglas Oakman correctly maintained that it was during these moments that elite exploitation was deeply felt by peasants and potential for various forms of social protest.[10]

Movements of protest against exploitation of farmers are echoed in the ministry of Jesus. His parables include various agrarian images and resulting interactions between elites and peasants (Mark 12:1–8; Matt 25:14–30; Luke 19:12–27).

the Sicarii . . . set fire to the house of Ananias the high priest, and to the palaces of Agrippa and Bernice; after which they carried the fire to the place where the archives were deposited, and made haste to burn the contracts belonging to their creditors, and thereby to dissolve their obligations for paying their

7. Strange, "Nazareth," 169. For a detailed discussion of vegetation in antiquity, see Irene Jacob and Walter Jacob, "Flora," 2. 804–17. Frick, "Palestine, Climate of," offers a helpful study of the climate of Palestine.

8. Oakman, "Debate," 352–53.

9. Pastor, *Land and Economy*, 2–3.

10. Oakman, "Debate," 348–49.

debts; and this was done in order to gain the multitude of those who had been debtors, and that they might persuade the poorer sort to join in their insurrection with safety against the more wealthy; so the keepers of the records fled away, and the rest set fire to them. (Josephus, *J.W.* 2.425–427, trans. Thackeray, LCL).

The burning of archives was not just a protest against exploitation, it was a cancelation of contracts many indebted and landless illiterate peasants were persuaded or forced to create.

Two opposite views of land tenure as Oakman maintains emerged[11]—the educated and wealthy elites who belonged to the social stratum experts call the Great Tradition and the Little Tradition made up of the less cultured, namely the illiterate and poor peasants. Members of the Little Tradition were likely to take their tenancy of God's land seriously and would have been the ones to observe the laws regulating land tenure, harvest, and festivals such as divine rest, Sabbatical, and Jubilee (Exod 23:10–11; Lev 25:2–40). Due to a disproportionate and limited rainfall in Roman Palestine, peasants developed strategic farming practices to keep the land moist to sustain healthy crops. Oakman observes, "The basic problem of agricultural production becomes the preservation of enough moisture in the soil to sustain crops every other year . . . Plowing stubble or green crops under occasionally, replenishes nitrogen and other nutrients."[12] The soil is as a result enriched with green fertilizers to ensure healthy crop growth.

The two Testaments, Josephus, second Temple literature, and Rabbinic Midrashim attested to laws governing agriculture. Biblical evidence also shows that the laws were at times observed (Exod 21:2–6; 23:10–11; Lev 25:2–7 and Deut 15:18), ignored (Lev 26:34–35; Jer 34:14; Neh 10:31) and reestablished, and by the time of Rabbi Hillel, debt releases were abrogated according to Fiensy.[13] The importance of the Jubilee in regulating land rights, tenure, and human servitude cannot be underestimated, especially in the memory of those who belonged to the Little Tradition who conceived of the land as a divine estate not for sale "in perpetuity" or as "a mere economic commodity but sacred trust."[14] To Fiensy the belief

11. Oakman, *Jesus and the Economic*, 38; Fiensy, *The Social History*, 2.

12. Oakman, *Jesus and the Economic*, 20–21. There isn't a uniform plowing method throughout Roman Palestine. Peasants developed and adapted farming techniques to high and lower lands.

13. Fiensy, *Social History*, 4.

14. Fiensy, *Social History*, 7.

that "one's inherited plot was inalienable is not only ancient in Israel but is also well attested for most peasant societies, where land is more 'a family heirloom' than an economic commodity."[15]

Animals have an important presence in the Torah, the prophets, and the writings. The myths of creation ascribe an important interdependent relationship the creator is determined to preserve through human vocational agency in the initial creative act (Gen 1–3), the flood (Gen 9), and beyond (Hosea, Isaiah, and Pss 148 and 104). Although much of this interdependent relationship cannot be fully discussed here, worthy of mention is human life as we know it would have been unthinkable without nonhuman creatures—the earth, the fauna, and the flora. That being the case, the distinction between clean and unclean animals in no way precluded the life of the unclean from being preserved from the flood [Gen 7:1–5, 7–8 (Yahwist) and 6:14–22; 7:9 (Priestly)].[16] The injunctions against consumption of creatures deemed unclean in Lev 11:1–6 and in particular eating pork or touching a pig's carcass cited in Lev 11:7–8 and Deut 14:8 might have been based on reasons other than the ones given.

It could be, as Milgrom insisted, that Israel's neighbors, especially archenemy, the Philistines, raised the animals for food and cultic sacrifices.[17] Over a decade ago, Israel Finkelstein and Neil Asher Silberman found the absence of pig and presence of goat and sheep bones in the dietary remains unearthed in Iron I settlements as evidence that these sites were settled by Israelites and offered the following interpretation.

> A ban on pork cannot be explained by environmental or economic reasons alone. It may, in fact, be the only clue that we have of a specific, shared identity among the highland villagers west of the Jordan. Perhaps the proto-Israelites stopped eating pork merely because the surrounding people—their adversaries—did eat it, and they had begun to see themselves as different. Distinctive culinary practice and dietary customs are two of the ways in which ethnic boundaries are formed . . . Half a millennium before the composition of the biblical text, with its detailed laws and dietary regulations, the Israelites chose—for reasons that are not entirely clear—not to eat pork.[18]

15. Fiensy, Social History, 7.

16. The summary is in Gen 7:14–16.

17. Milgrom, Leviticus, 116.

18. Finkelstein and Silberman, The Bible Unearthed, 119–20. See also Finkelstein, "Ethnicity," 206. Dever, "Ceramics, Ethnicity," 204, 200–213, thinks pottery remains rather than dietary remains are more accurate for retrieving Israelite identity.

Diana Edelman disagrees by citing the speculative nature in the inter-pretation of material culture.[19] Dietary evidence alone is good but insuf-ficient to determine Jewish identity, especially in late mixed Jewish and non-Jewish settlements. It is clear the prohibition against pork consump-tion was an issue Jews took seriously.

Philistines raised pigs for consumption and sale well before Rome conquered Palestine.[20] Pig bones found in the village of Ein Gedi of Ro-man Palestine and evidence from Rabbinic sources, according to Safrai, are good examples supporting the fact that some Jews might have raised pigs and sold them for profit—scriptural prohibition against eating pork is by no means an interdiction to raise and sell pigs by Jews.[21] Jesus' encounter with animals, namely pigs, are mentioned in the Gerasene Demoniac story (Mark 5:11, 13, 16; Matt 8:28–34; and Luke 8:32–33) somewhere in the Palestinian Decapolis.

> Now there on the hillside a great herd of swine was feeding; and the unclean spirits begged him, "Send us into the swine; let us enter them." So he gave them permission. And the unclean spir-its came out and entered the swine; and the herd, numbering about two thousand, rushed down the steep bank into the sea, and were drowned in the sea. Those who had seen what had happened to the demoniac and to the swine reported it. (Mark 5:11–17, NRSV)

Citing Rabbinic lampoons of Pharaoh and emperor Diocletian as being "swineherd," Roger David Aus[22] thinks this life restoration story symboli-cally echoes the drowning of the pigs with that of Pharaoh's army.[23] The dialogue between Jesus and the man with "unclean spirits" and the

---

19. Material culture is highly speculative and therefore yields insufficient evi-dence for the reconstruction of Israelite identity according to Edelman, "Ethnicity and Early Israel."

20. Yasur-Landau, *The Philistine Aegean Migration*.

21. Safrai, *The Economy of Roman*, 172–73; Safrai, "Agriculture and Farming," 258. The rabbinic texts cited by Safrai suggest that the Torah prohibitions of eating pork were late innovations to preclude and inhibit Jews raising pigs. To me, prohibi-tions are often not voiced in a vacuum and testify to the fact that some Jews might have raised pigs since Torah stipulations are on eating pork as Safrai suspects. That Jews raised pigs for economic reasons not consumption is possible given the ambiguous and scanty evidence.

22. Aus, *My Name Is "Legion,"* 45–48.

23. Carter, *Matthew and the Margins*, 213. See also Horsley, *Jesus and Empire*, 100–101, citing Carter.

resulting drowning of the pigs raises an important economic question. Did the pigs belong to a non-Jewish farmer? For instance, if a Galilean peasant were to understand Legion to mean a person associated with Roman colonial occupation and exploitation, might a non-Jewish swineherd be seen in the same light since the latter profited from Roman economy? Mark's telling silence about the economic question, though perplexing, is implicit in his telling of the story. The Roman economy is fair game as it is being displaced by the "good news of Jesus Christ the Son of God" (Mark 1:1).

The ubiquity of colonial Rome in all the aspects of Palestinian life was undeniable as it was evidenced "in trade, buildings, settled veterans, and troops."[24] Conflict between Jews and non-Jews of which Josephus spoke resulted from Rome's inescapable presence. In this colonial atmosphere colonial subjects would not have confused Legion (λεγιών) with anything other than the enforcer of the Peace of Rome[25]—Rome's army— the Tenth *Fretensis* Legion stationed nearby in Syria since the death of Herod the Great in 6 CE. and was instrumental in finally destroying and occupying Jerusalem. As scholars have noted, the mascot of this Roman Legion[26] was the image of a pig, which sheds much light on how much this animal might have been valued by many in antiquity. Unclean for Jews, pigs were lucrative for most of the pork-eating world. Carter reminds us that not only did Roman soldiers raise them for sustenance and sale (Tacitus, *Ann.* 13.54–55), pigs were often sacrificed during religious rituals associated with agriculture (Cicero, *Leg.* 2.55–57).[27] Authors such as Tacitus and Plutarch cited leprosy as the main reason the Jews abstained from eating pork (Tacitus, *Hist.* 5.4.2–3.; Plutarch, *Quaest. conv.*, 4.4–5.3). Epictetus knew that Greeks debated "whether the particular act of eating swine's flesh is holy or unholy" but was neutral on the issue (Epictetus, *Diatr.* 1.22.4c; ibid., 1.11.12–13).[28]

That some Jews and non-Jews raised pigs might have been problematic for Jesus since the sale of the animal contributed to the economy of

24. Carter, *Matthew and the Margins*, 211.

25. Wengst, *Pax Romana*, 66.

26. Carter, *Matthew and the Margins*, 212. See also Witmer, *Jesus, the Galilean Exorcist*, 171.

27. See Carter, *Matthew and the Margins*, 212, who cites Columella, *Rust.* 7.9–11 on farming pigs in towns.

28. See other classical authors such as Petronius, *Satyr. Frag.* 37; Strabo, *Geogr.* 16.2.37; Juvenal, *Sat.* 6.160.

Imperial Rome. Jesus' permitting "unclean spirits," Legion, (Mark 5:13) to occupy the swineherd might have been a counter-imperial performative life and economic restorative act—an alternative form of conquering Rome. Jesus' confrontation with Legion enshrined this multivalent battle of which Carter astutely writes. "The Conflict has multiple levels: *economic*, since the pigs are a source of food and income from sale and taxes; *political*, since Jesus has challenged their control and destroyed a symbol of Roman imperial control; *social*, since Jesus has taken the side of the expendables, at the expense of the elite; *ethnic*, since Jesus is a Jew asserting his authority among Gentiles; *religious*, since Jesus has destroyed an animal with important roles in religious rites."[29] Mark, having the unclean spirits ask not to be sent out of the country (χώρα), highlights the very heart of this tense conflict and bespeaks of imperial Rome's refusal to end the occupation as is common of empire to overstay in order to mutate its exploitative practices.[30]

Pigs are mentioned in Luke 15:13–16 in association with a character portrayed as a Jew, according to the narrative, hired by a non-Jewish pig farmer.

> A few days later the younger son gathered all he had and traveled to a distant country, and there he squandered his property in dissolute living. When he had spent everything, a severe famine took place throughout that country, and he began to be in need. So he went and hired himself out to one of the citizens of that country, who sent him to his fields to feed the pigs. He would gladly have filled himself with the pods that the pigs were eating; and no one gave him anything. (Luke 15:13–16, NRSV)

Readings of this story are often limited to either the incommensurable compassion of the father, the selfishness of the elder brother, the younger sibling disrespecting his father by wishing him dead, and wasting his share of the family estate, or for rendering himself unclean while feeding swine to earn a living.[31] To return to my earlier comment, Torah injunction against eating pork or touching its carcass (Lev 11:7–8 and Deut 14:8) says nothing about raising swine.[32]

---

29. Carter, *Matthew and the Margins*, 213–14.

30. Luke 8:31 redacts χώρα "country" with ἄβυσσος "abyss," while Matt 8:31 simply says "cast out" (ἐκβάλλω).

31. Meier, *A Marginal Jew*; Scott, *Hear Then the Parable*, 99–125.

32. Texts often cited by scholars also include 1 Macc 1:47.

> The pig, for even though it has divided hoofs and is cleft-footed, it does not chew the cud; it is unclean for you. Of their flesh you shall not eat, and their carcasses you shall not touch; they are unclean for you. (Lev 11:7–8, NRSV)

> And the pig, because it divides the hoof but does not chew the cud, is unclean for you. You shall not eat their meat, and you shall not touch their carcasses. (Deut 14:8, NRSV)

Missing in most interpretations of this parable I have read are farming realities that might have pressured a Jewish person to work for a non-Jewish pig farmer. The question is: might raising pigs for sale to non-Jewish people have been a contested issue? Might Torah prohibition against eating pork have been understood by some Jews to have precluded raising them for sale? Although the text does not provide readers with a clear geographical location, to focus on pig farming in Jesus' time, it may be helpful to translate Luke's "the younger son traveled to a distant village" (ὁ νεώτερος υἱὸς ἀπεδήμησεν εἰς χώραν μακρὰν) to mean somewhere in Roman Palestine.

Klyne R. Snodgrass and Arland J. Hultgren cite evidence from Torah, Isaiah, Maccabees, and Mishnahic texts as proof that Jews neither ate pork nor raised pigs.[33] These texts to me did not exist in a vacuum but appear to have been written in conversation with other texts that suggest some Jews might have farmed pigs, perhaps for sale, as Safrai convincingly writes citing additional Rabbinic texts both Snodgrass and Hultgren omit.

> The Mishnah in tractate Uktzin 3:3 states as a matter of fact that the carcass of a pig as well as that of a camel, hare and rabbit could be sold to a non-Jew any place in which there were non-Jews. Since the law is dealing with Jews, this would seem to indicate that pigs, after all, were raised by Jews. The Palestinian Talmud deals with damages caused by pigs (T Bava Kama 1:8; PT Bava Kama 1, 2a; BT Bava Kama 17b; 19b). The Talmudic

---

33. Snodgrass, *Stories with Intent*, 126; Hultgren, *The Parables of Jesus*, 75. See Hultgren's discussion of the parable, 70–91; 468–475. See also Scott, *Hear Then the Parable*, 114, who cites *m. B.Qam.7.7* (Danby, 342) and *b. B.Qam.* 82b (Soncino 10:470) as clear evidence that Jews did not eat or raise swine. Rohrbaugh, *The New Testament*, 99, noted in passing that the younger son degraded himself as "a Jewish person feeding swine." Donahue, *The Gospel in Parable*, 153, went so far as to say the young man took on an "occupation no Jew would assume" and as a result "has lost his family, ethnic, and religious identity."

tradition even mentions the law regarding the placing of food before a pig (BT Sahbbat 155b-it is not clear whether this *sugya* is Palestinian or Babylonian).[34]

Living memories of my grandparents and mother who raised swine have shaped my view of these creatures. I recall many times when I was trying to herd our pigs back to their barns and they often escaped by swimming across streams. I also observed them swimming across streams in search for food time and again. My grandparents' pigs are not unique. My point is pigs do swim and for them to drown as they did in Mark's story (Mark 5:13) raises intricate hermeneutical questions I cannot cover in this book. The point I am making is that some Jews might have raised pigs for sale as Safrai maintained. Given the pressures, the famine, and Roman Palestinian agrarian context assumed by the parable, it would not have been outlandish for a Jewish person in hardship to have herded swine. Diola people did and still raise pigs for consumption and religious ritual sacrifice but rice remains the sacred crop.

Many African groups share similar convictions including Diola people.[35] For the Sereer, Pélissier writes, the "earth is life"—"the body of a living woman, desirable and fecund to whom a feminine name is given, Kumba Ndiaye, rain fertilizes to bear fruit for human sustenance."[36] Most agrarian societies often develop resilient ways to adapt to manageable climate conditions and negotiate life with the earth. Senghor pointed out the African ability to farm successfully despite the warm and humid tropical climate which often extends over eight months—something he thought imperial geographers and agronomists failed to take seriously before they precipitously introduced new agricultural practices.[37] Instead they found the climate unhealthy for Europeans and then used their conclusions to construct the temperament of Africans. Climate conditions are but one aspect of how the African relates to nature. An important

34. Safrai, *Economy*, 172–3; Safrai, "Agriculture," 257.

35. Senghor, "Chants d'ombre," in *Oeuvres Poétiques*; Pélissier, *Les paysans du Sénégal*, 213–15; de Saint-Cheron, *Senghor et la terre*; Machingura, *The Messianic Feeding of the Masses*, 165–207.

36. Pélissier, *Les paysans*, 213, "La terre est vie. Aux yeux des Sérèr, 'la Terre est le corps d'une femme vivante, désirable et féconde. Ils lui ont donné un nom féminin, Kumba Ndiaye, et la pluie est la semence qui lui permet de donner son fruit.'"

37. Senghor, "Constructive Elements," 264–65, 282–83. I will return to this colonial practice in the last chapter and highlight Paul Lesourd's self-congratulating colonial argument.

dimension that affects African farming practices is the rhythmed faunal, floral, and soil/land/earth life that is integral to African myth based on the kinship between nonhuman and human creatures symbolized by totems. It is in this African imaginaire that Senghor spoke of the African-soil-cosmos mutuality.

Productive Powers of Earth and Empire

As Rome acted on the imperial prophecies of Jupiter expanding and occupying foreign lands, she learned the farming techniques of her vanquished nations, especially the husbandry insights of the Carthaginian Mago[38] which Varro, Columella, Pliny, and Palladius adapted as they deemed necessary for their works on agriculture.[39] As Rome expanded, imperially various plants and trees from other parts of the colonized world were studied and some brought to green and feed the empire.[40] Mago's love for farming is evident in his own words: "one who has bought land should sell his townhouse, so that he will have no desire to worship the household gods of the city rather those of the country; the person who takes greater delight in his city residence will have no need of a country."[41] This language appears to reflect Hesiod's concern for farming. Columella differs with Mago's precept, insisting that a nearby farm makes it easier to supervise and care for (Columella, *Rust.* 1.1.18–2.1). The ideas Mago offered on farming ranged from making organic fertilizers with a mixture of pressed grapes and dung, appropriate soil for certain plants, ideal cosmic conditions for related plants and trees, and raising animals.[42]

Jesus and the apostle Paul were born, lived, and died under imperial Rome and must have addressed human-nature relationship in many ways. A surface reading of the New Testament might write off most New Testament authors as unconcerned with nature. That reading may be misleading, especially when one explores texts such as Mark 1:13; 13; Matt 6:25–33; 12:11–12; Luke 12:23–28; 13:15–16; 14:5; John 1:1–14; I Cor 15:39–41; Rom 8:19–23; Col 1:15–20; 2 Peter 3:5–13; Rev 12; 21:1–22:2. These are the most explored passages for ecological concerns in the New

38. Pliny, *Nat.* 18.3.
39. Heeren, *Historical Researches*, 508–27.
40. Woolf, *Rome*, 58.
41. Quoted in Col. *Arb.* 1.1.18.
42. Heeren, *Historical Researches*, 511–12.

Testament,[43] due attention I affirm. I am limiting my discussion to five passages that I believe support my argument, namely Rom 8:18–25; Mark 4:26–29; Matt 13:24–30; John 1:1–18; and Rev 22:1–5.

Jews and non-Jews in antiquity, Louis Martyn writes, were "engaged in sustained and vigorous debates over questions of human autonomy and freedom, moral responsibility, divine providence, and determinism."[44] Greco-Roman literary traditions I explored earlier testify to Martyn's point. Until recently,[45] the Pauline and Johannine authors enjoyed a unique position in biblical studies as the theologians of the New Testament—a scholarly decision that reduced the content of the synoptic gospels to nothing more than a presupposition of New Testament theology.[46]

Productive Powers of Earth in the New Testament

Romans 8:19–22

In the Pauline traditions, Romans earned a lofty position as the embodiment of Pauline theology—a position maintained by many scholars except some such as Victor P. Furnish who argues that 1 Corinthians offers much of Paul's creative theology wrestling with difficult church issues.[47] That being said, in his epistolary conversation with the Romans, the apostle Paul informed them that human agency failed to exercise God's plan for creation, a plight with serious cosmic implications. As a result of this failure, human and nonhuman creatures were equally affected and in dire need of divine rescue. The only viable alternative is a divine response—buying back (ἀπολύτρωσις) God's creation—a process that began in Christ whose redemptive work is now transferred to his followers (Rom 5:11–17), God's revealed children (Rom 8:1–4, 19; cf. Gal 3:26–29). The chiastic structure of Rom 8:19–25 apostrophizes how both nonhuman and human creatures wait in hope as they groan for redemption. To

43. Habel and Balabanski, eds, *The Earth Story in the New Testament*; Horrell, Hunt, and Southgate, *Greening Paul*; Bauckham, *Living with Other Creatures*.

44. Martyn, "Epilogue," 173.

45. *Cambridge New Testament Theology* Series edited by Dunn offers the unique theology of each individual New Testament document.

46. Bultmann, *Theology of the New Testament*, 1:3 quoted by Schnelle, *Theology of the New Testament*, 41–2. See also Strecker, *Theology of the New Testament*, 1–4.

47. Furnish, *The Theology of the First Letter to the Corinthians*.

preclude human and angelic creatures from this event as Charles Talbert does, building on Wis 2:6; 16:24; 19:6,[48] is to overlook the cosmic dimension Paul's κτίσις language (Rom 8:19–22, 39; cf. Gal 6:15) aimed to convey. As a diaspora Jew, Paul reread Gen 1–4 against the backdrop of Roman imperial miniaturization of the earth—a point well-articulated by Jewett who sees Paul's use of the term κτίσις, especially with reference to nonhuman creatures, to counter:

> Graeco-Roman views of the eternal Mother Earth, the word implies purposeful creation of the natural order by God at a particular moment in time. The biblical creation stories are in view, but in contrast to Genesis, there is a striking measure of personification that may have been influenced by the Roman depictions such as the great Ara Pacis monument in Rome in which the earth is depicted as a female figure sitting with "two children and pomegranates, grapes and nuts on her lap; in front of her a cow and a sheep." The personified image Paul employs is given the mood of ἀποκαραδοκία ("eager expectation"), also employed for humans in Phil 1:20. This word, attested for the first time in Paul, conveys a positive connotation of "confident expectation," very much in contrast to the reclining depictions of Mother Earth in the Augustan Altar of Peace, which was emulated all over the empire. The attitude is contrasting, but the personification is similar.[49]

Building on Jewett's point, I would add another visual representation I believe shares themes of abundance and fertility symbolized in that Tellus panel. First, Paul engaged Rome in a mythological and apocalyptic battle in which God redeemed Eden from the failure of human agency proclaimed by the myths of creation (Gen 1–4)—a failure of human agency Imperial Rome symbolized. Second, the Augustan miniaturized cosmos captured in Ara Pacis and the cuirass shares similar key themes with the Garden Room of Livia at Prima Porta, especially fertility and abundance—a thematic thread I characterize as an imperial *condominiumization of a somewhat Roman Eden* (see frescos in the Villa of Livia).

48. Talbert, *Romans*, 214.
49. Jewett, *Romans*, 511.

FIGURE 9

The layout of the Garden Room of Livia with its paradisiacal themes. A plan
taken from Kellum's "Construction of Landscape," 216. It offers a very good
view of all the plants mentioned in Gabriel, *Livia's Garden Rome*—the third
pictures featuring plants, 2, 6, 17, 20, 26, and 33.

FIGURE 10

The walls of the Garden Room of Livia with its intriguing faunal and vegetal
paradisiacal themes on plate VI. Courtesy of David L. Balch.

The well-documented myth behind the garden begins with a laurel twig
in the beak of a hen said to have been dropped by an eagle on the lap of

Livia. She planted the laurel, as God was said to have planted a garden (Gen 2:8), and raised the hen. The laurel, like the seed in the parables of Jesus, grew to provide the imperial family with branches used to make wreaths for celebrating victories.[50] From Delphic Apollo to Julius Caesar and his nephew Augustus Caesar, the laurel symbolized not only purity, health, triumph, and peace, it enshrined the Augustan reign.[51] The garden, teeming with floral and faunal life that strikingly echoes faunal and vegetal life in Gen 1–2 was later publically displayed as "the paradisiacal state of the world brought about by the *Pax Ausgusta.*"[52] There are notable pictorial differences between the Garden Room and the Ara Pacis. The main elements missing in the Garden Room but present in the Ara Pacis I am emphasizing are the cow, sheep, and humans (divinities in human form—Tellus and aura velificans), and children (Romulus and Remus for some interpreters).[53]

FIGURE 11

Tellus is the Goddess of the Earth and the other two elements (air and water) are integral to the making of creation. She symbolizes human and nonhuman fertility. This image is integral to the Augustan Altar of Peace 13–9 BCE. Museum of the Ara Pacis, Rome, Italy. Courtesy of David L. Balch.

50. Klynne, "The Laurel Grove of the Caesars," in Frizzel and Klynne, *Roman Villas Around the Urbs*, 5. See also Kellum, "The Construction of Landscape in Augustan Rome," 213.

51. Kellum, "The Construction of Landscape in Augustan Rome," 214.

52. Zanker, *Roman Art*, 88; Zanker, *The Power of Images*, 172. See also Ling, *Roman Painting*, 149–50.

53. Zanker, *Power of Images*, 167–92; *Roman Art*, 125–28. For a detailed explanation on the Ara Pacis see Castriota, *The Ara Pacis*. See Gabriel, *Livia's Garden Room*; and Reeder, *The villa of Livia*, 45–91, for more insightful interpretations of the Garden Room. Rossini, *Ara Pacis*, 36–44.

Mabel M. Gabriel describes the actual plan of the room[54] and the landscape it depicts this way.

> The smoothly cut, formal little grass path between the two fences, where all is neat and trim, invites the visitor to stroll and admire the flowers and the wilderness beyond. The flowering plants, roses, chrysanthemums, periwinkles, and poppies, immediately behind the low stone fence, are still very tidy, but the middle ground is a wilderness of laurels, oleanders, myrtles, and fruit trees, growing in a tangled mass, with pines, cypresses, oaks, and palms in the background. Birds are flying in the shrubbery and perching precariously on branches. There are pigeons standing in the bushes and feeding on the grass path. Occasionally a sprig or vine hangs casually over the stone fence, inserting a very naturalistic detail. Not many varieties of trees and shrubs are represented. The trees are spruce, oak, pine, cypress, and palm. The fruit trees or bushes are quince, pomegranate, and *Arbutus unedo,* the fruit of which is called in Italian, *corbezrole.* For the shrubs, there are several varieties of laurel, myrtle, oleander, box, and viburnum. The flowers are pink roses, lavender poppies, blue periwinkles, yellow chrysanthemums, and white daisies. Violets and ivy, growing together, are planted at intervals in front of the balustrade, alternating with iris and hartstongue fern. An acanthus grows at the foot of the pine on panel V.[55]

Some of the vegetal species captured in the landscape of Livia's Garden Room reappear in the Ara Pacis. They are the laurel, grapevine, oak, pine, pomegranate, poppies, myrtle,[56] lilies, and acanthus (in the vegetal frieze)[57]—just to list a few. As for faunal life, the Ara Pacis has more

---

54. Gabriel, *Livia's Garden Room*, 10, notes, "In the lower foreground, enclosing the grass walk, is a yellow trellis of woven willow" with a rail above it. There is an opening in this fence in the centers of panels II and V, and one in the long wall between III and IV. The actual entrance to the room occupies the center of the opposite long wall, between panels VI and I. There is no opening in the willow trellis in front of the recesses in panels I, III, IV, and VI. Below the trellis is tucked a garland of very small plants with tiny white flowers, now mostly destroyed, which also is carried around the whole room forming a border. Below this garland, next to the floor, is painted a brown baseboard with an ochre top."

55. Gabriel, *Livia's Garden Room*, 10–11. Reeder, *Villa of Livia*, 84–107.

56. Castriota, *Ara Pacis*, 31.

57. Rossini, *Ara Pacis*, 80–81.

diverse animal species than Livia's Garden Room.[58] My point is not to enumerate all the species of the iconography but to highlight the thematic relationship between the two, especially the message they convey to viewers about Augustus Caesar, his role as son of god, and the significance of his reign. The presence of key deities is emphasized and symbolized in their respective sacred trees—Jupiter/oak, Diana/ilex, Venus/myrtle, Apollo/laurel, Liber/ivy.[59]

Associations a viewer might make between the panel of Tellus and the panoramic landscape of Livia's Garden Room would have included the varieties of vegetal and faunal species, fertility/abundance, peaceful scenes of human and nonhuman creatures, (poppies, fruits and fruit trees, the acanthus, laurel, grass, and animals just to name a few)[60] all marshaled to proclaim an eschatological world. In other words, nothing is missed as fecundity, growth and promissory world of plenty are visually captured in image and presence of the god of earth, Tellus, for Romans to see and believe—that "tokens surrounding the mother goddess illustrate how all creation of nature is a paradise blessed with this same fertility."[61] It is conceivable to argue that all the staged tokens in the garden, some of which have been incorporated in the making of the Ara Pacis (the towering laurel, other floral/faunal species, personified god of earth, and her progeny) are metaphors for Augustus' creative speech and acts ordering and creating a prosperous world. How might the Augustan propaganda affect Pauline eschatology in Romans?

In contrast to Caesar's, Paul's apocalyptic vision offers no visual representation of the future, but faith in the Crucified Son of God, Lord Jesus Christ, executed by Rome and raised from the dead (Rom 1:4).

> For the creation waits with eager longing for the revealing of the children of God; for the creation was subjected to futility, not of its own will but by the will of the one who subjected it, in hope that the creation itself will be set free from its bondage to decay and will obtain the freedom of the glory of the children of God. We know that the whole creation has been groaning in labor pains until now; and not only the creation, but we ourselves,

58. See Castriota, *Ara Pacis*; and Gabriel, *Livia's Garden Room* for detailed pictures of the various species being represented.

59. Reeder, *Villa of Livia*, 83.

60. Reeder, *Villa of Livia*, 82–83; Rossini, *Ara Pacis*, 36–43; Zanker, *Roman Art*, 125–28. Castriota, *Ara Pacis*, 70–72.

61. Zanker, *Power of Images*, 176, 172–81; Castriota, *Ara Pacis*, 13–57, 124–69.

who have the first fruits of the Spirit, groan inwardly while we
wait for adoption, the redemption of our bodies. (Rom 8:19–23,
NRSV)

In light of this, the would-be redeemed creation is not an object but a
corporate subject that shares the same strong verbs ["waits" ($\alpha\pi o\delta\acute{\epsilon}\chi o\mu\alpha\iota$)
in vv. 19–22 and groans ($\sigma\tau\epsilon\nu\acute{\alpha}\zeta\omega$ in v. 22)] as humans with the dire need
for liberation. Nonhuman creatures wait for the unveiling of God's chil-
dren. Why? Paul reads Gen 1–3 in Rom 1:20–23 and 8:19–25, speaking
of the restoration of humanity's initial role. He believes, as James D. G.
Dunn rightly observes, in the eschatological redemption of all creation to
the initial divine plan displaced by the failure of the human agency (Gen
1–3). In his use of the word "creation," Paul:

> presumably means the whole created order into which God set
> man, the context of man's present embodiment. This is implied
> by the clear allusion to the narratives of creation and of man's/
> Adam's fall (Gen 1–3), particularly in the next sentence (v
> 20)—creation understood in distinction from humankind (and
> from the creator), as also in 1:25. As (the rest of) creation in the
> beginning had its role in relation to man, the crown and steward
> of creation (Gen 1:26–30; 2:19), so creation's rediscovery of its
> role depends on the restoration of man to his intended glory as
> the image of God.[62]

Paul's concern is cosmic in scope as Dunn maintains. Central to Paul's
thought, I would argue, is not as much about restoring human status as
"crown and steward of creation"[63] as it is about the transformation of the
failed human agency through the redemptive work of the cross of Christ
into a mindful agent, namely those Paul identifies as "revealed children
of God" (Rom 8:1–3; 19). As Paul has come to understand the human
plight, it was not creation's fault that God cursed the earth (Gen 3:17–19)
but humans who abused and distorted their initial role from a mutual
relationship to domineering hierarchical agency (Gen 1:27–30; 2:25, 29).

By analogy the apostle Paul contrasts the failed human agency of
Gen 1–3 imperial Rome symbolized in his time, especially the Augustan reign (Rom 1:22–23) with the role of the revealed children of God;

62. Dunn, "Romans," 487.
63. Dunn, "Romans," 487.

namely the transformed human agency who will participate in the restoration of the suffering and groaning creation. On account of this, Jewett
observes:

> Paul implies that the entire creation waits with baited breath
> for the emergence and empowerment of those who will take re-
> sponsibility for its restoration, small groups of the υἱοὶ τοῦ θεοῦ
> ("sons of God") which the mission envisioned by Romans hopes
> to expand to the end of the known world, that is, to Spain. These
> converts take the place of Caesar in the imperial propaganda
> about the golden age, but they employ no weapons to vanquish
> foes. When Paul speaks of their "revelation/unveiling," there is
> a clear reference to God's glory advancing in the world, in this
> instance, through the triumph of the gospel. As the children of
> God are redeemed by the gospel, they begin to regain a right-
> ful dominion over the created world (Gen 1:28–30; Ps 8:5–8);
> in more modern terms, their altered lifestyle and revised ethics
> begin to restore the ecological system that had been thrown out
> of balance by wrongdoing (1:18–32) and sin (Rom 5–7).[64]

The contrived and fossilized *cosmization* of creation reflected in
the Garden of Livia, the Augustan Cuirass, and Ara Pacis was nothing
less than the core of Rome's imperial theology of creation as initially
portrayed in Livia's Villa on a much smaller scale. Building on David
Castriota and Paul Zanker, Jewett observes that the Ara Pacis enshrines
the Parousia of a "lost age of bounty and goodness that had pertained
in the mythical 'golden age.' . . . The Altar portrays a supernatural world
in which plants are larger than life and animals live in peace with one
another. This age has allegedly been ushered in by Caesar Augustus's triumph over his enemies."[65] This staged, to put it differently, performed
fossilization of creation tells the story of how empire conceives not only
of creation but also its constructed myth of an eschatological age. Besides
fertility and abundance, the Golden Age proclaimed a discontinuity and
continuity—this age and the one to come. Scholars, especially classicists,
point to the eschatological significance of the Augustan Golden age especially in the area of cancelation of sin, debt, and patronage but also
a return to "Virgin Justice, at least of Faith, Peace, Honor, Shame and

64. Jewett, *Romans*, 512.

65. Jewett, *Romans*, 512. See Castriota, *Ara Pacis*, 124–69; Zanker, *Power of Images*,
167–84; Zanker, *Roman Art*, 87–91.

Virtue."[66] Jesus' redemptive work in Pauline eschatology subverts and reorients itself away from imperial notions of the Augustan Golden Age proclaimed in text and image.

Andrew Wallace-Hadrill writes, "In Pauline Christianity, then it is Christ, not the emperor, who acts as the meditator between heaven and sinful mankind. It is Christ not the emperor who has the power to undo *scelus*, sin, by his grace or *clementia*, forgiveness. It is faith, allegiance, voluntary submission to Christ that will bring about or make ready for the return of paradise, original innocence."[67] Wallace-Hadrill, Phebe Lowell Bowditch, and Ian M. Le M. Du Quesnay draw on the Augustan poets' constructions of the Golden Age, especially Virgil and Horace, to expand on the multivalency of imperial propaganda.[68] The textual significance of both poets in promoting the Augustan reign cannot be underestimated. The creative link Wallace-Hadrill made is insightful, especially from a scholarly perspective that views some Greco-Roman literary traditions and domestic art invaluable for interpreting the New Testament. What does the Augustan Golden Age have to do with other New Testament voices? To this question I now turn.

Paul counters this elaborate construction of space with the message of the cross-event that changes an endangered creation—a decisive act only the God of creation can perform through the agency of the children of God, not Caesar. Since biblical and Greco-Roman imperial myths of creation are certainly in Paul's mind,[69] I wonder if there is evidence that Jesus said something about divine-human-nature relationship in the gospels. All passages cannot be discussed here, but it will suffice to focus on a concise reading of Mark 4:26–29; Matt 13:24–30; John 1:1–14; and Rev 22:1–5.

---

66. Wallace-Hadrill, "Golden Age and Sin," 27.

67. Wallace-Hadrill, "Golden Age and Sin," 33.

68. Wallace-Hadrill, "Golden Age and Sin," 19–36; Bowditch, *Horace*, 116–160; Ian M. Le M. Du Quesnay, "Vergil's Fourth Eclogue," 25–99. Other authors mentioned in this work such as Zanker and Castriota read the same texts along with other texts by both Greek and Roman writers.

69. Jewett, *Romans*, 511; 2 Cor 5:17 is an exception since it focuses on the human creature as evinced by the topic under discussion. The expression "sons of God" in this case applies to Christ followers as Dunn maintains.

Mark 4:26–29

The teachings of Jesus centered on the proleptic manifestation of the kingdom of God. In the first of his five teaching blocks in Matthew, Jesus talked about the character of those who will inherit the earth saying: "Blessed are the meek, for they will inherit the earth" (Matt 5:5). The language implies a journey of character transformation and formation given the identity of his audience—peasants and mostly Galileans alienated (Matt 4:23—5:15) by the Roman imperial presence (Mark 1:1; 12:17; Matt 9:35–36; 22:21; Luke 20:25).[70] The followers of Jesus must learn about the sustaining function of divine agency in their daily lives and their relationship with one another and with nature.

> Therefore I tell you, do not worry about your life, what you will eat or what you will drink, or about your body, what you will wear. Is not life more than food, and the body more than clothing? Look at the birds of the air; they neither sow nor reap nor gather into barns, and yet your heavenly Father feeds them. Are you not of more value than they? And can any of you by worrying add a single hour to your span of life? And why do you worry about clothing? Consider the lilies of the field, how they grow; they neither toil nor spin, yet I tell you, even Solomon in all his glory was not clothed like one of these. But if God so clothes the grass of the field, which is alive today and tomorrow is thrown into the oven, will he not much more clothe you—you of little faith? Therefore do not worry, saying, "What will we eat?" or "What will we drink?" or "What will we wear?" For it is the Gentiles who strive for all these things; and indeed your heavenly Father knows that you need all these things. But strive first for the kingdom of God and his righteousness, and all these things will be given to you as well. (Matt 6:25–33, NRSV)

Floral and faunal life of which Jesus spoke in this passage provides a good example of the mysterious ways in which divine agency and care for both human and nonhuman creatures works (Matt 6:26, 28–29). A clear illustration of divine-human and nonhuman agency is found in the seed and growth parables. The parables of Jesus, told in agrarian context, reflect vivid images busy with the everyday life of farming, harvesting, and economic transactions—a reality well-documented by New Testament scholars and especially interpreters of the parables of Jesus. Many

---

70. The language suggests an alternative reign—God's reign and not Imperial Rome.

parables present an intriguing world that manifests the very reign of God under imperial Rome by upsetting, as they often do, a comfortable and assured ordering of life that is incongruent with the daring alternative they provide, namely the reign of God. If scholars are right that the central message of Jesus on divine kingship/reign is enshrined in his parables, it is not surprising that they embody an inner working of divine and human-nature agency in Mark 4:26–29 and Matt 13:24–30 (cf. Gen 1:10–12). This could have been the reason many rabbinic parables draw living lessons from nature and farming. Most modern interpreters, with the exception of William R. Herzog and Richard L. Rohrbaugh,[71] tend to offer dazzling spiritual readings of the parables, clothing them with an eschatological aura that often precludes daily human–nature relationship. Such readings may be well-intentioned but they render the teachings of Jesus about the daily manifestations of the kingship/reign of God somewhat irrelevant to the daily lives of their hearers. A wait-and-see eschatology may be self-assuring but it tends to foster an unintended indifference to weightier daily human and environmental needs.

This brings me to Mark 4:26–29, a parable, I argue, that echoes much of the earth's agency in Gen 1:1–12 and a dimension of this story often overlooked by many interpreters. As in many parables, its content is very much reduced to eschatology (Mark 4:29 which parallels G. Thom 21.8 and Joel 3:9–14) and its concern for the earth's agency ignored. Bernard B. Scott reads the parable referencing the Sabbath in Lev 25:5 but then reverts to the eschaton.[72] The language of Mark 4:26–29 is about the daily manifestation of God's kinship/reign—a life force that enlivens nature. Building on Senghorian poetics, the farmer is a person of the soil and cosmos who negotiates life with the earth/land—a fact he learned to be reliable from his lived experience that the earth and the planted seed, given the right cosmic conditions, would respond to the initial divine command (Gen 1:11–12; Deut 11:11–12).

Beyond the eschatological reading I would argue that the parable conveys the agency of the farmer, the earth, and the seed. As John Dominic Crossan opines: "Most likely, however, the general context created by the preceding seed parable of the Sower in Mark 4:3–8 and the following one of the Mustard Seed in 4:30–32 has placed emphasis on the seed in 4:26–29 which was not there originally. The earlier version would have

71. Herzog, *Parables as Subversive Speech*; Rohrbaugh, *The New Testament*.
72. Scott, *Hear then the Parable*, 368–71. Hultgren, *Parables of Jesus*, 385–91.

kept the emphasis strictly on the farmer as in 4:26, 27, 29, before the addition of 4:28."[73] Unlike the expectations of modern interpreters to explain all there is about farming, an experienced farmer would have nursed the soil with manure prior to scattering the seed. The farmer of Luke 13:8 provides a good example of that in suggesting that the productive powers of the earth must have been undermined if the right conditions were not met—a lack of good husbandry (human participatory agency) would definitely have affected the plant's productivity. The aorist subjunctive βάλῃ "would cast" illustrates a possible action but one an experienced farmer would have exercised. Changes in tense from the aorist, present subjunctive to the perfect, serve to specify the distinct roles agency plays in this farming process. I concur with Robert A. Guelick that the act of sowing the seed "may describe the farmer's action of literally casting seed on the ground in a way that dissociates the seed from the farmer and eliminates any hint of his contributing to the seed's germination. The aorist subjunctive in contrast to the subsequent present subjunctives reflects the difference in activities. The seed is cast only upon the ground; the other activities are continued."[74]

To reiterate, I am not jettisoning the eschatological rationale of the parable (which Joel Marcus and other interpreters emphasize) nor am I ignoring the divine role. Quite the contrary, I am simply arguing for the symbiotic interrelationships among the distinct roles of agencies—that is the roles of God, the earth, farmer, and seed. The farmer's lack of knowledge about the mystery of the growth does not preclude or inhibit what experienced farmers do and always would have done during the farming season. Many modern readers would simply fill in the gaps inherent in this parable. The initial hearers of Jesus however, most of whom live in what social scientists call "'high-context' society"[75] would have gotten the point being made—a fact that would have rendered a detailed commentary on farming steps unnecessary.

> He also said, "The kingdom of God is as if someone would scatter seed on the ground, and would sleep and rise night and day,

73. Crossan, *In Parables*, 82–83.

74. Guelick, *Mark 1–8:26*, 240–41.

75. Malina and Rohrbaugh, *Social-Science*, 11; Malina and Pilch, *Social-Science*, 5–9. For a detailed discussion on social context, see Elliott, *What Is Social-Scientific Science*; Malina, *The New Testament World*; Theissen, *Social Reality*; Stegemann, Theissen, and Malina, eds., *The Social Setting of Jesus*; Stegemann and Stegemann, *The Jesus Movement*.

and the seed would sprout [βλαστάνω] and grow [μηκύνω], he
does not know how. The earth produces of itself [αὐτόματος],
first the stalk, then the head, then the full grain in the head. But
when the grain is ripe, at once he goes in with his sickle, because
the harvest has come. (Mark 4:26–29, NRSV)

My point is: Jesus was not addressing an audience oblivious about farming. Plants growing and bearing fruits by themselves (αὐτομάτη) as in our
parable are not unique phenomena in scripture and some Greco-Roman
literary traditions. The LXX version of Gen 1:11 uses the same term
βλαστάνω, "to grow," as Mark does to denote the agency of the sprout-
ing seed (Mark 4:27). Emphasis on the farmer's lack of knowledge on
how the planted seed grows helps delineate its agency that is very much
dependent on that of the earth—a point I have already made.

Matthew 13:24–30

Matthew 13:24–30 is a unique Matthean text (M) that appears to have
been worked out of Mark 4:26–29.

He put before them another parable: "The kingdom of heaven
may be compared to someone who sowed good seed in his field;
but while everybody was asleep, an enemy [ἐχθρὸς ἄνθρωπος]
came and sowed weeds [ζιζάνια] among the wheat, and then
went away. So when the plants came up βλαστάνω and bore
grain, then the weeds appeared [φαίνω] as well . . . 'Let both of
them grow together [συναυξάνω] until the harvest; and at harvest time I will tell the reapers, collect the weeds first and bind
them in bundles to be burned, but gather the wheat into my
barn.'" (Matt 13:24–30, NRSV)

In both parables, the farmer sowed the seed, the soil implicitly activated
its productive powers enabling the seeds to sprout (βλαστάνω) and yield
its fruits. In contrast to the Markan version, the farmer/householder
blames an enemy (ἐχθρὸς ἄνθρωπος) for sowing darnel (ζιζάνια) in the
same field, a crop that looks just like the wheat. Weeds grow naturally in
planted fields unless restrained or outwitted by farming techniques like
those practiced by Diola people. The parable is traditionally allegorized,
something the text itself invites as one reads on. The wheat stands for
believers and the weeds are unbelieving Matthean community members.
The master of the house advises his servants, perhaps community leaders,

not to excommunicate the unbelievers but leave that task to God's "reap-ers" at the eschaton (Matt 13:29). Reducing the parable to an allegory overlooks the symbiosis of agencies—that is the implicit fertility of the soil allows both crops to grow echoing the productive powers of the earth (Gen 1:11–12), especially the term βλαστάνω ("to grow").

Gen 1:11–12 does not speak of weeds or wheat; it simply emphasizes the creation and agency of each creature—that is human and nonhuman. Be that as it may, though the weeds and the wheat can be distinguished, the farmer believes uprooting the weeds is risky and might undermine the wheat as well. If wheat can be distinguished from the weeds, would a farmer not know how to restrain the weeds without affecting the wheat? Would a farmer not clear the weeds to protect the wheat unless there is an implicit agrarian reason that begs otherwise? As I noted earlier, in Diola farming practices, rice of a certain height is uprooted from nurseries and then planted in flooded fields to ensure that growing weeds will not af-fect the rice as both plants compete for height. Resilient weeds are often turned into green fertilizer once buried between the dikes. Strikingly, in Matt 13:24–30 the earth is impartial. She sustains the growth of both the wheat and weeds—a fact often overlooked by commentators. The agen-cies exercise their respective roles—the sowers, the seeds, the earth, and divine harvesters. I will now turn to the Johannine prologue and close the chapter with a brief discussion of Rev 22:1–2.

John 1:1–14

John 1:1–14 is often spiritualized with a strong anti-Judaism or stoic po-lemics. Seldom is there a reading that reflects divine and nature relation-ship. The prologue, John 1:1–18, as an echo of Gen 1:1–2 is undeniable. That the author of John was debating some community members on the nature of Jesus, namely his humanity, is well documented by Johannine scholars.[76]

> In the beginning [ἀρχῇ] was the Word [λόγος], and the Word
> was with God, and the Word was God [θεός]. He was in the be-
> ginning with God. All things [πάντα] came into being [γίνομαι]
> through him, and without him not one thing came into being.
> What has come into being in him was life, and the life was the
> light of all people . . . The true light [φῶς], which enlightens

76. Keener, *Gospel of John*, 377–412; Beasley-Murray, *John*.

everyone, was coming into the world [κόσμος]. . . And the Word became flesh [σὰρξ] and lived [σκηνόω] among us, and we have seen his glory, the glory as of a father's only son, full of grace and truth. (John 1:1–14, NRSV)

For God so loved [ἀγαπάω] the world [κόσμος] that he gave his only [μονογενῆς] Son [υἱός], so that everyone who believes in him may not perish but may have eternal life. (John 3:16, NRSV)

A close analysis of the semantic fields of the words *archē, lógos, théos, zōē, phōs, kōsmos,* and *sārx* yields fascinating insights into a Johannine ecojustice. If John meant to say that the *lógos* became *sārx* with reference to Jesus,[77] then ὁ λόγος σὰρξ ἐγένετο can be translated to mean "the *lógos* became human" (John 1:14). Exegetically, *lógos* as subject of the verb *ginomai* bespeaks an ontological transformation from one state of being to another. Scholars speak of this change as either the "Word of God enters" the "sphere of mortality and frailty,"[78] "becomes something it was not before . . . *flesh*,"[79] or "became . . . a person among persons."[80] Given these renditions, it is conceivable therefore to translate the "Word became flesh" to the Word became human—living being through birth (Gal 4:4).[81] According to Gen 2:7, God made humanity (*'adamah*)—earth matter. Reading John through the optics of Senghorian Négritude, *archē* "beginning" signals an incipient process during which the *lógos* "word" becomes *sārx* "flesh, material." Jesus is the *lógos* "word" that became *sārx* "flesh, material" who cannot be fully understood and experienced outside the *kōsmos* "nature/world" (John 1:2–4, 14, 3:16). Reading the prologue this way has profound ecological implications. Many readings

77. *LSJM*, "σάρξ," 1585. This word is translated to mean flesh and has various meanings. By "material" I mean physical human form which according to Gen 2:7 is made from *'adamah*. In Pauline writings, the word "flesh" covers a range of meanings most of which, depending on the context, range from the physical human form to negative behavior.

78. Thompson, *John*, 32; Keener, *Gospel of John*, 408.

79. Beasley-Murray, *John*, 12–13.

80. Haenchen, *John*, 119. To Haenchen, John is simply staying clear of Pauline anthropology in Phil 2:6.

81. I am aware of the debates discussed in Keener, *Gospel of John*, 377–419, that echo my early discussion of De Mundo or Ps-Aristotle where the author reflected centuries of debates on divine transcendence to maintain divine *immanence* only in divine power. Conclusions drawn by this author suggest that Johannine community members might have been aware of or even influenced these debates.

of John 3:16, especially of the term *kōsmos,* preclude creation reducing its meaning to just humans. John, unlike Ps-Aristotle, was arguing that Jesus was both divine and human.

John takes ecological issues seriously, in particular the human-nature relationship because *lógos* ("word") has a *sārx* ("material") dimension. Most Johannine scholars have paid little to no attention to this ecological significance of the Johannine prologue until now. Rereading John 1:1–14 in a West African Diola village, one would have to consider first the people's firm belief in the sacred relationship between humans and nature—human life is inextricably linked to earth and God. A Diola exposed to a reading of John 1:1–18 that emphasizes the connection of Jesus to the cosmos [Jesus as *lógos* "word" that became *sārx* "flesh, material" (John 1:2–4, 14, 3:16)] would have readily affirmed it as a reality that pervades Diola lived experience.[82] In contrast to most conservative publications that tend to focus only on spiritualizing the message of John 1:1–18, this passage should also be read to emphasize the ecological dimension, namely God and human-nature relationship.

Revelation 22:1–5

A surface reading of the book of Revelation soon reveals the author's deep concerns for creation and her future. In spite of the gory and cryptic images of destruction and dreadful beasts that permeate much of the book, the closing chapters (Rev 21–22) present God's new beginning—new creation.

> Then the angel showed me the river of the water of life, bright as crystal, flowing from the throne of God and of the Lamb through the middle of the street of the city. On either side of the river is the tree of life with its twelve kinds of fruit, producing its fruit each month; and the leaves of the tree are for the healing of the nations. Nothing accursed will be found there any more. But the throne of God and of the Lamb will be in the city, and his servants will worship him; they will see his face, and his name will be on their foreheads. And there will be no more night; they need no light of lamp or sun, for the Lord God will illuminate them [φωτιζω], and they will reign forever and ever. (Rev 22:1–5)

82. Diatta, "Le Prêtre et les députés"; Diatta, "Demain, le dialogue des religions?"; Diatta, "Et si Jésus était initié?"

God's new beginning is sustained by God's living water and the tree of life that yields twelve kinds of fruit monthly (Rev 22:2; cf. 2:7, 14, 19). The idea of "living water" and "tree of life" recalls the visions of Ezek 47:12 and Zech 14:8 as well as the Eden river (Gen 2:10). That these trees produced fruits emphasizes their participatory agency, namely their vocation to sustain creation. This is supported by the present active participle ποιοῦν "producing"—a role that echoes that of the trees of Eden, Livia's Garden Room, and the Ara Pacis. The trees of Rev 22:1–2 carry on their customary activity that precludes human participation, a phenomenon we already encountered in some of the parables of Jesus where seeds (Matt 13:26; Luke 8:8), and plants (Mark 4:32; Matt 3:10; Luke 3:9; 7:17–18; 13:9; Jas 3:12; Rev 22:2) have productive powers. As we have seen earlier, the self-productive capacity, αὐτόματος, of earth and plants in creation myths (Gen 1:11–12) and the Greco-Roman world (Hesiod, *Op.* 118; and Diodorus 2.57.2) is implicit in John's vision (Rev 22:1–2).

Since God did not plant new trees, the "tree of life" in Rev 22:2 might have been the same tree first mentioned in Gen 2:9. Enoch's vision of trees from which holy ones (probably the first humans of Gen 1:27–2:25) ate (ἐσθίω) lends strong support to this conclusion (1 Enoch 32:3–6; cf. 29–33). For our purpose, John's eschatological vision echoes Gen 1:1–3, 11–12, 28, 2:15 creation myths; especially their emphasis on Divine-nonhuman agency. The sacred forest provides food for humans and the trees' foliage has medicinal properties said to be for the healing (θεραπεία) of the nations. The "tree of life" represents "numerous trees"[83] and functions as *a divine pharmaceutical grove par excellence* empowered by divine eternal presence (Rev 22:3–5). Divine agency permeates God's new creation. This is why I render κύριος ὁ θεὸς φωτίσει ἐπ' αὐτούς as "the Lord God will enlighten them"[84] instead of "the Lord God will be their light" (Rev 22:5, NRSV) to emphasize divine enlightenment of the human agency in the new creation.

David E. Aune is probably correct in interpreting the absence of curse in Rev 22:3 in light of Israelite and Judahite ḥērem tradition (Gen 9:1–11; Zech 14:1–11) as absence of war[85]—an important reading when juxtaposed with the Augustan Golden Age discussed above. The vision

---

83. Aune, *Revelation 17–22*, 1177; Koester, *Revelation*, 835; Blount, *Revelation*, 397.

84. I prefer the NASV 1977 and 1995 rendition of κύριος ὁ θεὸς φωτίσει ἐπ' αὐτούς as "the Lord shall illuminate them."

85. Aune, *Revelation 17–22*, 1179.

of future tranquility emanates from divine eternal presence that will effect divine–nonhuman and human mutuality of which the apostle Paul spoke, insisting that "God may be in all" (1 Cor 15:27–28)—a presence that replaces a physical temple (Rev 22:3; cf. 21:22). A Diola would have been at home with the language of trees with leaves endowed with healing properties, fruits for food, and the divine role in effecting symbiosis between nonhuman and human creatures. In precolonial Diola country, food (game), medicine (tree leaves, fruits, roots, and bark), and shelter (wood and grass used to build houses such as impluviums) are gifts of the forest, a sacred milieu where rites of passage (*bouhout*) were customarily held. The crux of the *Bouhout* retreat in the sacred forest was to teach initiates the practice of mutuality, transition to adult life, and leadership.

As scholarly opinion has it, the tree of life symbolizes floral life, and, I would add, redeemed vegetation. This language suggests something strikingly responsive to the Roman imperial message enshrined in both the Garden of Livia and Augustus' Altar of Peace as I have discussed. It is clear that the author of Revelation is building on Gen 1–3, which was yet another response to the imperial (Assyrian and Babylonian) construction of the world.[86] The (J) account locates both the "tree of life" and the tree of knowledge of good and evil in the middle of Eden (Gen 2:9). Gen 3:3 suggests that only the latter is planted in Eden. John has the former placed on each side of the river from which flows water of life (Rev 22:2) to symbolize a divine grove. Livia's garden room, about 10 feet wide x 39 feet long, has two spruces equidistantly planted on each of the longer sides, a pine on one width and an oak on the other and there was no river in between. Though the placement of the trees in the Garden of Livia does not reflect exactly those in Gen 1–2 or Rev 22:2, the scene remains paradisaically secure and promissory.

My initial take is that biblical scholars concerned about human relationship with nature can learn from Diola agricultural practice and other autochthonic cultures. Biblical and extrabiblical literature and oral traditions have a wealth of information for a healthy and mystical repositioning of ourselves with nature. Diola expressions of African and Native American and some non-western faith traditions[87] believe their deity

---

86. Perdue and Carter, *Israel and Empire*.

87. See Palmeri, *Living with the Diola*; Berghen et Manga, *Une introduction*; Taringa, *Towards an African-Christian*; Taringa, "How Environmental Is African Traditional Religion?" 191–214; LaDuke, "In Time of Sacred Places"; See also J. C. Scott, "Protest and Profanation," 9.

is the source of all life and a dynamic force that moves in and sustains nature. The author of Revelation would concur as he places the life of the world and everything in it resting in God and the lamb,[88] an implicit response to imperial Rome's claim—Augustus Caesar's claim to be the source of life that enlivens the whole empire and lavishes her with abundant water supply and vegetation.[89] The tree of life in Rev 22:2, according to many scholars, symbolizes many trees, a reading that draws from Ezek 47:7, 12 and especially Gen 1:11–12 and 2:9–10. The throne on which the lamb sits (Rev 22:1), however, echoes God's planted garden, Eden (Gen 2:9), from which humanity has been exiled. Eden reclaims her mutual vocational agency with God to sustain life forever. Greco-Roman authors echo ideas of trees with medicinal leaves and edible fruits.[90] God's new city (Rev 22:2), the New Jerusalem, is not Rome. Revelation provides a counter imperial message conveyed not through gardens planted by humans and friezes commissioned by Caesar but a reimaged transformed world that reinscribes the very imperial paradisaical symbolism in Livia's Garden Room and the Ara Pacis it seeks to subvert.

Agriculture in Rabbinic Literature

Agriculture and Daily Life

Agricultural imagery pervades rabbinic literature[91] but evidence for how the land was nursed is lacking except for incidental allusions to manure.[92] As is evident in the Midrashim, the aim is not so much about the making of agriculture but to illustrate figuratively daily responsible living by drawing on images familiar to hearers from their agrarian world. Rabbinic similes address a wide range of issues dealing with agriculture, economy, and socioreligious concerns. This could have been the reason Feldman insists that "the field as such, and not merely its cultivation and ingathering of its increase, suggested several figurative ideas."[93] Working

88. Koester, *Revelation*, 834.

89. Hartswick, *The Gardens of Sallust*.

90. Koester, *Revelation*, 834–35; Aune, *Revelation 17–22*, 1177–78.

91. Feldman, *The Parables and Similes*; Safrai, "Agriculture and Farming."

92. Feldman, *The Parables and Similes*, 45, 47, 50–52.

93. Feldman, *The Parables and Similes*, 27.

the land is often a task relegated to tenant farmers—a practice also reflected in the Gospels (Mark 12:1–8; Luke 16:1–8; Matt 20:1–15).

In spite of the symbolic nature of rabbinic references to agriculture, the figurative embodies what rabbis observed and exercised as farmers and found to have a human-nature relational dimension. The connection between acts of clearing fields, fertilizing, watering, cultivating or hoeing, sowing seed, weeding, harvesting and faith undergirded by ethics bespeaks the spiritual dimension of farming. There are "several other similes drawn from the domain of agricultural life and used to emphasize the importance of religious belief and religious practice."[94] It is conceivable to argue that in drawing similes from farming practices to illustrate spiritual responsible living (moral and ethical), rabbis, most of whom were farmers, suggest there is something important about the relationship among God, humans and the earth/land.[95]

According to some rabbinic illustrations,[96] even thorns and thornbushes a farmer might uproot do serve a good purpose, such as fencing, in the great scheme of farming. To summarize, people in antiquity were aware of the divine and human-nature relationship—an awareness that evolved over time. Evidence from Mesopotamian material and Israelite cultures (biblical and extrabiblical traditions) and Greco-Roman literary and domestic art show crucial innovations from deified humans, the fauna, the flora, the waters, the land to a supreme deity who governs creation (Gen 1–2; Lev 25:23; Rom 1:20). Divine and human-nature relationship, either explicit or implicit, was very much in the mind of most people in antiquity whether they exercised it or not.

Farming and Rainmaking

Rabbinic similes drew instantly a strong relationship between farming and the practical side of human interrelationships. There are however some Rabbinic Midrashim that are not agricultural similes. The multivalency of the sacred in Rabbinic Midrashim is such that it does not preclude the concrete existential need for rain as is clearly the case in the Midrash of Deut 11:11–15 known as the *Bavli Tractate Taanit*.[97]

94. Feldman, *The Parables and Similes*, 75.

95. Feldman, *The Parables and Similes*, 190.

96. Feldman, *The Parables and Similes*, 190.

97. BT, *Taanit* 2a–15a in Neusner, *Babylonian Talmud*; Neusner, *Jerusalem Talmud*;

But the land that you are crossing over to inherit[98] is a land of hills and valleys, watered by rain from the sky, a land that the LORD your God looks after. The eyes of the LORD your God are always on it, from the beginning of the year to the end of the year. If you will only heed his every commandment that I am commanding you today—loving the LORD your God, and serving him with all your heart and with all your soul—then he will give the rain for your land in its season, the early rain and the later rain, and you will gather in your grain, your wine, and your oil; and he will give grass in your fields for your livestock, and you will eat your fill. (Deut. 11:11–15, NRSV)

The importance of land, rain, and crops in this pericope cannot be underestimated. Land, rain, and food are foundational to ancient Israel's subsistence based on an intentional relationship conditionally marked by obedience and love for the deity. God irrigates Israel's farms with divinely regulated rain as a blessing to sustain her, the fauna, and the flora—a blessing the deity threatens to withhold if Israel disobeys.

As noted above, the *Bavli Tractate Taanit* provides insightful ways some rabbis reread Deut 11:11–15 for their Late Temple Judaism. I reiterate that the importance of Tannaitic literary tradition lies in the fact that this "literature was written and edited by people who were mainly occupied with agriculture and the agrarian economy."[99] The rabbinic lens invaluably sheds light on the reception of Deut 11:11–15. Julia Watts Belser's reading of the *Bavli Tractate Taanit* shows how rabbis interpreted Deut 11:11–15 theologically and ethically responding to drought as an ecological disaster.[100] Rabbinic innovations speak about rainmaking rituals that actualize the vision of Deut 11:11–15 tempered with a nuanced critique against the Deuteronomic covenant theology of piety-reward.[101] In spite of their innovative rereading of biblical traditions, rabbis were cautious about the role of human agency in negotiating rain with the deity. Put differently, piety does not necessarily translate into abundant rainfall. Belser writes:

"Ta'aniyot," in Neusner, *The Tosefta*; "Taanith," in Danby, *Mishnah*, 194–201, variations of this reading appear in a shorter form in the Mishnah, Jerusalem Talmud, and Tosefta.

98. The word יׁרש should be rendered as "inherit" rather than "take possession" or "dispossess." To inherit does not imply driving *out* those who are already in the land.

99. Safrai, "Agriculture and Farming," 247.

100. Belser, *Power, Ethics, and Ecology*, 1–3.

101. Belser, *Power, Ethics, and Ecology*, 4.

> Bavli Ta`anit demonstrates a striking willingness to critique
> and challenge its own culture-heroes, to expose flaws and fail-
> ings within rabbinic character and cultural practice . . . I argue
> that Bavli Ta'anit evinces a striking propensity to recognize and
> critique rabbinic ethical failings, to reveal the moral pitfalls of
> rabbinic power . . . Through its aggadic narratives, Bavli Ta'anit
> challenges a foundational premise of Deuteronomy's covenantal
> ecology: the claim that exemplary piety or ethical virtue will
> guarantee divine reward . . . Bavli Ta'anit's complex narratives
> decouple human virtue from divine reward, asserting that even
> exceptional merit cannot guarantee miraculous rescue in times
> of distress. When rescue *does* come, Bavli Ta'anit's narratives
> suggest that it often comes from an unlikely or unconventional
> source. Bavli Ta'anit valorizes the holiness of ordinary men
> (and occasionally women) whose piety and connection to God
> trump that of the most illustrious sages . . . Though many narra-
> tives in Bavli Ta'anit still assume a link between misfortune and
> divine rebuke, its tales rarely center on the problem of human
> sin . . . While ancient rainmakers might have rescued their com-
> munities in times of trouble, the present generation's attempts
> to access charismatic power are more likely to reveal human
> arrogance and a dangerous inclination toward strict, measure-
> for-measure justice.[102]

Belser's take on the rabbinic self-critical stance is well taken as it echoes similar critiques ancient Israelite wisdom leveled against covenant theology, especially Proverbs, Qohelet, and Job. My interest however rests on the idea that biblical and rabbinic traditions do agree on maintaining a divine-nature-human relationship. Clearly Belser is aware of the fact that rabbinic self-critique does not preclude or inhibit this relationship. She distinguishes the Bavli Ta'anit from the Mishnah, insisting that the former emphasizes stories of how charismatic holy rainmakers inter-vened on behalf of their communities while the latter centers on fasting rituals.[103]

One of the rainmakers and miracle workers of the Second Temple Judaism period was Ḥoni-Ha-Me` Aggel, also called the Circle-Drawer or Roof-Roller.[104] He was a law-observing Jew known for his piety and his miracle-working prayers in healing and rainmaking. The Mishnah states:

---

102. Belser, *Power, Ethics, and Ecology*, 4–5.
103. Belser, *Power, Ethics, and Ecology*, 212.
104. Gottleib, "Ḥoni-Ha-Me` Aggel," 335–36.

> Once they said to Onias the Circle-maker, 'Pray that rain may
> fall'. He answered, 'Go out and bring in the Passover ovens that
> they be not softened'. He prayed, but the rain did not fall. What
> did he do? He drew a circle and stood within it and said before
> God. 'O Lord of the world, thy children have turned their faces
> to me, for that I am like a son of the house before thee. I swear
> by thy great name that I will not stir hence until thou have pity
> on thy children'. Rain began falling drop by drop. He said, 'Not
> for such rain have I prayed, but for rain that will fill the cisterns,
> pits, and caverns'. It began to rain with violence. He said, 'Not
> for such rain have I prayed, but for rain of goodwill, blessing,
> and graciousness'. Then it rained in moderation [and continued]
> until the Israelites went up from Jerusalem to the Temple Mount
> because of the rain. They went to him and said, 'Like as thou
> didst pray for the rain to come, so pray that it may go away!' . . .
> (*m. Ta'an.* 3:8)

To me the ways Bavli Ta`anit and the Mishnah responded to drought are
two sides of the same coin. They provide different ways of negotiating the
same human need to elicit divine action. The expression of vulnerability
before the deity is the best human response to the divine–nature–human relationship. Both the Babylonian and Palestinian Talmud clearly
evidence the ritualization of the interconnectedness between rain and
harvest. This *imaginaire* implies that fertile land is life and moderate rain
is life-giving, moved by divine agency in tandem with human obedient
participatory agency.[105]

That being said and for the purpose of this book, acts of responding
to disasters as something precipitated by some individual or corporate
communal ethical failures are not unique to biblical and rabbinic worlds.
Most agrarian cultures whose livelihood rests on rain or some type of
irrigation tend to view severe crop failures as divine punishment. Diola
and Shona people reading Deut 11:1–15 would have heard echoes of
their own beliefs and practices. In Shona, Diola, and many of the Senegambian cultures, rain is a divine gift and can be withheld by God as a

---

105. What I am meaning here is that land without nutrients needs fertilizer. Earlier I
discussed how Diola people negotiate life with the land by making green fertilizer as
well as manure. Every culture is keenly aware of the natural disasters such as floods,
fires, strong winds, and earthquakes. Clearly our modern era has its share of disasters
caused by floods. Rabbis were familiar with the disastrous dimension of rain as evidenced by Bavli *Ta'anit*, 6. Belser, *Power, Ethics, and Ecology*, 34–58, offers an insightful take on how rabbis understood the divine role in providing rain with covenantal
relationship.

punishment for individual or communal moral failures that range from various socioreligious matters such as violation of some communal interdicts, and failure to revere ancestors or perform appropriate rituals associated with each phase of the agricultural cycle.[106] Like many people in antiquity, we must always scrutinize and test our vocation to see whether its effect translates into a sustainable participatory symbiosis or destruction to nature. Life as we know it is inextricably linked to how sustainable humans relate to nature as a subject—a vocation some voices in antiquity and much of Diola life and thought enshrine. To abuse nature is to abuse humans. Building on the Senghorian notion of human-nature-cosmos interconnectedness, I turn to the French colonial relevance and its effect on Diola farming practices.

---

106. Palmeri, *Living with the Diola*, 98–101; Berghen et Manga, *Une introduction*, 197–200; Machingura, *Messianic Feeding of the Masses*, 165–207; Taringa, *Towards an African-Christian*; Taringa, "How Environmental Is African Traditional Religion?"

5

Empire in Senegal West Africa

I see a white man coming, accompanied by black men who will
help him undermine the power of our leaders and make many
suffer in the land of our ancestors. All the country of rice fields
will be tired. All will end one day, at God's appointed time. —
AHOUMOUSSEL DIABONE, a Diola Prophet[1]

Oh God! You must have pity on us, your children.
We wish that the Europeans will not return any more.
Why do the Europeans want to do nothing but squander our lands?
But we wish all the more that God will hold their spirits in God's hand
So that they will not have the idea of returning to Africa. —ALINE SITOÉ
DIATTA[2]

When the white man came to our country he had the Bible and
we had the land. The white man said to us "let us pray." After

---

1. Quoted by Father Diamacoune Senghor in Bassène, *L'abbé Augustin Diamacoune Senghor*, 145, "Je vois venir un homme blanc, accompagne d'hommes noirs qui
l'aideront à nous arracher le Pouvoir de nos autorités et à faire beaucoup souffrir la
terre de nos ancêtres. Tout le pays des rivières sera fatigué. Tout finira au jour et à
l'heure de Dieu."

2. Poem 19, collected by Girard in his *Genèse*, 352.

  "Oh, Dieu! il faut avoir pitié de nous, vos enfants.
  Nous souhaitons que les Européens ne reviennent plus.
  Pourquoi les Européens ne font-ils que gaspiller nos terres?
  Mais nous souhaitons en plus que Dieu retiene, leurs esprits, en sa main
  Afin qu'ils n'aient pas l'idée de revenir en Afrique."

the prayer, the white man had the land and we had the Bible. —
TAKATSO MOFOKENG[3]

Cosmization of Empire

This chapter argues for the incompatibility of Diola farming practices
with the new cash crop introduced by imperial France. I reemphasize
the great care exercised by Diola people not to destroy the land, namely
the fauna and flora. The beliefs and practices that undergirded a kinship
between humans and nature were significantly altered by new land tenure laws introduced by imperial France. In other words, French colonization altered much of the Diola subsistence-based agriculture. The spread
of foreign religions (Islam and Christianity) also helped destabilize the
Diola sacred cosmos. While some meetings are worthless, others have a
profound way of altering the course of history for good, ill or both. One
such crucial meeting spearheaded by the Transatlantic Slave Trade with
its so-called "Code Noir" reduced African slaves to nothing more than
"'de meuble' et de 'bétail humain'" ("'furniture' and 'human cattle'"):[4] The
West African Conference held in Berlin in 1884–85. A second, the Bretton Woods Conference, took place in Bretton Woods, New Hampshire,
in 1944.

Agreement in both meetings can be framed this way: the world and
its human and nonhuman resources are fair game. First, they must be
divided and shared among those who mastered "the art of conquering
without being in the right,"[5] an example of which is colonization or the
so-called scramble for Africa, which in many ways was the outcome of the
transatlantic slave trade. Second, the Bretton Woods Conference on the
other hand engendered the International Monetary Fund and the World
Bank. From these two financial structures, subsistence-based agricultural
"communities across the developing world experienced the adverse effects

3. Quoted by Mofokeng, "Black Christians, the Bible and Liberation," 34.

4. Beslier, Le Sénégal, 68, writes "la pratique de l'esclavage coexista en antinomie
avec la brillante civilisation de la seconde moitié du XVIIe siècle . . . La thèse de l'
infériorité de la race noire s' était accréditée facilement auprès des chefs des nations
exploitant 'le bois d' ébène.'" "The practice of slavery coexisted as an antinomy with the
brilliant civilization of the second half of the seventeenth century . . . the thesis of the
inferiority of the black race was easily sanctioned by leaders of nations exploiting the
ebony wood." See Sala-Molins, Le Code Noir, 172, Article 44.

5. Kane, Ambiguous Adventure, 37.

of our current world-economic system of corporate globalization."[6] As Matthew Coomber observes, "From structural adjustment programmes to conditionality loans, the world's wealthiest nations have been able to use their sizable governing influence in the IMF and World Bank to create a trade environment that is beneficial to their own interests while often neglecting the interests of the world's poorest countries."[7] Ironically as in the biblical story of Job (1:1–2:13), Africans knew little if nothing about how much decisions reached in Berlin and later in New Hampshire by world powers would forever affect their land, culture, economy, and very existence. I understand some Western and African readers may object to my take and even discard it as passé since Africans are now independent and have their destiny in their hands or believe they can no longer blame the transatlantic slave trade, colonization or influences of some financial institutions. These views, I would argue, ignore the persistent effect of trauma experienced by Africans from centuries of displacements.[8]

As Berger reminds us, humans are in fact world builders by nature who would do anything to create necessary conditions that ensure their survival—a process of ordering their lived experience in such a way that it also informs how they define or differentiate themselves or present their civilization and ways of doing things as normative for all people. Some French colonial administrators thought Senegalese people should be grateful for being colonized by France. The rationale was that colonization made it possible for some Senegalese people to be taught profitable agricultural practices and French cultural ways which the French deemed normative and deeds of goodwill.[9]

Capitaine Frœlicher, a French colonial administrator, describes the French effort as a three-phase process that began with the actual "conquest, pacification and exploitation."[10] Three types of colonies would underpin the entire project—colonies of settlement, exploitation, and a combination of both. Exploitation in this case recalls aspects of Roman colonization very much informed by Greek imperialism in particular.

6. Coomber, "Subsistence and Greed," 14; Coomber, "Prophets to Profits."

7. Coomber, "Subsistence and Greed."

8. Smith-Christopher, *A Biblical Theology of Exile*, 89–94; Smith-Christopher, "Ezekiel on Fanon's Couch."

9. Péter, *L'Effort Français au Sénégal*, 244–45, 367–76; Beslier, *Le Sénégal*, 221–22; Frœlicher, *Trois Colonisateurs*, 343–61. See also Michelet, *Autobiographie*, 221, 231–32, who views France's civilizing role in the world as a divine mandate.

10. Frœlicher, *Trois Colonisateurs*, 11.

Greg Woolf observes that empires in antiquity were "funded from the agricultural surplus."[11] As the Roman Empire expanded with agricultural handbooks at hand, plants, trees and various crops (vegetable, grains) were studied, brought back and farmed in appropriate soils. Romans carefully "learned from the agricultural regimes they incorporated"[12] to ensure a greater yield that would satisfy imperial needs. Some of the main imperial visual representations such as the cornucopia held by Tellus and the Ara Pacis capture this reality.

Having grown up in a culture where oral storytelling, religion, and ritual mask-wearing[13] are integral to the Diola construction of reality, I learned that the ear sees as much as the eye does. What the ear sees the mind conceptualizes, memorizes, and reimages—a process that invigorates the faculty of memory with the kind of vividness often missing in scripted texts—what literary scripts (texts) fail to communicate paintings, sculptures, and monuments proclaim to inquiring viewers. In other words, the failure of the ear to make sense of a heard text may be corrected by sight and vice versa. In the act of reading a visual representation, the eye engages the mind to reimage, appropriate, and contextualize the message being conveyed by literary scripts (texts), paintings, maps, sculptures, and monuments.

As David Lee Balch once observed, the Jewish Christian author of the gospel of Matthew reinterpreted Exod 20:3–4 to allow the use of coins with human images (Matt 5:1–7; 22:19–20) perhaps for didactic reasons since images in the Lucian *imaginaire* helped interlocutors visualize words—a communication traceable back to apostle Paul's interpretation of Jesus crucified on the cross (Gal 3:1, 13; cf. Deut 21:23).[14] On reading a visual representation, Paolo Berdini theorizes that:

> a text cannot exist outside its reader, it is because I believe—and this is my thesis—that fundamentally painting visualizes a reading and not a text . . . the painter reads a text and translates his

11. Woolf, *Rome*, 180.

12. Woolf, *Rome*, 56–61, observes that animals were also studied and some brought back to the empire.

13. For other perspectives based on direct observations of Diola visual representations see Mark, *Wild Bull and the Sacred Forest*; de Jong, *Masquerades of Modernity*. For meanings of Diola performance of visual representations, see Diatta, *Le Taureau*.

14. Balch, "Paul's Portrait of Christ Crucified," in Balch and Osiek, *Early Christian Families in Context*, 85–87. For insightful readings of images, see Kahl, *Galatians Reimagined*; and Lopez, *Apostle to the Conquered*.

reading into a problem in representation, to which he offers a solution—the image. In that image, the beholder encounters not the text in the abstract, but the painter's reading of the text, so that the effect the image has on the beholder is a function of what the painter wants the beholder to experience in the text. This process could be called the trajectory of visualization . . . My point is that painting does not aim at simply substituting the narrative of the text, at showing what the text tells as a story, but rather at presenting the beholder with an experience that, like reading for the reader, exceeds the narratival aspect of the text and proposes itself as a form of exegesis, a visual exegesis.[15]

Berdini's take on visual exegesis sheds much light on how one might interpret the Augustan Cuirass, the British maps, Pierre Henri Ducos de la Haille's "La France et les Cinq Continents." The three epigraphs at the beginning of this chapter share key elements—the land and her people. J. B. Harley saw imperial maps as dynamic powerful imperial tools in colonial geopolitics. He writes:

As much as guns and warships, maps have been the weapons of imperialism . . . Insofar as maps were used in colonial promotion, and lands claimed on paper before they were effectively occupied, maps anticipated empire. Surveyors marched alongside soldiers, initially mapping for reconnaissance, then for general information, and eventually as a tool of pacification, civilization, and exploitation in the defined colonies . . . They helped create myths which would assist in the maintenance of the territorial *status quo*. As communicators of an imperial message, they have been used as an aggressive complement to the rhetoric of speeches, newspapers, and written texts, or to the histories and popular songs extolling the virtues of empire.[16]

Harley's words powerfully illustrate how colonial cartography succeeds in effectively laying claim on human bodies and their environment[17]— a reality that shaped colonial and postcolonial Senegal; and especially, Diola life and thought as we shall see. My question is: what might the Roman, British, and French empires have wanted to convey to the colonized

15. Berdini, "Jacopo Bassano," 170–71; Berdini, *Religious Art of Jacopo Bassano*, 35, cf. 1–35. There are other ways visual representations have helped communicate meaning since antiquity, as Hughes demonstrates, to illustrate "exegetical texts," "exegetical writing and thought" and actual "visual exegesis" (Hughes, "Art and Exegesis," 180–87.

16. Harley, *The New Nature of Maps*, 57–58.

17. Harley, *The New Nature of Maps*, 59–60.

with these images and how might colonial subjects read them? To this question, I now turn.

Observing the Augustan statue found at Prima Porta, the cuirass provides a visual representation of the wealth Rome drew from her colonies—ironically attributed to the emperor as master of the world and dispenser of abundance symbolized in the cornucopia or horn of plenty. The spherical earthlike picture on the cuirass is populated by deities.

FIGURE 12

The Augustan Cuirass also known as the Prima Porta offers an imperial divinization and condominiumization of space. Its theme is of divine legitimation of conquest and extraction of abundance from Tellus, the tireless mother earth who always provides in spite of the violence directed against her. © Art Resource, NY

The cornucopia placed at the stomach of Augustus, and held by Tellus herself with children seated by her side and a wreath of grain on her head, symbolizes peace, abundance, and fertility.[18] Tellus, the earth mother goddess, is Augustus' womb birthing and sustaining the world—in this case, his gigantic empire.

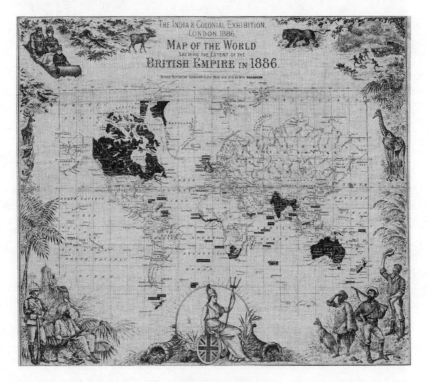

FIGURE 13

The India and Colonial Exhibition 1886 Map of the World proclaimed the Extent of the British Empire in 1886. British colonies are highlighted in blue. Courtesy of the British Library.

18. Zanker, *Power of Images*, 175, 190–92; Zanker, *Roman Art*, 88, 91.

FIGURE 14

The Imperial Federation Map shows the extent of the British Empire in 1886.
This map was cited by Brian Harley who argues that maps communicate power.
Courtesy of Boston Public Library.

If images, like Augustus' Prima Porta, embody imperial language of
power so do maps and paintings—another form of language that reveals
and conceals. What is fascinating about this cornucopia is its appropriation by the British imperial cartography. John Brian Harley (1880) found
its symbolism fitting for imperial Great Britain. Whereas Augustus' cuirass has one cornucopia, the map of the British Empire in 1886 has two,
perhaps to capture the inexhaustibility of the plenty the empire drew from
her colonies around the world—that is India, Africa, and the Americas.
The map according to Pippa Biltcliffe is meticulously

> framed by lavish illustrations of flora and fauna; down both
> sides depictions of inhabitants of the colonies evoke the exoti-
> cism of the empire's distant lands. All co-exist under the ban-
> ner of freedom, fraternity, and federation that are emblazoned
> along the top of the map. Along the bottom, and the focus for
> the colonist's gaze, Britannia is enthroned on the world with her
> trident and shield . . . the very manifestation of imperialism.

Seated on the world, upheld by mythical figure of Atlas, and accompanied by her regalia of a shield bearing the Union Jack flag and a trident that strikes into the heart of the world, Britannia would seem to portray the all-powerful civilizing force of Great Britain. As her subservient subjects look towards her for leadership, she in turn, represents the power that places the colonial population under surveillance and control.[19]

The imperial Federation painting has only one cornucopia.[20]

Both however represent the world under imperial Britain highlighting the wealth or plenty she was able to draw from British colonies—agricultural goods as well as raw materials. Another intriguing picture echoing the idea of abundance flowing from France's colonies is captured by Pierre Henri Ducos de la Haille's work known as "La France et les Cinq Continents." This picture has vivid colors and themes similar to those reflected in the British Imperial maps mentioned above. Although there are many differences that cannot be discussed here, I will highlight one key difference I think is crucial for my argument. In Ducos de la Haille's work, there is no cornucopia, instead humans carry the plenty to empire. Here I argue that plenty does not flow from empire's orchestration or concealment of its actual discourse; rather, the colonized bodies replace the cornucopia—the very embodiment of the theme of abundance that Empires (the Roman and British) drew from their colonies. The abiding message Ducos de la Haille conveys is that the world belongs to France and she is the center of the world. Strikingly, the cornucopia under imperial France becomes human so to speak—colonial subjects bearing and carrying abundance to empire. This is a dreadful and yet honest portraiture of what empire was after.

In context, *France and the Five Continents* is a contrived picture of a world conquered by France symbolized by a fully dressed woman at its center who gives her right hand to powerful Europe. The continents are represented by women. Here one cannot help but recall the symbolism intended by Louis-Sébastien Mercier who presented the king's cabinet and library as a miniaturized world controlled by monarchy.[21] I argue that enshrined in *France and the Five Continents* is the heart of France's propagandist *mission civilisatrice* (civilizing mission) or *paix Française* (peace of France) symbolized by the white dove at the woman's left hand.

19. Biltcliffe, "Walter Crane," 63–64; Harley, "Maps, Knowledge, and Power."

20. Biltcliffe, "Walter Crane."

21. Mercier, *Memoirs*, 1–7, 61–68.

She is the personification of France who lavishes the vanquished with the gift of civilization and peace. Cupid, son of Venus, sits by her "feet perched on a grapevine that gives wine to France"[22] rather than a dolphin as in the Augustan cuirass.

FIGURE 15

La France et les Cinq Continents "France and the Five Continents" by Pierre Henri Ducos de la Haille (1889–1972). This fresco from the Hall of Celebrations in the Museum of African and Oceanic Arts created for the Musée des Colonies (Musée des Arts d'Afrique et d'Océanie, Paris, France) captures how Imperial France related to her colonies. © Art Resource, New York.

The presence of Cupid stands for divine presence and love that conquered nations should exercise towards the occupying empire as Patricia A. Morton observes.[23] This divine presence of Cupid also displaces or demotes Eastern spirituality enshrined by the main Asian female and the cobra. Similarly, the French Catholic missionary version of Christianity also displaces Diola Faith Traditions as unworthy of reverence and outright satanic.[24] The other Asian and African women are living cornucopias as they carry plenty to empire. My interest however is not to read all the aspects of these crucial visual representations but to focus on the theme of abundance associated with the cornucopia. This, to me, stands

22. Morton, *Hybrid Modernities*, 299–300.

23. Morton, *Hybrid Modernities*, 300.

24. Baum, "Emergence"; Mark, "Fetishers, 'Marybukes.'"

for agricultural yields the French Empire assiduously tried to wrest from Diola rice farmers. As I noted, all the images do emphasize abundance symbolized by the cornucopia (the statue of Augustus and the two British maps). In the case of Ducos' *"France and the Five Continents,"* there is no cornucopia. It is replaced by living cornucopias, namely colonial subjects carrying plenty to empire. Imperial France exploited not only the Senegalese agricultural sector, but also the Tunisian and Algerian as well.

Imperial France in Tunisia and Algeria

As previously stated, Africans experienced a succession of events that forever changed the face of their continent, peoples, and cultures. From trading goods that escalated into trading humans objectified as being nothing more than movable goods, to the actual act of occupying the continent eventually led to the control of resources of much of continental Africa. Imperial France in West Africa profoundly altered the culture and the agricultural practices of the people of Senegal. It is surprising that as a colony of exploitation, the country shares much in common with the French settler colonies of Tunisia and Algeria as they were both forced to adopt laws that altered their traditional agricultural practices.[25] So much for the distinctions Frœlicher makes between French colonies. The Tunisian agricultural sector, like that of Diola people, has seen its traditional farming practices reshaped by imperially sponsored laws most of which were introduced at the dawn of independence.

Leaders of independent Tunisia in 1956, especially President Habib Bourguiba, a good friend of the then-President of Senegal Senghor, was instrumental in implementing these changes that nearly reduced subsistence-based economy to extinction. The intention behind these changes was to promote economic growth so Tunisians could compete in the world market shrewdly governed by the World Bank and IMF.[26] This move endangered the livelihood of smallholding traditional farmers as land tenure of precolonial Tunisia regulated by the *Habous* "or endowment, was a religiously sanctioned and fixed land in a perpetual

25. Powers, "Orientalism, Colonialism, and Legal History," shows that changes to the *habous* precipitated by imperially enforced laws are not limited to Tunisia. Maghrebia and other Muslim countries were also affected in many ways. See also Coomber, "Prophets to Profits," 226, on the *habous*.

26. Ashford, "Succession and Social Change in Tunisia," 23–39.

mortmain status"[27] and was being displaced. Like land tenure in pre-monarchial Israel and precolonial Diola contexts, the *habous* secured land tenure by usufruct—an Islamic system of land tenure rooted in Islamic Faith Traditions traceable back to the beginning of Islam. David S. Powers writes:

> Religious endowments (*awqāf*, plural of *waqf*; in North Africa *ḥubūs*, plural of *ḥabs*, popularly known as *habous*) have provided for both the spiritual and material needs of Muslims since the first century A.H. To create a religious endowment, a founder (*waqif*) would assign the usufruct of a revenue-producing property to either a person or an institution in a way considered "pleasing to God," while sequestering the property itself in such a manner that it became inalienable in perpetuity and could not be sold, given away as a gift, or inherited. Religious endowments are of two basic types: public and familial. A public endowment (*waqf khayrī*) is one in which the founder dedicates property to a religious or charitable institution. Public endowments have been used to supply weapons to warriors fighting in the path of God (*fī sabīl allāh*), to provide funds for the establishment and maintenance of mosques, schools and hospitals, and to pay the salaries and stipends of scholars, religious functionaries, and students. A familial endowment (*waqf ahlī*) is one in which the founder dedicates property to his/her children and descendants (upon extinction of the family line, entitlement to the usufruct passes to a religious or charitable institution). Endowments of this type made it possible for Muslim property owners to preserve their wealth (1) by removing it from the operation of the Islamic law of inheritance, which, when it is applied, tends to fragment property into large numbers of small and awkward shares; and (2) by rendering it immune - in theory, at least - from seizure by rapacious and predatory rulers.[28]

As I noted earlier, Tunisian independence in 1956 came at a heavy expense for many Muslim farmers who still believed in exercising usufructuary land tenure rights. Bourguiba, then president of Tunisia, managed to persuade many religious leaders to innovatively interpret the *habous* with deference to his government-backed land management

---

27. Lemel, "A Land Tenure Profile for Tunisia," 1.

28. Powers, "Orientalism, Colonialism, and Legal History," 536. See also Coomber, "Prophets to Profits," 224–25. The acronym A.H. means *After the Hijra*, an expression used in the Muslim lunar calendar to date the migration of Mohammad from Mecca to Medina—that is AD 622.

laws. As a result of this, new land tenure laws were adopted and "the collectively managed lands known as *habous*, which operated some public services, such as hospitals and schools, were abolished and privatized."[29] Relinquishing the *habous* facilitated rechanneling "the benefits of the Tunisian agrarian economy from the religious establishment to the new ruling elite."[30] Empires appeared to have developed an aversion to traditional farming based on *habous* land tenure, denouncing it for its perceived hindrance to the advancement of modern agriculture and economy as shown by Powers and others.[31] As Coomber observes, the new imperial laws regulating land tenure and the resulting economic changes gradually engendered disproportionate landownerships as the wealthiest confiscated land from smallholding Tunisians—a situation that give rise to an increase in poverty and poor health amongst rural Tunisian peasants by the early 1990s.[32] The point I am making here is analogical. I am arguing that imperially introduced policies that undermined traditional usufructuary land rights in Maghrebian and other Muslim countries under Imperial France are analogous to those that nearly obliterated land endowment rights in most of the Diola townships of Senegal.

Imperial France in Senegal

As I mentioned earlier in this chapter, Frœlicher conceives of French colonization sequentially as a three-phase movement beginning from the initial act of conquest and pacification followed by the exploitation

29. Zaibet and Dunn, "Land Tenure," 834.

30. Coomber, "Prophets to Profits," 224.

31. Powers, "Orientalism, Colonialism, and Legal History," 535–571; Coomber, "Prophets to Profits," 225–6.

32. Coomber, "Prophets to Profits," 227–28, citing Zaibet and Dunn, "Land Tenure," 835; Coomber shows how rapidly the turn of events occurred for Tunisians, noting that, "As is often the result of cultural-evolutionary shifts like the one that Tunisia experienced, by the end of the 1980s the wealthiest 3% of Tunisians controlled one-third of the country's farmlands while the poorest 46% held only 8% and to devastating effect. . . In 1989, citing increased food costs, decreased family wages, and a serious lack of access to medical facilities, UNICEF filed a complaint against the Tunisian government and the World Bank, blaming their developmental policies for the nation's rising infant mortality rate (United Nations Children's Fund 1989). As has often occurred during the waxing of previous world systems, the land consolidation and wealth-hoarding policies of this modern-day agrarian society's ruling elite had devastating effects on the country's rural producers."

of vanquished and their lands. To clarify what he meant by the three-dimensional colonial process, he proudly writes:

> Cet effort s'est accompli en Algérie, au Sénégal, au Soudan, au Tonkin, à Madagascar, au Congo et en Tunisie . . . Ce que nous devons envisager, c'est la mission civilisatrice de la France. La grandeur de la France, en matière colonial, c'est son puissant rayonnement intellectuel que n'arrête aucun obstacle, qui pénètre les obscurités des régions les plus éloignées et les sauvages de la surface du globe. C'est la colonisation au vrai sens du mot (*colere*-cultiver), c'est à-dire la culture des esprits autant que celle des terres productives.[33]

> [This effort was accomplished in Algeria, Senegal, Sudan, Tonkin, Madagascar, Congo and Tunisia . . . What we must consider is the civilizing mission of France. The greatness of France, when it comes to colonization, is her powerful intellectual influence that no obstacle could stop that penetrates the darkness of the most remote and savage on the surface of the globe. It is colonization in the true sense of the word (*colere*—educate), that is the cultivation of minds as well as productive land.]

By *colere*, Frœlicher means educating or civilizing the vanquished as well as exploiting their land, especially extraction of raw materials and agricultural produce. To achieve this, colonists would have to introduce laws governing the education of the people and the exploitation of resources. If Frœlicher is correct, Senegal was a colony of exploitation, not of settlement, as were Algeria, Tunisia, and New Zealand. Only some of the conquered, Frœlicher claims, would be trained in French to work and be paid lower wages for their work, improve their acumen and morality as they were being introduced to civilization, and eventually be assimilated to French. Of course, the French imperial ideological policy was based on the belief that African peoples were well suited for progress because the intellectual differences between them and French people were due to nurture and could be righted through assimilation.[34]

By Frœlicher's estimation, French colonial effort, especially in Senegal, was not just cultural and intellectual, it was agricultural as well.[35] Since the country was not found to have many raw material reserves,

---

33. Frœlicher, *Trois Colonisateurs*, 6–7.

34. Péter, *L'effort Français au Sénégal*, 201.

35. Frœlicher, *Trois Colonisateurs*, 12–13.

the French would have to depend on the agricultural sector and fisheries. I conceive of the intellectual colonization to be an atonement for the violence of colonial occupation. It also bewitches and woos colonized African Negroes to embrace words of peace and their mutation into persons with black skin guised with a white mask. It also conceals the real colonial intent—that is the colonization of the agricultural sector. I will return to this colonial dimension of French presence in Mof Avvi.

Prior to the French arrival, Dinis Diaz of Portugal sailed to the Island of Gorée in 1444. Gorée was a strategic location that made it a fiercely and violently contested site by European traders. For instance the Dutch wrested it from the Portuguese in 1588 and renamed it Goede Reede ("Good Port") that later became Gorée. The British took it from the Dutch from 1664 to 1667 but were displaced by the French who occupied it from 1677 well into the colonial period. The initial entry point into Senegal is the Island of Saint Louis—founded in 1659 as the first trading post. Gorée Island was visited by many Europeans and Americans, especially of African descent, for its role in the transatlantic slave trade rather than its significance as one of the key assimilation centers under imperial France.[36] French colonization of my home country, Sénégal, West Africa, led to the creation of the *Quartres Communes* "four towns": Saint-Louis and Gorée (1872), Rufisque (1880), and Dakar (1887).[37] There, assimilation, a policy that underpinned France's *mission civilisatrice* "civilizing mission" or ironically *la paix Française* "the peace of France" was carried out.

On what Rome meant by Roman peace, Woolf warns that "what '*pax Romana*' did claim to mean was an end to the civil war. Threats to the credibility of this claim came not from crime and banditry, but from provincial revolts and civil wars. Both existed, of course, just as they had under the Republic. A number of provincial revolts are reported by literary texts, more from the West than the East and more from the first century than from subsequent ones."[38] The process of empowering these towns to fully exercise the assimilation experiment took fifteen years (from 1872 to 1887). The policy unfortunately did much to divide Senegalese people into civilized citizens of the towns called *originaires* and

36. Niang, "Postcolonial Biblical Theology," 320.

37. Diouf, "The French Policy of Assimilation and Civility."

38. Woolf, "Roman Peace," in Rich and Shipley, *War and Society*, 186. The French peace was in many ways terror for many Diola people, especially those on the southern shores of the Casamance River.

uncivilized subjects living in the *protectorat* (protectorate) engendering an identity crisis.

Most protectorate dwellers and some of their leaders, including some of the most powerful Muslim clerics, who refused to collaborate with French colonial officials, employed both nonviolent and violent resistance to imperial policies and inland incursions; but due to an overwhelming firepower differential, they resorted to various oppositional tactics ranging from violent confrontations, daring defiance by refusing to pay taxes, to sabotaging forced labor.[39] Though divisive, the assimilation policy had its supporters, especially the so-called *originaires* and a handful of schooled elites to whom some of the fictional characters of Ousmane Sembène—probably some protectorate dwellers, directed their ire.

> Look at the inhabitants of the towns, Saint-Louis, Dakar, Rufisque, Gorée . . . Because of their long period of contact with Europeans, they thought themselves more "civilized" than other bush Africans living in the forest or savanna. This arrogance grew when they alone were given the vote and considered French citizens. People from these four *communes*, and their descendants, were proud of being the equals of Europeans. They began to parody them, and acquired a pretentious mentality . . . How many times have we heard a man from Dakar, Gorée, Rufisque or Ndar (Saint Louis) say contemptuously to his country cousin: "I was civilized before you were." These alienated, rootless people, enslaved from within—of whom I was and still am one—were unconsciously the most faithful and devoted servants of the then prevailing system of occupation . . .[40]

This is not the whole story, as even the so-called civilized were still wondering what would become of the future of the country—a concern that not only preoccupied those in the protectorate, but dwellers of the towns as well. The following conversation between two of Sembène's characters capture this reality:

> In the years 1945–50, Léon Mignane would say during his election campaigns: "I will free you from serfdom of native status . . . I will make you . . . French citizens." That was why the peasants supported him. Twenty years after our independence, our thinking still bears the marks of serfdom. When we talk

39. Niang, "Postcolonial Biblical Theology," 322–23.
40. Sembène, *The Last of the Empire*, 134–35.

of foreign goods . . . we never mean French cars or goods. The foreigners in our country are English, American, Japanese, Chinese, Russian. Similarly, I've known Africans who were highly critical of certain regimes or ideologies, without realizing that their opinion was based on the European system, their gold standard, concluded Kad. Exactly, exclaimed Djia Umrel. What model of society are we offered through the media? English, We're made to swallow outdated values, no longer accepted in their countries of origin. Our television and radio programmes are stupid. And our leaders, instead of foreseeing and planning for the future, evade their duty. Russia, America, Europe and Asia are no longer examples or models for us. It would be a dangerous step backwards to revert back to our traditions . . . "That is not what I am saying, *Joom Galle*," she interrupted. "We must achieve a synthesis . . . I don't mean a step backwards . . . 'New type of society,' she ended blinking."[41]

By "country cousin," Sembène, born a Diola in the Casamance in 1923,[42] is revealing sentiments some northern Senegalese people held towards most Diola people—a rice farming group of people who lived in the then-called protectorate as I noted in the earlier chapters. Saying to one's country cousin, "I was civilized before you were" is a clear example of how the Senegalese of the "Towns" re-inscribed the very stereotypes/invectives that led to their assimilation into French ways. Péter proudly lists the Diola first among those he thinks are culturally less evolved and belligerent peoples of the Casamance whom France pacified.

> Depuis que la France a ramené le calme dans cette région, ces peuplades mènent une existence laborieuse. Si tous ces peuples forment encore des groupes distincts, du moins la paix française les fait vivre en bonne intelligence . . . la paix Française a eu pour conséquence l'accroissement de la population du Sénégal. La fin des guerres civiles et les famines d'une part, d'autre part la lutte menée vigoureusement contre les épidémies et l'amélioration de l'hygiène publique ont abouti à préserver la population des dangers qui la menaçaient et à accroitre sa valeur humaine.[43]

> [Since France has restored calm in the region, these tribes live a laborious existence. If all these people still form separate groups,

41. Sembène, *Last of Empire*, 135.

42. Gadjigo, *Ousmane Sembène*, xix.

43. Péter, *L'Effort Français au Sénégal*, 13–14.

at least the French peace makes them live in harmony . . . The French peace has resulted in increasing the population of Senegal. The end of the civil wars and famine on the one hand, and on the other hand the vigorous fight against epidemics and improving public hygiene has resulted in protecting the population from dangers that threatened her and increased its human value.]

The language of pacifying Senegalese people and ending civil wars echoes the Augustan claim (*Res Gestae*, VI.34a). Some Diola people collaborated with empire and facilitated the permanency of French hegemony in many ways that echo the famous African dictum: "When the white man came to our country he had the Bible and we had the land. The white man said to us 'let us pray'. After the prayer, the white man had the land and we had the Bible."[44] One of Sembène's films called *Émitai* tells of how French colonists and African collaborators tried to intimidate and force the Diola to give up their rice for empire, an abuse Diola prophet Aline Sitoé Diatta, overtly denounced. At any rate, Imperial France in Senegal imposed one cash crop under the pretense that it would benefit and develop the country.

Peanut: The Queen of Imperial Crops

To recall the words of Frœlicher, Senegal was meant to be a colony of exploitation simply because the country lacks natural resources. After studying the land of their West African colonies, French colonists decided to develop the Senegalese agricultural sector with peanut monoculture. Of course, this French determination to develop the country, so to speak, antedates the Berlin Conference evinced by the fact that the French were already exploiting many West African countries, including Senegal. They found peanuts to be easier to farm, rich in oil and thus lucrative for the country. From 1841 to 1853, peanut exportation increased from 266 to 3000 tons leading the colonists to conclude that "peanuts would save the country."[45] Péter and Besslier concluded that colonized Senegalese people should be thankful rather than negatively critique the empire and that potential critics should first consider imperial accomplishments like French education, agronomy, and infrastructures.[46]

44. Mofokeng, "Black Christians, the Bible and Liberation," 34.

45. Péter, *L'Effort Français au Sénégal*, 55, "les arachides doivent sauver le pays."

46. Besslier, *Le Sénégal*, 221–222; Péter, *L'Effort Français au Sénégal*, 367–76. See

As I discussed in chapter two, peanut farming was not introduced into Diola country (southern region of Senegal) until much later. It is important to clarify that peanut farming was introduced much earlier in the north, east, and the central regions of Senegal. Peanut farming began in the northern ridge of the Casamance River and gradually made its way to the south where it changed from local consumption to mass production to satisfy Imperial demands. Put differently, the agricultural fate of Senegal was decided and she will number among the main peanut producing countries in the name of economic development.[47]

France's decision to have Senegal cultivate peanuts as the main cash crop affected Diola agricultural practices, especially Diola rice farming, to an extent that cannot be underestimated. Peanut infiltration into the southern rice farming Diola country is blamed on the so-called Diola *mandingized* Muslim—dwellers of the northern ridge of the Casamance River. Though debated, French colonial officials seemed to have persuaded Diola Muslims to cultivate the crop in the area. Peter Mark places the beginnings of peanut farming between 1900 and 1940, especially among the Diola of Boulouf.[48] Migration to cities, trading, and selling peanuts for cash inspired financial autonomy and a sense of agency in the newly introduced economy. Overwhelming experiences of natural disasters and rapid economic changes in the area created a sense of powerlessness precipitating increasing conversions to Islamic faith with the majority of Diola people becoming Muslim by World War II.[49] In contrast to the north, Islam had yet to reach most of the Diola subgroups in the southern ridge, namely the Brin-Séléki, Esulalu and the Kabrousse Diola townships.

Modern agricultural practices associated with French colonial presence were first introduced in northern and much of central Senegal as documented in Roland E. Portères' and Pélissier's encyclopedic works.[50] There is not a consensus among anthologists and ethnographers as to who might have introduced peanut farming to the Diola. Thomas and Linares point to the Mandinka Muslims. Thomas opines that since we are not sure who is responsible, it must have been the Diola mandingized Muslim. He diffidently points to other perspectives rather than blame the

---

also Frœlicher, *Trois Colonisateurs*, 143–361.

47. Diabone, *Les ressources foncières*, 32–33.

48. Mark, "Urban Migration," 1–14.

49. Mark, "Urban Migration," 1.

50. Portères, *Aménagement de l'économie*; Pélissier, *Les paysans du Senegal*.

entire enterprise on the French colonial dawn—a convenient and under-standable move since he was somewhat associated with imperial France. What is clear however is the lucrative nature of peanut growing, of which Thomas and other ethnographers spoke, comes at a heavy expense for many Diola people. Its introduction into Diola subsistence-based rice farming became news of terror for many Diola people steeped in centu-ries-old rice farming practices they believe manifested and maintained the healthiest symbiosis with nature. As is evident in the problems that come with farming peanuts, the community's subsistence-based econo-my will never be the same. The status of the earth/land, the fauna and the flora will gradually be changed from a subject to an object by many Diola people attracted to the imperial promises of wealth. I will return later to this agricultural displacement and its lasting effect.

Land as Sacred Subject in Diola Country

That most Diola people believe in the sacredness of the land is undeni-able, a belief shaken to its very core since the dawn of imperial France in Diola country. Diola people of the southern shore of the Casamance River, even four years after the independence of Senegal, were subjected to French-backed laws on land tenure that were passed and altered land endowments in Diola country through centrist political jousting that permeated the socioeconomic and agrarian sectors. The stipulation of Law 64–44 states:

> *toutes les terres non classées dans le domaine public, non imma-triculées ou dont la propriété n'a pas été transcrite à la convention des hypothèques à la date d'entrée en vigueur de la présente loi, constituent le domaine national. L'État détient les terres du do-maine national en vue d'assurer leur utilisation et leur mise en valeur rationnelles conformément aux plans de développement et aux programmes d'aménagement. Les terres du domaine national ne peuvent être immatriculées qu'au nom de l'État ou des occu-pants qui ont réalisé des constructions, installations ou aménage-ments constituant une mise en valeur à caractère permanent . . .[51]*

[all unclassified land in the public domain, not registered or whose ownership has not been transcribed to the conven-tion mortgages on the effective date of this Act, constitute the

51. Text cited in Manga, *La Casamance*, 166. The italicized text is his.

national domain. The state owns the lands of the national domain in order to ensure rational use and development plans in accordance with development and management schemes. The lands of the national domain can only be registered to the state or to occupants who have made constructions, installations or facilities constituting a character development permanent . . .]

Like his friend Bourguiba of Tunisia, Senghor told the Senegalese people that the content of this law is an actual return to African land tenure rights from imperial law regulating tenure.[52] This is where Senghor fell short and should have been critiqued for misleading many Senegalese peasants. The title of a monograph, *Sacred Rice*, recently published by Joanna Davidson[53] captures the magnitude of rice as the most treasured crop in the broader Diola culture. It is true that most Diola people believe rice to be sacred as is the land. The Diola cannot speak of rice without land and rain the deity sends. The land to a Diola is a subject with a sacred dimension that requires respect and care because of its salient role in sustaining human and nonhuman life. Manga observes rightly:

> La terre est le lieu de prédilection et d'affirmation des liens sociaux et de leur sacralité au sein des communautés casamançaises; elle reste à la fois un lieu de reproduction économique pour la survie de la famille et de la communauté et l'espace où se trouvent préservées la mémoire des ancêtres ainsi que les *djalang* et les *ukiine,* c'est-à-dire les fétiches dont la représentation est source de cohésion au sein des différents groupes sociaux.[54]

> [The land is the place of predilection and affirmation of social bonds and their sacredness before the communities of the Casamance. She remains both a place of economic production for the survival of the family and the community and a place where ancestral memories are preserved as well as the shrines, that is fetishes whose representation is a source of cohesion among different social groups.]

The sacredness of the land among most Diola people that Manga is referring to is well documented but I take issue with his description of Diola sacred spaces as fetishes. As I noted in the previous chapters, a Diola who has not encountered this Western objectification of their

52. Cited by Ki-Zerbo, *Les sources du droit,* 142; See also Manga, *La Casamance,* 165–66.

53. Davidson, *Sacred Rice.*

54. Manga, *La Casamance,* 166–67.

sacred space would not have referred to a Diola shrine in that manner. That does not obviate Manga's point that the land "enables the individual to settle and identify with other community members through mutual relationships that truly express themselves in time of crisis."[55] The sacredness of the land bespeaks to her agency as a living subject that makes life possible and demands respect and delicate care. In Diola cosmology, the sacredness of the land, *Etam* or *Etam ai* as a creature is derived from the intrinsic divine being, Ala Émit.[56] In chapter two I focused on Diola Myths of origins, community, leaders, nature-human relationship exercised through rice farming with particular attention to the Diola of Mof Avvi.

Newly introduced land tenure laws were shaped by colonial motivation that tended to be "secular, static and monolithic with stereotypical characteristics" that did little to dissuade most Diola people from observing their customary land endowment as Gerti Hesseling convincingly maintains.[57] Olga Linares, on whose work Hesseling builds, provides a good illustration of how land tenure in Diola country still retained traditional elements in spite of foreign colonial influence.[58] One of the influences however in the Esulalu townships is that the responsibility of the king to oversee land endowments and settle land disputes is now placed in the hands of individual families. The land passes from fathers to their newlywed sons to support their new families. The outsider must exercise caution not to conclude that women are at the losing end in the Diola land tenure rights. Women's rights to property ownership are in many ways far greater than those of their husbands. Husbands often end up with less property than their wives since they must turn over their land to their married sons.[59]

Frequent mistakes foreign anthropologists made and still make in their studies of Diola people is their inability to recognize their own

---

55. Manga, *La Casamance*, 167.

56. Julliard, "Droit du sol en Guinée-Bissau," in François-George Barbier-Wiesser, *Comprendre la Casamance*, 142–47. I do not think the Diola subgroup equates sacredness with divinity as Julliard appears to argue on page 142.

57. Hesseling, "La terre, à qui est-elle?" in François-George Barbier-Wiesser, *Comprendre la Casamance*, 244.

58. Linares, *Power, Prayer and Production*, 15–79; Hesseling, "La terre, à qui est-elle?," 245–49.

59. Linares, *Power, Prayer and Production*, 17–51, 211–13; Hesseling, "La terre, à qui est-elle?," 245–46. That the culture is changing is a fact both authors document.

subjectivity unconsciously mistaken for objectivity. The Western lens shapes their conclusions about the making of Diola culture. That is an undeniable fact. Having lived in America since 1990, I sympathize with them as I have come to recognize how difficult it is to bracket out one's subjectivity. I also recognize the persistent temptation to demote the cultural values that shaped me for those Western values I find more progressive than mine. When studied closely one can clearly see subtle differences between Diola subgroups. In matters of land tenure, Mof Avvi dwellers share what all Diola people believe regardless of their subgroup that land and all creation (human and nonhuman creatures) belong to Ala Émit and everyone else is a tenant—a concept held by some biblical authors as well (Gen 1–2; Lev 25:23; Isa 66:1–2). Diola people are known for leading an egalitarian life anchored on their notions of liberty for each individual community member—male or female. Again, caution should be exercised not to compare this Diola worldview with Westernized values; instead one can compare the Diola with their neighbors yet to be influenced by other cultures.

Earlier I noted the fact that husbands and wives in Mof Avvi own their separate rice fields and farm them together. A married woman possesses her own rice fields and granaries in the same way her husband does. In this light marriage is not an economic transaction. The wife is fully engaged in the political as well as economic life of her household and community at large. Her input in socioreligious and economic matters is taken seriously as an equal, free, and responsible human agent.[60] During the farming season her husband cultivates the rice fields and she plants the rice. This division of labor between male and female should not be construed in terms of Western notions of gender power differential; rather this is a sort of *mutual productivity* in Diola eyes.

To return to my initial point, land, more precisely the environment, and rice (as a crop), are both sacred. As a Diola of Mof Avvi, I was socialized to uphold and exercise the conviction that rice farming is a sacred journey. I learned to build lasting dikes and sophisticated drainage systems in between field plots in my grandparents' rice fields. There is a fundamental kinship between humans and nature that directs rice farming in Diola community, most of which can be traced back to the first ancestor and shrines. This Diola subsistence-level farming was forever altered since the dawn of imperial France in Senegal—a reality similar

60. Palmeri, *Living with the Diola*, 181–82; Berghen and Manga, *Une Introduction*, 165.

to what happened in Tunisia. Diola country gradually changed from its initial encounters with imperial France during World War I and World War II and much more during the independence era.

Rice as Sacred and Queen Crop

As most Senegalese in the north turned their attention to the imperially sanctioned crop, peanuts, many Diola people kept farming their rice. The importance of rice and environment-sensitive farming techniques is highlighted in chapter two. I reiterate that to the Diola the earth/land, the fauna and the flora are sacred. To say that something is sacred does not mean that it is divine. For instance, in Exod 3:5 Moses learned from God that the place where he stood was sacred. God's creation is sacred. This means both human and nonhuman creatures that live in it are also sacred. Creatures communicate with their creator in speeches inaudible to humans—an insight the Psalter clearly understood (Ps 19:1–4b). Gen 1:1–3, 10–12 depicts creatures as agents (land, vegetation, and animals) responding to divine address in ways only the deity who caused their existence knows. The hovering or incubating (Gen 1:2) role of the spirit affects all creatures causing them to exist and respond to their creator. Seen from this vantage point, it is conceivable to argue that creatures like trees and plants would not only relate to God but also to humans.

I will return to this point in the next chapter. In the meantime, it suffices to note that the Diola believe trees and plants do have "a vital energy" or spirit that makes them useful to humans for sustenance and healing of various diseases.[61] This divinely endowed sacredness also applies to the rice plant—a divine gift to humans for sustenance and not for sale.

During the ministry of Aline Sitoé Diatta in 1942–43, she opposed French colonists for their attempt to wrest Diola rice to feed empire—a concern she voiced in messages. I believe Girard is the first to have provided a written account of her story, followed by Baum and Wilmetta J. Toliver-Diallo.[62] Aline Sitoé Diatta was born to a Diola family in the 1920s

---

61. Diédhiou, *Riz*, 210, talks about how roots, tree bark, and foliage are used by Diola people to heal various diseases. Trees possessed by evil spirits are often struck by lightning.

62. Girard, *Genèse*, 181–267, 347–56; Baum, "*Alinesitoué*"; Baum, *West Africa's Women of God*; Toliver-Diallo, *Aline Sitoé Diatta*. Waldman and Baum, "Innovation as Renovation," 248–53.

in Kabrousse, part of the protectorate. French colonial presence created a sense of bewilderment that pressured many Diola people to question the effectiveness of their shrines before the birth of Aline Sitoé Diatta. The presence of the Roman Catholic Holy Ghost Fathers as early as 1880 in the area led to a handful of Diola conversions to Christianity. Whereas some of the converts maintained some aspects of their traditional faith, others rejected it.[63] The French thought Diola people were primitive, forest dwelling savages, anarchists,[64] drunkards and fickle[65]—invectives that can be heard to this day. She was called by the Diola supreme deity Ala Émit to rainmaking and delivering her people from French occupation.

French colonial officials found her messages threatening and arrested, tried, and exiled her to her death in Mali. Being interrogated by Colonel Sajous during her trial, Aline Sitoé Diatta unflinchingly responded: "God, who appeared to me many times, sent me. I am just transmitting the orders he dictated to me." Ala Émit (God) taught and sent her. Of the thirty-five songs Girard recorded, thirteen overtly denounced the French imperial occupation that aimed at wresting Diola land and rice.

> Oh God! Have mercy on us, your children.
> We hope the Europeans do not return.
> Why do Europeans keep on wasting our land?
> And we also wish that God retains their spirits in God's hand
> so that they will not have the idea to come back to Africa. (*ASDP* 19)

Her question, "why do Europeans keep on wasting our land?" was aimed at denouncing peanut farming that drains the soil's nutrients. She calls Diola people to continue to farm their sacred crop—the Diola brown rice.[66]

> We are pressured to take our canoe.
> The French approach,
> Behold, rice is thrown at us from all sides,
> Behold the bird which flies high among the clouds and the sky.
> Oh God! Forgive us,
> Give us water because of our charity,
> For the French have plunged us into famine. (*ASDP* 21)

63. Baum, "Emergence," 375–76.

64. Méguelle, *Chefferie coloniale et égalitarisme diola*, 48; Mark, "Fetishers, 'Marybukes,'" 95–97.

65. Roche, *Histoire*, 34–35.

66. Baum, *West Africa's Women*, 143–44.

These lines reflect her deepest sentiments on the entire colonial enter-prise. The rice she is referring to here could be the Asian rice that has a greater yield, but farming it would displace the Diola preferred rice con-sidered as sacred. She blames the French for causing the famine which is a hidden way of saying that the French confiscated Diola rice. The ques-tion, however, is why Aline Sitoé Diatta discouraged peanut farming.

First, the peanut crop impoverished the soil and required forest clearing that undermined sylviculture; and to an extent, rice growing was jettisoned—a fact even Jean-Claud Marut could not refute in spite of his blistering attack on the late Father Augustin Diamacoune Seng-hor's socioreligious and cultural memory.[67] Second, it disrupted domestic life by introducing power differentials in Diola households. In the once egalitarian precolonial Mof Avvi and other Diola townships, gendered labor emerged as most men turned to peanut farming leaving women to work the rice fields. Barter, the basic mode of economic exchange or transaction and maintenance of community solidarity, was displaced by the newly introduced currency-based economy associated mostly with growing peanuts.

Though the Mandinka might have been responsible for spreading peanut farming, colonial officials must have introduced and accelerated the cultivation of the crop and Asian rice (faster growing and higher yields) as a cash crop (traded for other foreign products) to support im-perial economy in metropolitan France or to feed empire, especially dur-ing the war years. The Diola cannot conceive of the idea of selling their sacred rice or paying taxes with currency to empire. A third issue has to do with labor division where there was none in precolonial Mof Avvi and most other Diola townships. The corporate labor the Diola exercised was threatened.

As I noted earlier, men and women once equally owned rice fields which they cultivated together, but with the advent of peanut farming most men grew and sold peanuts for cash in accordance to the newly in-troduced imperial economy. Women, on the other hand, were left to cul-tivate, plant, and harvest the rice to feed their families.[68] In this imperially caused situation, men often controlled the money earned and women were reduced to a subordinate status as they became economically de-pendent on their husbands, precluded from a fair share in the new French

67. Marut, *Le conflit de la Casamance*, 67. See also Cheneau-Loquay, "Demain, encore le riz ?" in François-George Barbier-Wiesser, *Comprendre la Casamance*, 373.

68. Diédhiou, *Riz*, 165.

controlled market economy.[69] While many Mof Avvi dwellers and their neighbors might have considered this new economy disastrous, many northern Senegalese people, especially the Mourides, did not.[70] As a result, they became the most powerful and rich religious group in Senegal. Other Diola groups negotiated life as they deemed necessary but without completely compromising their traditions.[71] Colonization affected Senegalese people intellectually, culturally, religiously, and agriculturally.

The Diola were among the people of the protectorate considered uncivilized—an ethnic group (with subgroups[72]) living in the southwestern region of Sénégal (Casamance). Although my focus is on dwellers of the territory known as Mof Avvi "Royal Land," my grandparents' homeland, the French presence did not spare any subgroup. The Diola of Kabrousse were also affected, especially by French taxation and rice confiscations in the early 1940s. Aline Sitoé Diatta confronted the French and her movement spread to other Diola townships. In Girard's account, Queen Sibeth of Siganar and especially Jiñaabo of Séléki in Mof Avvi took part in the Diola resistance to the French occupation.[73]

In sum, Péter and Besslier concluded that the colonized Senegalese people should be thankful instead of negatively critiquing the empire. To them, potential critics should first consider imperial accomplishments that benefitted the people such as French education, agronomy, and infrastructures.[74] Although many Diola people were affected and some did farm peanuts, many tried to negotiate life in terms of give and take. Changes to Diola culture are obvious throughout Diola country but the belief in the sacredness of nature remains in the hearts of many.

69. Thomas, Les Diola, 107. See also Baum, West Africa's Women of God, 162, 167–68.

70. Foster, Faith in Empire.

71. Diédhiou, Riz, 166–68.

72. Diola of Bliss-Karons and Fonyi who dwell on the northern shore of the Casamance River and those of Oussouye (Floup), Youtou/Effoc (Diamat), Diembering (Dyiwat), Kabrousse (Her/Haer), Kagnout/Mlomp (Pointe Saint-Georges), and of Brin-Seleki. See Thomas, Les Diola, for more details.

73. Girard, Genèse, 217–267; Roche, Histoire, 40, 284–86.

74. Beslier, Le Sénégal, 221–222; Peter, L'Effort Français au Sénégal, 367–76. See also Frœlicher, Trois Colonisateurs, 143–361.

6

Conclusion

Human–Nature Relationship and Négritude

> . . . By the power of the Creator God,
> I ask you to please grant me the water of rain.
> Like all the villagers, I raise my hand
> To ask you for rain.
> We greet you with our devotion,
> Grant us our request . . ." —ALINE SITOÉ DIATTA[1]

. . . the land that you are crossing over to inherit is a land of hills and valleys, watered by rain from the sky, a land that the LORD your God looks after. The eyes of the LORD your God are always on it, from the beginning of the year to the end of the year. If you will only heed his every commandment that I am commanding you today—loving the LORD your God, and serving him with all your heart and with all your soul—then he will give the rain for your land in its season, the early rain and the later rain, and you will gather in your grain, your wine, and your oil; and he will give grass in your fields for your livestock, and you will eat your fill. —DEUT 11:11–15

Then the angel showed me the river of the water of life, bright as crystal, flowing from the throne of God and of the Lamb through the middle of the street of the city. On either side of the

---

1. Poem 10 collected by Girard in his *Genèse*, 350.

river is the tree of life with its twelve kinds of fruit, producing its fruit each month; and the leaves of the tree are for the healing of the nations. —REV 22:1–2

Senghorian Négritude as Postcolonial Repositioning

This concluding chapter shows how the initial thesis is bolstered and explains how Senghorian Négritude, *a poetics of postcolonial biblical criticism*, did much to reposition especially Diola Christians to celebrate their faith traditions that once informed their interrelationships, sustainable rice farming practices and thus inculturate the biblical message. The encounter between imperial France and Diola people altered life and agricultural practices in ways that threatened the very ecosystems Diola once embraced symbiotically and worked hard to maintain since time immemorial.

Négritude presented a monumental challenge to its founders who agonized over the appropriateness of the term itself. The French word *nègre*, which is derived from the Latin *niger,* carries a negative connotation derogatorily applied by the French to the people of African descent. Although they acknowledged their discomfort in using it, both Senghor and Césaire embraced it as a repositioning trope.[2] During the first conference of black writers and artists from Africa and the diaspora, Senghor stood in front of his brothers and sisters and reminded them that the "Negro is the person of Nature who traditionally lives of and with the soil, in and by the *cosmos.*" These words come from a Christian, who happened to be an African, very much concerned about what European colonization did to Africans and their traditional faith expressions, namely the objectification of Africans, well before Senghor was born. The centuries-long process on how this happened is clearly illustrated by Mark in the following words:

> English and French attitudes toward Africans in the Senegambia developed and became well-defined during the late sixteenth, seventeenth, and early eighteenth century. These attitudes were influenced by three main factors: European ethno-centrism, the commercial relations which governed European-African intercourse, and the growth of the slave trade. During this period, Europeans expressed increasingly negative characterizations of Africans and their way of life. An ideology of African inferiority

2. Diagne, "Négritude," 4–5, citing Césaire, *Discours sur le colonialisme,* 80.

served, in part, to validate the Atlantic slave trade. It was easier
to justify the enslavement of people who were considered less
civilized or even a lower form of humanity. The formation of this
ideology was facilitated by ethnocentric perceptions which led
to a bias in favor of more westernized peoples. One important
parameter by which Senegambians came to be judged inferior to
their European counterparts was in the area of religious beliefs
and practices.[3]

In contrast to Diola traditionalists, Muslims received a better treatment because they could write and read. Hearing their God-oriented
prayers and Qur'anic parallels to the Bible, the French and English colonists concluded that Muslims were civilized but their Diola neighbors
were primitive, animist, and idolatrous.[4]

Returning to Senghor, his words were informed by his lived experience as a young boy in his agrarian Sereer village of Joal, which he spoke
of often in his writings as his *childhood kingdom*. To Catholic missionaries, the Sereer, Senghor's ethnic group, were animists like Diola people.
The depth of his spirituality permeates his poems where he constantly
echoes the encounter between two sacred dimensions that shaped his
life—the sacred arising from his ancestral land and the one imported by
Catholic missionaries. He writes:

> Bénis ce peuple qui m'a apporté Ta Bonne Nouvelle, Seigneur,
> et ouvert mes paupières Lourdes à la lumière de la foi.
> Il a ouvert mon cœur à la connaissance du monde, me montrant
> l'arc-en-ciel des visages neufs de mes frères . . .
> Ah! je sais bien que plus d'un de Tes messages a traque mes prêtres
>   comme gibier et fait un grand carnage d'images pieuses.
> Et pourtant on aurait pu s'arranger, car elles furent,
> ces images, de la terre
> à Ton ciel l'échelle de Jacob . . .[5]

> [Bless this nation that brought me Your Good News, Lord,
> And opened my heavy-lidded eyes to the light of faith.
> It has opened my heart to knowledge of the world, showed me
> The rainbow of the new faces of my brothers . . .
> Ah! I know that more than one of Your messengers

3. Mark, "Fetishers, 'Marybuckes,'" 91.

4. Mark, "Fetishers, 'Marybuckes,'" 95–96.

5. Senghor, "Prière de Paix," in Dixon, 71–72, 349–50. For a detailed discussion of
Senghor's spirituality, see Diop, *La multivalence du sacré*, 47.

Hunted down my priests like wild game and slaughtered
Sacred Images. We might have had understanding,
For those images were our Jacob's ladder
From earth to your heaven . . .]

This poem, according to Diop, reflects Senghor's idea of the sacred. It is the lens through which he sees both the world and African Faith Traditions, not just his Sereer ones, etched in the revealed religions, especially in Christian cosmology, which he believes defines the sacred for him.[6] As Senghor understands it, colonization aimed to obliterate African culture and could not see that God was always in Africa—a reality exercised in the love of nature, namely "self-giving to the OTHER."[7] Most colonial missionaries failed to build on African spirituality—that is "Soyez nègres avec les Nègres afin de les gagner à Jésus-Christ," "Become negroes with the Negroes in order to win them to Jesus Christ"—something Father Francis Liebermann, founder of the Order of the Catholic Holy Ghost Fathers, sternly advised. In effect, Father Liebermann uncovered the proper method to what Senghor terms "la méthode négro-africaine de connaissance: *con-naître*, c'est mourir à soi pour renaitre dans l'AUTRE," "the black African method of knowledge: born-with is to die to self to be reborn in the OTHER."[8] Of course much of this advice was not followed and Africans were forced to adhere to Faith Traditions that reflected little if nothing of their culture—a situation that led to a cultural as well as religious alienation. The only option left is to reposition Africans to be Christians in their own milieu.

Just as Senghor, Césaire, and Damas were forced to formulate Négritude to reposition themselves from colonial alienation so too must Africa and her church after independence. For Senghor, repositioning Africans as well as the church from Western cultural hegemony is imperative. He is reacting to the experience of being alienated, a fact shared by most colonized people—the experience of being between two cultures: African and European. He writes:

> Mais, aujourd'hui, il est, essentiellement, question de mener une action cohérente et efficace. Celle-ci peut se résumer par les mots libération et réhabilitation. Libération de la domaine

6. Diop, *La multivalence du sacré*, 47.
7. Senghor, *Liberté 1*, 414.
8. Senghor, *Liberté 1*, 414.

culturelle de l'Occident, réhabilitation des valeurs de la Négritude. L'action est double, qui est de s'affirmer et de s'assumer.[9]

> [But today, it is essentially a question of conducting coherent and
> effective action. This can be summarized by the words liberation
> and rehabilitation—liberation from Western culture, rehabilita-
> tion of the values of Negritude. The action is twofold, which is to
> be assertive and to be responsible for one's own action.]

Colonization alienated both African culture and the church and
both must be de-alienated. Whether one appeals to Said, Bhabha, or Spivak, the goal is the same: repositioning. Once Africans are freed from
imperial trappings and then rehabilitated, they will be able to reclaim
their once objectified faith traditions and practices. Elements of Western
culture confused for scripture must be removed from both the culture
and the church and replaced with the African cultural lens. Just as Europeans were able to use tradition and exegesis to bring scripture to bear on
their own context, Africans should be able to do the same.[10] Unfortunately
much effort was expended to debunk Senghor's language about the African mode of knowing—"l'émotion est nègre, comme la raison est hellène"
(emotion is negro as reason is Greek). His cardinal sin however was his
attempt to redeem the distorted African image arguing that emotion is
integral to reason. Most blistering attacks on this sentence were directed
at his political and philosophical ideas rather than Christian faith. Senghor, who once wanted to become a Catholic priest, ended up being a
teacher, poet, politician, and president of a country newly independent
from imperial France. It is difficult to understand the breadth and complexity of his many ideas. To focus solely on the ambiguity of some of his
ideas[11] instead of building on those that are clear and readily actionable is
a waste of time the continent cannot afford.

What does Négritude have to do with Diola agricultural practices?
In his discussion of black contributions, Senghor returns to his own saying: "Negro is the person of Nature who traditionally lives of and with the
soil, in and by the *cosmos*" in conversation with Father Liebermann's advice to the Holy Ghost Fathers: "Become negroes with the Negroes to win
them to Jesus Christ." Whereas the former highlights the human-nature
relationship, the latter focuses on human mode of knowledge which is

9. Senghor, *Liberté 1*, 417.

10. Senghor, *Liberté 1*, 419.

11. Mazrui, "Négritude, the Talmudic Tradition," 300–325.

very much connected to the former. Human interrelationship, equality, and human-nature relationship pervade Senghor's underlying thought on humanism. Relationships between human and nonhuman creatures are symbiotic—a life connectivity that echoes much of Diola belief and practices.[12] Images of solidarity, communalism, and abiding interrelatedness are central to what Senghor considers to be black people's contribution to universal civilization. This is not only a response to colonialism but in many ways a rehabilitation of black people which is a foundational repositioning dimension of his Négritude. Whether he is using the designation black African, Sereer, Wolof, or Toucouleur as examples to illustrate his argument, the practices he described are also exercised by Diola people from agriculture, collectivism, to attitude toward nature.[13]

As a farmer by nature who is very much in tune with nature, the African is well adapted to the African milieu using agricultural techniques suitable to tropical climate. Senghor critiques European colonists, I suspect French, for having introduced farming practices in West Africa that did not improve agricultural production as they had projected. He writes:

> Mais, peut-être, plus que le climat, plus que les forces cosmiques, plus que le soleil et la lune, ont agi les environnements végétal et animal. De l'importance de l'arbre et de l'animal dans la mythologie négro-africaine, dans l'élaboration des totems et thèmes. Les Négro-africains se sont adonnés, très tôt, à l'agriculture, et c'est le milieu agricole qui explique le mieux leur société. Je le répète, le Négro-africain est un paysan qui vit de la terre et avec la terre ... Les ingénieurs agronomes s'en sont aperçus après avoir introduit, trop hâtivement les méthodes culturales de l'Europe. Leurs science avait échoué, dans un premier temps, là où la pratique des Négro-Africains avait réussi sans "isme" ni "logie" ni charrue. Mais ceux-ci étaient les familiers de la nature; ils cultivent, dans tous les sens, nous le verrons l'arbre et l'animal.[14]

[But, perhaps, more than the climate, rather than cosmic forces, more than the sun and moon, acted the plant and animal

12. Senghor, *Liberté 1*, 27–29.

13. Senghor, *Liberté 1*, 28–30. It is important to note that there are differences in farming practices between the Sereer, Wolof, Toucouleur or the Diola, especially in the areas of rituals associated with farming and harvesting. However, Senghor is correct in highlighting equality between the sexes, communism, solidarity, and human-nature relationship.

14. Senghor, *Liberté 1*, 255.

environments, from the importance of *tree* and *animal* in the
Black African mythology, in the development of totems and
themes. The black Africans were given, very early, agriculture,
and it is the agricultural sector that best explains their society. I
repeat, the African Negro is a farmer who lives of and with the
land . . . agronomists realized after having introduced too hastily European farming methods. Their science had failed, at first,
where practices of black Africans have succeeded without "ism,"
"logy" or plow. But these were familiar with nature; they farm in
all directions, we shall see the tree and the animal.]

Senghorian Négritude helped many Senegalese people reposition
themselves from the trauma wrought by the alienating effect of French
colonization and empowered them to reclaim their culture and traditional practices. It helped resurrect national pride in being black and
members of a vibrant black culture. In the case of Diola people, many
who converted to Christianity and were once encouraged by the Catholic
Holy Ghost Fathers to abandon faith traditions as primitive and supersti-
tious began to reclaim the same beliefs and practices as something worth
celebrating. One can hear Diola people respond to their northern brothers and sisters who still think of them as savages, *Je connais les coutumes,
I know my customs*. Baum is correct in saying that Négritude reinvigo-
rated Diola pride in being African and reclaiming ancestral practices.[15] I,
myself, echoed these words time and again in the late 1980s when I was
attending school in Dakar.

Diola–Nature Relationship and the Bible

In chapter two, I argued that the Diola developed a unique way of farming rice. To this day, the sacredness of rice is a belief most Diola people
share in spite of the major transitions precipitated by French colonialism. The *hil* of the Diola of Mof Avvi, as I noted earlier in chapter 2, is
their *sacred devotion to cultivate the sacred land and plant the sacred rice*.
Reverence for God and God's creation in Diola lived experience manifests itself in meticulous rituals spread out from before rice planting to its
harvest. Everything begins with the first (*garumò*) of seven indispensable
farming rituals during which the Diola community is made ready for the
arduous labor.[16]

15. Baum, "Emergence," 391.
16. Palmeri, *Living With the Diola*, 97.

I will summarize the rituals built around rice farming in Mof Avvi recorded by Palmeri.[17] Palm wine is poured on the altar of the *ufulungs* (shrine of the spirit of the ancestor of the family). Families with children renegotiate child care. The father assumes child care. Domestic problems like divorce have to wait until the end of the cycle to take effect. Seasonal migrants must return to cultivate their rice fields. Shortly after *garumò*, the second ceremony called *ebùn* follows in late June to early July. Men prepare the fields by seed bedding, and by creating ridges and diking to ensure drainage is all in place waiting for the actual rice planting task. For rice planting to begin, the rainmaking priest pours libation on the altar of the same shrine, offers prayers, and everyone present shares meals of rice. This ritual is performed to ensure that the deity lavishes the community with abundant rain and harvest. Individual family shrine rituals are officiated by other priests performing the same ritual. Rice seedling in nurseries begins as soon as ebùn was observed—a ritual performed even to this day. As I mentioned in chapter one, the Diola, especially those whose fields had Acacia Albida trees, knew the benefits of cultivating rice nurseries close to these trees for their natural ability to dispense good nutrients for the paddy.[18]

The third ritual (*galilò buròk*) is performed from late July to mid-August by the wives of the king in a rice paddy nursery close to the sacred forest. They pour libation and transplant the royal paddy believed to be sacred and therefore reserved for special rainmaking rituals performed only at the *ufulung* of the king. As soon as this observance is complete, other women begin transplanting the paddy from their own nurseries. The sacredness of the king's paddy is symbolic for all the Mof Avvi paddies. Seedlings are carried to the already cultivated rice fields for planting from mid-August to about the end of September. At this time the people hope the rituals performed to that point are accepted by Ala Émit who

17. Palmeri, *Living With the Diola*, 97–101. *Garumò* (Diola people gather and prepare to start rice farming), *Ebùn* (rain priest pours the libations at the altar of his *ululungs* and announces the beginning of rice planting), *Galilò buròk* (end of rice transplantation by the rain priest, community members then start transplanting theirs), *Gahùl Émit* (ceremony of conciliation intended to bring the rains), *Uutés* (the last transplanting announces the end of rice cultivation), Béng (beginning of harvest), and *Gaffilò* (rain priest proclaims the end of the farming season).

18. Berghen and Manga, *Une Introduction*, 76–77. See also Diédhiou, *Riz*, 108. This underscores the point Senghor made about the African knowledge of agriculture in tropical climates and also knowing how to use the land in ways foreigners do not. See Senghor, *Liberté 1*, 255.

will send rain and secure a life sustaining abundance of rice. The rationale for these rituals echoes God's promise to Israel that the deity would send rain to the believing and obedient community (Deut 11:10–15).

The fourth ritual (*gahùl emìt*) focuses on human–nature relationship that might engender a divine response to lavish the obedient community with abundant rain. Here, Diola appropriate response to the divine intention to provide rain is similar to the biblical voice as I noted above (Deut 11:11–12). This ritual is also performed by women who pour water tempered with prayer for God to send abundant rain. A black bull symbolizing black clouds is sacrificed and meals are shared. At Aline Sitoé Diatta's shrine, a black bull is often sacrificed during rainmaking rituals.

By the end of October, a fifth ritual (*uutés*) concludes paddy planting proclaimed by the shrine keeper located in one of the Mof Avvi townships known as Batignère. This ritual observed with wine libations marks not only the end of rice paddy planting but also lifting of the ban on divorce enforced by the initial observance of *garumò*. A wife who finds her marriage unbearable could leave and return to her parents' household. The ritual marked the end and beginning of new relationships. Activities suspended during *garumò* must now be resumed. Community members could now do other tasks like fishing, tapping palm wine and the like. The sixth ritual, in November, marks the beginning of harvest, and is celebrated with wine libations to the spirit of the *béng*, who protected the rice fields. The arduous rice farming season finally ends with the seventh ceremony (*gaffilò*).

During this ritual performed in the sacred forest, the rainmaking priest extends gratitude to *Gaffilò*. Other priests join the rainmaking priest in the forest and there they pour palm wine libation and share meals of rice cooked with fish. Families also celebrate this end of rice farming in their own households. Every ritual is based on the deity-human-nature relationship. Senghor alluded to this abiding relationship saying, "la religion négro-Africaine est une religion *agriare* . . . La religion négro-Africaine est aussi une *religion familiale*,"[19] "black African religion is an *agrarian* religion . . . The black African religion is also *a family religion.*" To build on Senghor's words, I would say that rice farming to Diola people is a spiritual journey that seeks to maintain a deity-human-nature relationship. A violation of this relationship threatens both the environment—that is life itself of human and non-human beings. Diola

19. Senghor, *Liberté 1*, 267. The italicized words are his.

people find their role participatory with the performance ritual believed to maintain a sustainable equilibrium that does not disrupt the rhythm of life. This is done by maintaining two interrelated symbolic worlds: one "is based on the man-god-land relationship, at once an ontological explanation of the life cycle and the ideological manifestation of the culture" and the other "on the set of rituals that organize relations between people and spirits, creating what is from a symbolic point of view a single coherent universe."[20] Palmeri observes:

> The Diola feel that they are part of a totality in which they, the objects around them, the things that happen, and nature itself are elements within a single and all encompassing context. This is why the elements needed for survival, like the land and its products, the forests and animals, are not considered to be available to anyone who happens to be the first to take possession of them. Nature is not seen as an object to be exploited, but rather as a subject that meets people on equal terms. This view of nature as a protagonist in its own right calls into question an entire body of concepts that position traditional society within a logical framework of production, consumption and exchange, and which is in fact only typical of the West . . . nature is a partner that can be both good and evil. It gives people life, but can also abandon them and withhold life as well. . . There is a symbolic unity between the group, the gods and nature within which the harvest is experienced not as the equivalent of labor, but as offered by nature as part of the continuing process of the symbolic exchange/gift relation linking man, nature and god.[21]

The fauna and the flora are central to this journey. The sacred forest is not just a place for rituals such as *buhut* and *gagnaleen*,[22] *it is a living pharmacy.* Like Diola people, many ethnic groups also depend very much on nature for food and medicines.[23] Mof Avvi healers are first and foremost rice farmers. Healing is an art exercised not for making money but service to community members in need. The healer does not expect

20. Palmeri, *Living With the Diola*, 199.

21. Palmeri, *Living With the Diola*, 195–96.

22. *Bukut* is the men's initiation rite during which initiates learn about adulthood and responsibility. *Gagnaleen* is a ritual exclusively performed by women on behalf of other women who have difficulty bearing children or raising one to adulthood.

23. Connor and Keeney, *Shamans of the World*; Somé, *The Healing Wisdom of Africa.* See also Keener, *Miracles*, who offers an extensive account of healings from around the world.

anything in return. The healed are left to choose any means by which they wish to extend gratitude.[24] Special tree leaves, roots, and bark are used by many healers of Mof Avvi for the healthcare of the community. In fact, my grandmother was very gifted in this art and often served the entire village of Tranquille Adéane as a midwife. To my knowledge, she charged nothing for her services. She named most of the children she delivered at the parents' request.

Human-Nature Relationship in the Bible and Other Traditions

I was stunned when I came across the work of Nisbert Taisekwa Taringa in which he engages his Shona Faith Traditions through a Christian lens. He recognizes some important aspects of Shona culture that are sensitive to the environment and worthy of exploration for interfaith conversation. Debates on the importance of Shona Faith Traditions in postcolonial Africa I mentioned earlier have something to do with the fact that they share similar elements found in what I am calling a Diola cosmotheology and its encounter with colonial missionary Christianity. Religion as lived experience is not unique to Diola people or most Africans and is an integral part of daily life in biblical times. Recent scholarship in Zimbabwe has been devoted to divine governance over nonhuman and human creatures; in particular, exploring how humans relate ecologically to nature in Shona Faith Traditions and Christianity. As in the case of Diola people, colonialists and colonial Christian missionaries failed to respect and learn from the socioreligious and spiritual practices of Zimbabweans, especially agricultural practices of the devotees of Shona faith traditions. Shona Faith Traditions are in many ways similar to those Diola people practiced before the dawn of colonization. Some recent publications have shown how Robert Mugabe built on traditional Shona beliefs in land as divine estate. As Niekerk sees it:

> The symbolism of land played a central role in mobilizing the rural communities to support the war for liberation from white domination and occupation in the time when Zimbabwe was still Rhodesia, with a white government. In Zimbabwe, "(L) and belongs to God, the ancestors and, particularly, to the founders of the lineage, clan or tribe interred therein." Mwari is the Shona High God, the creator. The spirit mediums are the link between

24. Berghen and Manga, *Une Introduction*, 241–42.

the people and the different tribal spirits and the lesser spirits. At the end of the 19th century the mediums played a vital role in the uprisings of 1894 and 1896–1897 against the colonial occupation of the land.[25]

Losing land to colonists, many Zimbabwean subsistence farmers resorted to traditional religious rituals for answers. As in Aline Sitoé Diatta's rainmaking rituals, direct appeals to the divine were made. The process is such that "god is addressed more directly as an insider, one who is present at the ceremony . . . (the) ceremonies affirm Mwari's traditional role as ecological liberator, that is, as rain-giver, who periodically liberates selected regions or entire country from crippling droughts."[26]

French imperial policies in Senegal affected long held Diola relations to the land and much of the country's agricultural sector. Peanuts, as a cash crop, were not the only threat to traditional agricultural practices. Logging gradually threatened the sacred forest on either side of the Casamance River and recent studies evinced how much deforestation and natural factors related to climate contributed to the degradation of rice fields. As Mouhamadou Diémé documents, the shortage of rainfall from 1918 to 2008, coupled with a steady rise in temperature in the region, spiked at an alarming rate from the 1970s to this day.[27] Clearly, climate change, the increasing effect of clandestine deforestation[28] and the need for modern professional careers such as nursing, agronomy and the like[29] are seriously changing Diola culture. Diémé hopes enlisting local authorities to conserve nature might help reverse this spiraling danger— the very thing Diola people did for centuries before colonization.[30]

What struck me as I read Taringa's work was his insistence that African Traditional Religious attitude toward nature lies in fear of or reverence to ancestral spirits instead of respect for nature.[31] I suspect he

25. Niekerk, "The Lost Land and the Earth Mother," 196–97.

26. Niekerk, "The Lost Land and the Earth Mother," 201.

27. Diémé, *Déforestation, dégradation de terres*, documents the deterioration of rice field soil due to clandestine logging as well as measures taken to reverse deforestation. Dia, *Lowland Rice and Climate*, explored the effect of climate change on rice farming in Sédhiou, Casamance.

28. Diémé, *Déforestation, dégradation de terres*, 70–84.

29. Barbier-Wiesser and Preira, "Demain, les jeunes? " *in Comprendre la Casamance*, 321–35.

30. Diémé, *Déforestation, dégradation de terres*, 133–63.

31. Taringa, *Towards an African-Christian*, 191–214.

is generalizing based on his Shona Faith Traditions rather than African Traditional Religion. I object to his generalization because my Diola expression of African Traditional Religion is certainly not based on fear, but on the idea that nature is not an object but a subject humans meet on equal terms, and that there is kinship between human and nonhuman creatures who owe their existence to God—Ala Émit for Diola people. Even if one were to agree with Taringa, the Bible neither precludes fear from faith nor inhibits it. Biblical language is highly metaphorical because it is the human voice testifying about human experiences of the divine—something that cannot be done in any other way than through human words.

The creation myths discussed in chapter 3 reveal that human-nature relationship is ambivalent in the Hebrew Bible and Ancient Near Eastern texts. *Enuma Elish* and *Atrahasis* provide a view of human-nature relationship different from the biblical account. Also noted were other ancient texts that highlight a keen relationship between humans, the fauna, and the flora—a reality well-illustrated in the works of Lang, Keel and Schroer, and Keel and Uehlinger.[32] The biblical narrative reflects the kind of relationship Diola people would readily recognize, especially as framed in Gen 1–2. Creatures (the earth, the fauna, and the flora) God made responded to the divine command. Only the human response gave rise to a host of complex issues captured through intriguing myths (Gen 1–11). What is clear from the text is the failure of human agency to act in accordance with divine creative intention. Gen 3–4 assumes an altered relationship between deity-human-nature on the divinely cursed earth. The relationship model initiated by the deity for humans to emulate is somewhat distorted—the outcome of which significantly affected the cosmos and everything in it (human and non-human).

Whether the divine intent was for humans to rule over and dominate God's creation or not, the result proved catastrophic. The divine determination to redeem creation is clearly voiced by these biblical myths because the divine vision echoed in them pictures humans as co-creators with God (Gen 1–11). The human relational responsibility to care, rather than dominate, is also evinced (Gen 2:15). The language of "knowledge of good and evil," land, hard labor, mortality, and violence seems to reflect exilic community introspections and hopes for newness. This is the

---

32. Keel and Uehlinger, *Gods, Goddesses*; Lang, *The Hebrew God*; Keel and Schroer, *Creation*.

central biblical vision for creation—a reality some Hebrew prophets[33] proclaimed and sages[34] keenly upheld as the divine intention for creation and the human role in it. Israel's response to exercise the divine role in creation was stymied by imperial interference from the Assyrians to the Romans.[35]

Classical literature provides a mixed picture of human attitude toward nature. Some emphasize the human destructive hand on both flora and fauna[36] while other types provide a more relational picture that is sensitive to nature and its relationship to the divine. This is well-illustrated in the work of Dillon on sacred groves and trees.[37] Influenced by their Greco-Roman world, New Testament authors often used apocalyptic language to speak about the roles of two diametrically opposed empires on creation: God's empire in the redemptive work of Jesus Christ and Rome's empire in Jupiter's son, Caesar. The parables, though highly figurative, reveal the inner work of nature and provide models for humans to emulate. Farming scenes do not have a ritual dimension, as in the Diola world, but focus on the human and nature roles familiar to peasants. What is important to highlight here is the similarity between Diola and New Testament peasantry—sowing under the right conditions and reaping. Read with Gen 1:11–12 and Deut 11:11–15 in mind, a clear picture emerges. Jesus' parable (Mark 4:26–29) highlights the roles agents like the farmer, the earth, and the seed play. Luke 13:8 offers an additional clue missing from the Markan version. It leaves open the possibility that either the productive powers of the earth must have been undermined or the right conditions were not met in the first place. The failure of human agency to act appropriately rendered the plant unproductive.

The author of John offers yet another intriguing take on human-nature relationship by connecting Jesus to creation. Many interpreters simply overlook the materiality of Jesus of which the author persistently spoke (John 1:1–14; 3:20). The expression "God so loved the world" should not be reduced to humans but includes the entire creation—human and non-human creation (John 3:16). The logos enters into human history and becomes human (John 1:2–4; 14; 3:16), that is Jesus, who

33. Wilson, *Prophecy and Society*; Petersen, *Prophetic Literature*.

34. Perdue, Wisdom *and Creation*; Perdue, *Wisdom Literature*.

35. Perdue and Carter, *Israel and Empire*.

36. Nollé, "Boars, Bears, and Bugs"; Toner, *Roman Disasters*.

37. Dillon, "The Ecology of the Greek Sanctuary."

still maintains his divinity. A Diola would have affirmed this relationship. The apostle Paul anticipates the reversal of the failure of the human agency in those who are in Christ—a process initiated by God in the cross of Christ Jesus (Rom 8:1–2, 19–23). Human and non-human creatures also await divine redemption. Against Ps-Aristotle, who believes in a harmonious cosmos sustained by divine power active in pairs of opposites (air, fire, water, and earth), Paul anticipates God, not Caesar, will transform divine-human-nature relationship through the participatory agency of God's children. The imperially staged paradisiacal images of fertility, abundance, and newness, which conceal imperial exploitation of humans and nature, will be subverted. The author of Revelation also takes on empire, subverting its staged paradisiac images with God's new city and garden (Ara Pacis). There humans would have access to water and inexhaustible abundant food from trees year round whose healing leaves sustain an everlasting divine healthcare for all people.

These images resonate with Diola people who have always tried to maintain a symbiotic life with nature for sustenance and healthcare. I reiterate this is an analogical attempt to understand how Diola Faith Traditions might be conversant with the biblical notions on divine-human-nature relationship. Analogically, I argued that learning from non-biblical traditions would help Christians deal with global warming. I am not calling for Diola people to make a return to their traditional farming practices or western Christians to adopt them. I am hoping that twenty-first century Diola and western Christians will learn and draw from them actionable elements for our age threatened by human indifference to the agency of nature. The point is to see how we might build on these insights to negotiate life with nature as Native Americans and other cultures have always done without much interruption to the life of nature. The biblical text encourages Christians to respond to God's creation as participatory agents. Recent publications are calling for a change in lifestyle that does not harm the environment but relates to it as a subject[38] worthy of reverence not as a deity but as sacred creature like us.

Mof Avvi Diola Today

The French-backed land tenure law introduced in 1964 shook the foundation of traditional views of land tenure amongst the various ethnic

---

38. Bauckham, *Living with Other Creatures*; Tonstad, *The Letter to the Romans*.

groups of Senegal. In spite of Senghor's effort to attenuate the people's angst about this tenure law, especially Diola people, insisting that it would in no way undermine traditional practices, the Diola saw it as yet another imperial intrusion on their very religious agrarian life.[39] The law, in many ways, was to many Diola people another colonial ploy to seize their land for the purpose of farming peanuts. That was, in fact, the initial objective of colonial administrators: to make Senegal one of the main producers of peanuts as stated by Péter and Besslier.[40] As it turns out, the colonists were wrong. Peanuts did little to grow the Senegalese economy; instead the opposite appears to be true according to Diédhiou and Diabone.[41] To Diédhiou, Senegal's economy:

> reste toujours dépendante des structures qui ont été mises en place depuis la colonisation. Les politiques économiques et agricoles appliques depuis l'indépendance n'ont pas amélioré les conditions de vie des populations rurales et urbaines, dont beaucoup restent nostalgiques de la période colonial durant laquelle les conditions de vie leur semblaient meilleures . . . la structure fondamentale de l'agriculture sénégalaise est soumise à une tyrannie de l'arachide. À l'interne, cette tyrannie a étouffé le développement des culture vivrières dont, l'externe les débouchés restent encore dépendants du contexte mondial qui lui fournit ses intrants et ses principaux marches.[42]

> [remains dependent on the structures that have been set since the colonization. Economic and agricultural policies applied since independence have not improved the living conditions of rural and urban populations, many of which remain nostalgic for the colonial period in which the living conditions appear their best . . . The fundamental structure of Senegalese agriculture is subjected to "a tyranny of peanuts." Internally, this tyranny has stifled the development of subsistence farming of which the external opportunities are still dependent on the world context which provides its inputs and its main steps.]

The outcome of this reliance on imperial structures that takes the land away from traditionalists led to the Diola decision to fight for their

---

39. Berghen and Manga, *Une Introduction*, 278; Manga, *La Casamance*, 165–69; Ki-Zerbo, *Les sources du droits*, 141–58; Diabone, *Les ressources foncières*, 128.

40. Péter, *L'Effort Français au Sénégal*, 55; Besslier, *Le Sénégal*, 221–22.

41. Diédhiou, *Riz*; Diabone, *Les ressources foncières*, 128.

42. Diédhiou, *Riz*.

freedom and manage their own affairs as they did for centuries before the colonial dawn. Although Diola people were not immune from family feuds and intergroup skirmishes over land, imperial intrusion, according to many observers, led to a war for independence that started in the early 1980s, which severely displaced my family and led to the eventual death of my stepfather. In fact, most ethnographers believe antecedents of this war can be traced back to the colonial era.[43] As it was with their brothers and sisters of the northern banks of the Casamance River, changes wrought by France in Senegal finally affected Diola traditions related to political leadership, land tenure, and agricultural practices. These changes precipitated Linares' comments in which she made fun of the idea that the so-called Diola timeless Faith Traditions and farming practices were in fact anything but timeless.[44]

Educated and assimilated Senegalese elites, like Senghor and many Diola people, turned to Négritude as a repositioning trope to reaffirm their identity as black Africans while advocating a cultural symbiosis. Besides the destabilizing effects of the government tenure law decreed in 1964, the French portrayal of the Diola as uncivilized and irreligious is alive and well; however, it failed to deter most Diola people from observing some of their socioreligious traditions as illustrated by the words of a Diola Catholic priest, Father Nazaire Diatta. Sometime in the mid-1990s, Father Diatta wrote a letter to government officials serving in the Casamance region insisting that "participation and communion for the promotion of collective and individual life" is the touchstone of the Diola socioreligious world.[45]

The Diola can neither be *othered* to submission nor assimilated to French ways but can only be won through dialogue and a quest for "a common solution" leading to "peace, harmony, and communion." To Father Diatta, participation in traditional religious practices is a necessary act for a Diola Christian—a much needed "return to native land" that should not be viewed as a renunciation of Christian faith.[46] The actions

---

43. Marut, *Le conflit de la Casamance*; Diédhiou, *L'identité Joola*; Manga, *La Casamance*. The war broke out in 1982 and the cease fire introduced in 2004 was often interrupted by nagging flare-ups culminating with independence advocates suing the Senegalese government in 2014.

44. Linares, *Power, Prayer, and Production*, 213.

45. Diatta, "Le Prêtre et les députés," in François-George Barbier-Wiesser, *Comprendre la Casamance*, 268.

46. Diatta, "Participation du Joola chrétien aux rites Traditionnels," 77–8. A

of Robert Sagna,[47] a well-educated uninitiated Diola Catholic serving in the Senegalese government for many years, corroborate Father Diatta's argument when Sagna recently decided to undergo initiation (*Bouhout*) as a way of reclaiming his identity. During the summer of 2016, a Diola professional soccer player, Bakary Sagna, left the French national team for the same initiation rite in the Casamance—Diola country. Upon his return to France, his teammates received him with respect.

According to Adrien Manga, Mof Avvi dwellers found ways to adjust to the inevitable reality. The once-treasured rice farming practices are being relinquished, leaving rice fields flooded with salt water as modern agricultural practices are being adopted. Like the Tunisian Muslims who once upheld *habous* tenure practices just to see them slipping away under imperial sway, so are most of Diola agrarian customs. Manga, who reflects on the many changes happening in Enampor, Séléki and other townships of Mof Avvi, advises accommodation and innovation—that is building on the positive elements of both the Diola and French cultures. He admits that Diola Faith Traditions should be kept but rejects remarks made by "foreigners who believe that the animists are pagans, that is they attribute power to carved statues instead of God" as false.[48] The Diola, Manga maintains, knows God and the afterlife. French colonial influences are so monumental that many Diola people are abandoning their rice fields. Architectural changes in the Mof Avvi townships are forever altering the Diola habitat. The new houses being built with zinc roofing are replacing the traditional Diola impluviums and attract many pests that were once absent in the traditional impluviums. These changes precipitated Linares' remarks on how things changed since the first time she visited Diola country including the increasing use of machines to cultivate fields.

The mandingized Diola, the first to farm peanuts to my knowledge, on the northern ridge of the Casamance River, did not abandon most of their traditional beliefs whether Muslim or Christians. Some have

---

handful of Diola Christians however believe their socioreligious traditions are satanic and call for their repudiation.

47. de Jong, *Masquerades of Modernity*, 78–80, sees a political dimension to his initiation—an argument I dispute.

48. Manga, "Conclusion," in *Une Introduction*, 282, "étrangers qui croient que les animistes sont des païens, c'est, à dire qu'ils attribuent un pouvoir a des statuettes et non à Dieux. Ce qui est faux. Nous savons que Dieu est en nous et que nous sommes éternels, forme d'un corps, d'un double et d'une âme." See pages 275–83.

adjusted to life in independent Senegal without completely abandoning their faith traditions. The post-independence developments in the agricultural sector became great cause for concern for many. Sagna's re-embrace of Diola traditional ritual of initiation testifies to an increasing attempt by many Diola people to accommodate to the new realities without abandoning central Diola beliefs. This is also true for their brothers and sisters of the southern bank. Innovative change is part of human life but does not necessarily mean the obliteration of one's faith traditions. In spite of the gradual changes wrought by neocolonialism and globalization, important Diola Faith Traditions persist and their resurgence is pervasive. Rice remains a sacred crop for many Diola people and the land, the forest and animals are sacred creatures made by Ala Émit.

Senghorian Negritude as a *Poetics of Postcolonial Biblical Criticism* is a repositioning trope to liberate and rehabilitate colonized people of African descent. In this sense, it is much more a prophetic than apostolic voice calling intellectual people of African descent to do the right thing for themselves by reclaiming who they are—humans *who traditionally live of the soil and with the soil, in and by the cosmos*. The agency of nature to sustain human and other forms of life is enshrined not only in the biblical myths of creation, wisdom, and prophetic utterances, she permeates Sereer and Diola faith traditions. In light of this, what does this mean for ecologically minded people faced with an impending ecological disaster as we are are experiencing? Might *living of the soil and with the soil, in and by the cosmos* be the answer? Probably.

Bibliography

Primary Sources

Aristotle. *Metaphysics, I–IX*. Edited by Jeffery Henderson. Translated by Hugh Tredennick and G. Cyril Armstrong. LCL. Cambridge: Harvard University Press, 1933.

———. *Metaphysics, X–XIV, Oeconomica, Magna Moralia*. Edited by G. P. Goold. Translated by Hugh Tredennick and G. Cyril Armstrong. LCL. Cambridge: Harvard University Press, 1936.

———. *Physics*. Translated by Philip H. Wicksteed and Francis M. Cornford. 2 vols. LCL. Cambridge: Harvard University Press, 1929–1934.

———. *Art of Rhetoric*. Edited by G. P. Goold. Translated by J. H. Frese. LCL. Cambridge: Harvard University Press, 1926.

Cato and Varro. *On Agriculture*. Edited by G. P. Goold. Translated by W. D. Hooper and H. B. Ash. LCL. Cambridge: Harvard University Press, 1934.

Cicero. *Ad Quintum fratren*. Edited and translated by D. R. Shackleton Bailey. LCL. Cambridge: Harvard University Press, 2002.

———. *De Republica*. Translated by Clinton Walker Keyes. LCL. Cambridge: Harvard University Press, 1928.

Columella. *On Agriculture X–XII*. Edited by Jeffery Henderson. Translated by E. S. Foster and Edward H. Heffner. LCL. Cambridge: Harvard University Press, 1955.

Diodorus. *Diodorus of Sicily*. Edited by T. E. Page. Translated by C. H. Oldfather. 12 vols. LCL. Cambridge: Harvard University Press, 1933–1967.

Diogenes Laertius. *Lives of Eminent Philosophers*. Edited by G. P. Goold. Translated by R. D. Hicks. 2 vols. Loeb Classical Library. Cambridge: Harvard University Press, 1925.

Dionysius of Halicarnassus. *Critical Essays*. Edited by Jeffrey Henderson. Translated by Stephen Usher. Vol. I. LCL. Cambridge: Harvard University Press, 1974.

Hesiod. *Theogony, Works and Days, Testimonia*. Edited and Translated by Glenn W. Most. LCL. Cambridge: Harvard University Press, 2006.

Horace. *Odes and Epodes*. Edited by Jeffery Henderson. Translated by Nail Rudd. LCL. Cambridge: Harvard University Press, 2004.

Isocrates. Volume I and II. Edited by Jeffery Henderson. Translated by George Norlin. LCL. Cambridge: Harvard University Press, 1929.

Josephus. *Jewish Antiquities*. Translated by H. St. J. Thackeray et al. 9 vols. LCL. Cambridge: Harvard University Press, 1930–1965.

———. *The Life Against Apion*. Edited by G. P. Goold. Translated by H. St. J. Thackeray. LCL. Cambridge: Harvard University Press, 1926.

———. *The Jewish War*. Edited by G. P. Goold. Translated by H. St. Thackeray. 3 vols. LCL. Cambridge: Harvard University Press, 1927–1928.

Livy. *Histories: From The Founding of the City*. Edited by T. E. Page. Translated by Evan T. Sage. LCL. Cambridge: Harvard University Press, 1955.

Ovid. *Fasti*. Translated by Sir James George Frazer. LCL. Cambridge: Harvard University Press, 1931.

Pausanias. *Description of Greece*. Translated by W. H. S. Jones. Vol. I. LCL. Cambridge: Harvard University Press, 1918.

Philo. *Questions and Answers on Exodus*. Edited by G. P. Goold. Translated by Ralph Marcus. Vol II. LCL. Cambridge: Harvard University Press, 1953.

———. Translated by F. H. Colson and G. H. Whitaker. 10 vols. LCL. Cambridge: Harvard University Press, 1929–1942.

Plato. *Les Lois: Livres III–VI*. Collection des Universités de France: Association Guillaume Budé. Texte Etabli et Traduit par Eduard des Places. Paris: Les Belle Lettres, 1994.

———. *Epinomis*. Edited by T. E. Page. Translated by W. R. M. Lamb. LCL. Cambridge: Harvard University Press, 1927.

———. *The Laws*. Edited by G. P. Goold. Translated by R. G. Bury. Vol I & II. LCL. Cambridge: Harvard University Press, 1926.

———. *Menexenus*. Edited by G. P. Goold. Translated by R. G. Bury. LCL. Cambridge: Harvard University Press, 1929.

———. *Republic*. Translated by Paul Shorey. 2 vols. LCL. Cambridge: Harvard University Press, 1930/1935.

———. *Symposium*. Translated by W. R. M. Lamb. LCL. Cambridge: Harvard University Press, 1925.

Pliny. *Natural History*. Edited by T. E. Page. Translated by H. Rackham. Vol. II. LCL. Cambridge: Harvard University Press, 1942.

———. *Letters and Panegyricus*. Translated by Betty Radice. LCL. Cambridge: Harvard University Press, 1969.

Plutarch. *Moralia*. Edited by Jeffrey Henderson. Translated by Frank Cole Babbitt. Vol IV. LCL. Cambridge: Harvard University Press, 1936.

Polybius. *The Histories*. Edited by Jeffrey Henderson. Translated by W. R. Paton. Vol. II. LCL. Cambridge: Harvard University Press, 1922.

Pseudo-Aristotle. *On Philosophical Refutations, On Coming-To-Be and Passing Away, On the Cosmos*. Edited by Jeffery Henderson. Translated by E. S. Forster and D. J. Furley. LCL. Cambridge: Harvard University Press, 1955.

Seneca. *Epistles*. Edited by G. P. Goold. Translated by Richard M. Gummere. LCL. Cambridge: Harvard University Press, 1920.

———. *On Benefits*. Edited by G. P. Goold. Translated by Richard M. Gummere. LCL. Cambridge: Harvard University Press, 1920.

Strabo. *Geography*. Translated by Horace L. Jones. Vol. VI. LCL. Cambridge: Harvard University Press, 1929.

———. *Geography*. Translated by Horace L. Jones. Vol. VII. LCL. Cambridge: Harvard University Press, 1930.

Strabon. *Géographie.* Tome II. Livres III et IV. Collection des Universités de France Text Établi et Traduit par François Lasserre. Paris: Les Belles Letters, 1966.

———. *Géographie.* Tome IX. Livres XII. Collection des Universités de France. Text Établi et Traduit par François Lasserre. Paris: Les Belles Letters, 1981.

Suetonius. *Claudius.* Edited by Jeffrey Henderson. Translated by J. C. Rolfe. Vol II. LCL. Cambridge: Harvard University Press, 1914.

Tacitus. *Annals.* Edited by E. H. Warmington. Translated by John Jackson. Vol. IV. Loeb Classical Library. Cambridge: Harvard University Press, 1956.

———. *The Histories.* Edited by G. P. Goold. Translated by Clifford H. Moore. Vol. II. Books IV-V. Loeb Classical Library. Cambridge: Harvard University Press, 1956.

Virgil. *Eclogues, Georgics Aeneid I-IV.* Edited by Jeffery Henderson. Translated by H. Rushton Fairclough. Loeb Classical Library. Cambridge: Harvard University Press, 1916.

Secondary Works

Albertz, Rainer. *A History of Israelite Religion in the Old Testament.* Vol. 1, *The Beginnings of the End of the Monarchy.* Translated by John Bowden. Old Testament Library. Louisville: Westminster John Knox, 1994.

Appiah, Anthony K. *In My Father's House: Africa in the Philosophy of Culture.* New York: Oxford University Press, 1992.

Ashcroft, Bill, Gareth Griffiths, and Helen Tiffin. "Third World (First, Second, Fourth)." In *Post-Colonial Studies: The Key Concepts,* 212–13. 2nd ed. Routledge Key Guides. New York: Routledge, 2007.

Ashford, Douglass E. "Succession and Social Change in Tunisia." *International Journal of Middle East Studies* 4 (1973) 23–39.

Aune, David. *Revelation 17–22.* Word Biblical Commentary 52C. Nashville: Nelson, 1998.

Aus, Roger David. *My Name Is "Legion": Palestinian Judaic Traditions in Mark: 5:1–20 and Other Gospel Texts.* Studies in Judaism. Dallas: University Press of America, 2003.

Bâ, Sylvia. *The Concept of Négritude in the Poetry of Léopold Sédar Senghor.* Princeton: Princeton University Press, 1972.

Balch, David L. "Paul's Portrait of Christ Crucified (Gal 3:1) in Light of Paintings and Sculptures of Suffering and Death in Popmeiian and Roman Houses." In *Early Christian Families in Context: An Interdisciplinary Dialogue,* edited by David L. Balch and Carolyn Osiek, 84–108. Religion, Marriage and Family. Grand Rapids: Eerdmans, 2003.

Balz, Horst. "Κόσμος." In *EDNT* 2 (1991) 309–13.

Barbier-Wiesser, François-George, and Antoinette Preira. "Demain, les jeunes?" In *Comprendre la Casamance: Chronique d'une intégration contrasté,* edited by François-George Barbier-Wiesser, 321–35. Paris: Karthala, 1994.

Barr, James. "Man and Nature—The Ecological Controversy and the Old Testament." In *Biblical Interpretation: The Collected Essays of James Barr,* edited by John Barton, 2:344–60. New York: Oxford University Press, 2013.

Bassène, Alain-Christian. *Morphosyntaxe du jóola banjal: Langue atlantique du Sénégal.* Grammatical analyses of African languages 32. Cologne: Kôppe, 2007.

Bassène, René Capain. *L'abbé Augustin Diamacoune Senghor: Par lui-même et par ceux qui l'ont connu.* Paris: L'Harmattan, 2013.

Bauckham, Richard. *Living with Other Creatures: Green Exegesis and Theology.* Waco, TX: Baylor University Press, 2015.

Baum, Robert M. "*Alinesitoué*: A Diola Woman Prophet in West Africa." In *Unspoken Words: Women's Religious Lives,* edited by Nancy Auer Falk and Rita M. Gross, 179–95. 3rd ed. Belmont, CA: Wordsworth, 2001.

———. "Crimes of the Dream World: French Trials of Diola Witches in Colonial Senegal." *International Journal of African Historical Studies* 37 (2004) 201–28.

———. "Diola Prophets." In *Encyclopedia of African and African-American Religions,* edited by Stephen D. Glazier, 116–18. New York: Routledge, 2001.

———. "Emergence of Diola Christianity." *Africa* 60 (1990) 371–98.

———. "Shrines, Medicines, and the Strength of the Head: The Way of the Warrior among the Diola of Senegambia." *Numen* 40 (1993) 274–92.

———. *Shrines of the Slave Trade: Diola Religion and Society in Precolonial Senegambia.* New York: Oxford University Press, 1999.

———. *West Africa's Women of God: Alinsitoué and the Diola Prophetic Tradition.* Bloomington: Indiana University Press, 2016.

Baumgarten, Jörg. "καινός." In *EDNT* 2 (1991) 229–32.

Beale, G. K. *The Book of Revelation.* New International Greek Testament Commentary. Grand Rapids: Eerdmans, 1999.

Beasley-Murray, George R. *John.* Word Biblical Commentary. 2nd ed. Dallas: Nelson, 2000.

Belser, Julia Watts. *Power, Ethics, and Ecology in Jewish Antiquity.* New York: Cambridge University Press, 2015.

Berdini, Paulo. "Jacopo Bassano: A Case for Painting as Visual Exegesis." In *Interpreting Christian Art: Reflections on Christian Art,* edited by Heidi Hornik and Mikeal Carl Parson, 169ff. Macon, GA: Mercer University Press, 2004.

———. *The Religious Art of Jacopo Bassano: Painting as Visual Exegesis.* New York: Cambridge University Press, 1997.

Berghen, Constant Vanden. *La végétation des plaines alluviales et des terrasses sablonneuses de la basse Casamance (Sénégal Méridional).* Liège: Lejeunia, 1997.

Berghen, Constant Vanden, and Adrien Manga. *Une introduction à un voyage en Casamance: Enampor, un Village de riziculteurs en Casamance, au Sénégal.* Paris: L'Harmattan, 1999.

Berger, Peter L. *The Sacred Canopy: Elements of A Sociological Theory of Religion.* New York: Anchor, 1967.

Berry, R. J., ed. *Environment Stewardship: Critical Perspectives-Past and Present.* New York: T. & T. Clark, 2006.

Beslier, G. G. *Le Sénégal.* CEDTSHT. Paris: Payot, 1935.

Beyerlin, Walter, ed. *Near Eastern Religious Texts Relating to the Old Testament.* Louisville: Westminster John Knox, 1975/1978.

Bhabha, Homi. "The Third Space: Interview with Homi Bhabha." In *Identity, Community, Culture, Difference,* edited by Jonathan Rutherford, 207–21. London: Lawrence & Wishart, 1990.

———. *The Location of Culture.* New York: Routledge, 1994.

———. "The Other Question: Difference, Discrimination and the Discourse of Colonialism." In *Out There: Marginalization and Contemporary Cultures,* edited by Russell Ferguson, Martha Gever, Trinh T. Minh-ha, and Cornel West, 71–88. New Museum of Contemporary Art New York. Cambridge, MA: MIT Press, 1990.

Biltcliffe, Pippa. "Walter Crane, and the Imperial Federation Map: Showing the Extent of the British Empire (1886)." *Imago Mundi* 57/1 (2006) 63–69.

Bishau, David. *Reign With Him for Thousand Years (Rev 20:6): A Socio-Hermeneutical Exposition of Biblical and Contemporary Millenarian Movements in Zimbabwe as Radical Responses to Deprivation.* Bible in Africa Studies 2. Bamberg: University of Bamberg Press, 2010.

Blount, Brian K. *Revelation: A Commentary.* New Testament Library. Louisville: Westminster John Knox, 2009.

Boer, Roland. *The Sacred Economy of Israel.* Library of Ancient Israel. Louisville: Westminster John Knox, 2015.

————, ed. *Tracking the Tribes of Yahweh: On the Trail of a Classic.* Journal for the Study of the Old Testament Supplement Series 351. Sheffield: Sheffield Academic, 2002.

Boring, M. Eugene, Klaus Berger and Carsten Colpe, eds. *Hellenistic Commentary to the New Testament.* Nashville: Abingdon, 1995.

Bowditch, Phebe Lowell. *Horace and the Gift Economy of Patronage.* Berkeley: University of California Press, 2001.

Brown, Colin, ed. *New International Dictionary of New Testament Theology.* 4 vols. Grand Rapids: Zondervan, 1975–85.

Brueggemann, Walter. *Genesis.* Interpretation. Louisville: Westminster John Knox, 1982.

————. *The Land: Place as Gift, Promise, and Challenge in Biblical Faith.* Overtures to Biblical Theology. 2nd ed. Minneapolis: Fortress, 2002.

————. *Prophetic Imagination.* 2nd ed. Minneapolis: Fortress, 2001.

————. *Theology of the Old Testament: Testimony, Dispute, Advocacy.* Minneapolis: Fortress, 1997.

Bultmann, Rudolf. *Theology of the New Testament: Complete in One Volume.* Translated by Kendrick Grobel. New York: Scribners, 1951, 1955.

Burri, Renate. "The Geography of De Mundo." In *Cosmic Order and Divine Power: Pseudo-Aristotle, On the Cosmos,* edited by Johan C. Thom, 89–106. Sapere 23. Tübingen: Mohr/Siebeck, 2014.

Carr, David. "The Politics of Textual Subversion: A Diachronic Perspective on the Garden of Eden Story." *Journal of Biblical Literature* 112 (1993) 577–95.

Carter, Warren. *Matthew and the Margins: A Sociopolitical and Religious Reading.* Sheffield: Sheffield Academic, 2000.

————. "Postcolonial Biblical Criticism." In *New Meanings for Ancient Texts: 55 Recent Approaches to Biblical Criticisms and Their Applications,* edited by Steven L. McKenzie and John Kaltner, 97–116. Louisville: Westminster John Knox, 2013.

Castriota, David. *The Ara Pacis Augustus and the Imagery of Abundance in Later Greek and Early Roman Imperial Art.* Princeton: Princeton University Press, 1995.

Césaire, Aimé. *Discourse on Colonialism.* Translated by Joan Pinkham. New York: Monthly Review Press, 1972.

————. *Discours sur le colonialisme suivi de Discours sur la Négritude.* Paris: Présence Africaine, 1955/2004.

————. "An Interview with Aimé Césaire conducted by René Depestre." In *Discourse on Colonialism,* 81–94. Translated by Joan Pinkham. Introduced by Robin D. G. Kelley. New York: Monthly Press, 1955, 1972, 2000.

Cheneau-Loquay, Annie. "Demain, encore le riz?" In *Comprendre la Casamance: Chronique d'une intégration contrasté*, edited by François-George Barbier-Wiesser, 351–83. Paris: Karthala, 1994.

Chitando, Ezra, Masiiwa Ragies Gunda and Joachim Kügler, eds. *Prophets, Profits and the Bible in Zimbabwe: A Festschrift for Aynos Masotcha Moyo*. Bible in Africa Studies 12. Bamberg: University of Bamberg Press, 2013.

Choi, Agnes. "Never the Two Shall Meet?" In *Galilee in the Late Second Temple and Mishnaic Periods*. Volume 1: *Life, Culture, and Society*. Edited by David A. Fiensy and James Riley Strange, 297–311. Minneapolis: Fortress, 2014.

Cone, James H. "Whose Earth Is It Anyways?" *CrossCurrents* 50 (2000) 36–46.

Connor, Nancy and Bradford Keeney. *Shamans of the World: Extraordinary First-Person Accounts of Healings, Mysteries, and Miracles*. Boulder, CO: Sound Truth, 2008.

Coomber, Matthew J. M. "Prophets to Profits: Ancient Judah and Corporate Globalization." In *The Bible and Justice: Ancient Texts, Modern Challenges*. Edited by Matthew J. M. Coomber, 212–37. London: Equinox, 2011.

———. "Subsistence and Greed: Revisiting the Eighth-Century Prophets in an Age of Corporate Globalization." *Masihi Sevak* 24/3 (2009) 14–30.

Crossan, John Dominic. *In Parables: The Challenge of the Historical Jesus*. 1973. Reprint, Eagle Books. Sonoma, CA: Polebridge, 1992.

Crüsemann, Frank. *The Torah : Theology and Social History of Old Testament Law*. Translated by Allan W. Mahnke. Minneapolis: Fortress, 1996.

Culpepper, R. Alan. "Children of God: Evolution, Cosmology, and Johannine Thought." In *Creation Stories in Dialogue: The Bible, Science, and Folk Traditions*, edited by R. Alan Culpepper and Jan G. Van der Watt, 3–31. Radboud Prestige Lectures in New Testament. Boston: Brill Academic, 2013.

Culpepper, R. Alan, and Jan G. Van Der Watt eds. *Creation Stories in Dialogue: The Bible, Science, and Folk Tradition: Radboud Prestige Lectures by R. Alan Culpepper*. Boston: Brill Academic, 2016.

Darbon, Dominique. *L'administration et le paysan en Casamance: Essai d'anthropologie administrative*. Paris: Pedone, 1988.

Davidson, Joanna. *Sacred Rice: An Ethnography of Identity, Environment, and Development in Rural West Africa*. New York: Oxford University Press, 2016.

Davies, W. D. *The Gospel and the Land: Early Christianity and Jewish Territorial Doctrine*. Berkeley: University of California Press, 1974.

Davis, Ellen F. *Scripture, Culture, and Agriculture: An Agrarian Reading of the Bible*. New York: Cambridge University Press, 2009.

de Jong, Ferdinand. *Masquerades of Modernity: Power and Secrecy in Casamance, Senegal*. Bloomington: Indiana University Press, 2007.

de Maistre, Joseph. *Les Soirées de Saint-Pétersbourg ou Entretiens sur le Gouvernement Temporel de la Providence*. Vol 2. Paris: Pélagaud, 1854.

de Saint-Cheron, François. *Senghor et la terre*. Paris: Sang de la terre, 1988.

Depestre, René. *Bonjour et Adieu à la Négritude*. Paris: Laffont, 1980.

Dever, William G. "Ceramics, Ethnicity, and the Question of Israel's Origins." *Biblical Archaeologist* 58 (1995) 200–213.

Dia, Massylla. *Lowland rice and climate change in Senegal* (Casamance). Moldova: Éditions Universitaires Européennes, 2017.

Diabone, Clédor. *Les ressources foncières, forestiè res et le développent en Casamance: Regard de l'anthropologie du développement sur l'agglomération de Houlouf*. Germany: Éditions universitaires Européennes, 2010.

Diagne, Souleymane Bashir. "Negritude." In *Stanford Encyclopedia of Philosophy*. http://
plato.stanford.edu/archives/spr2014/entries/negritude

――――. *Léopold Sédar Senghor: L'art Africain comme philosophie*. France: Riveneuve,
2007.

Diatta, Nazaire Ukëyëng. "Demain, le dialogue des religions? Religions révélées et
religion traditionnelle des Diola." In *Comprendre la Casamance: Chronique d'une
intégration contrastée*, edited by Francois-George Barbier-Wiesser, 429–53. Paris:
Karthala, 1994.

――――. "Et si Jésus était initie?" *Téléma* 57 (Jan–Mar 1989) 49–72.

――――. "Femme joola a traves proverbes et rites." *Téléma* 49 (Jan–Mar 1978) 47–71.

――――. "Participation Du Joola Chrétien aux rites traditionnels." *Téléma* 46 (Apr–June
1986) 67–81.

――――. "La personne entre individu et communauté." *Téléma* 70 (Apr–June 1992)
18–27.

――――. "Le Prêtre et les députés: Lettre d'un prêtre catholique aux députés de
Casamance." In *Comprendre la Casamance: Chronique d'une intégration contrastée*,
edited by Francois-George Barbier-Wiesser, 263–76. Paris: Karthala, 1994.

――――. *Proverbes Jóola de Casamance*. Paris: Karthala, 1998.

――――. "Rites funéraires joola et liturgie chrétienne." *Téléma* 67–8 (July–Dec 1991)
61–72.

――――. *Le Taureau symbole de Mort et de Vie dans l'initiation de la circoncision chez les
Diola (Senegal)*. Mernoire pour l' obtention du Diplome de l' Ecole des Hautes-
Etudes en Sciences Sociales. Paris: Mai 1979.

Diédhiou, Lamine. *Riz, symboles et développement chez les Diolas de Basse-Casamance*.
Laval: Les Presses de l'Université Laval, 2004.

Diédhiou, Paul. *L'identité Joola en Question (Casamance)*. Paris: Karthala, 2011.

Diémé, Mouhamadou. *Déforestation, dégradation de terres rizicoles et stratégies de
gestion: dans la communauté Rural de Tenghory, en Base Casamance, au Sud du
Sénégal*. Berlin: Éditions Universitaires Européennes, 2012.

Dillon, Matthew P. J. "The Ecology of the Greek Sanctuary." *Zeitschrift für Papyrologie
und Epigraphik* 118 (1997) 113–27.

Diop, Mamadou. *La multivalence du sacr dans l'œuvre de Léopold Sédar Senghor*:
Négritude, *Universalité, Géopoétique*. Berlin: Éditions Universitaires Européennes, 2010.

Diouf, Mamadou. "The French Policy of Assimilation and Civility of the Originaires
of the Four Communes (Senegal): A Nineteenth Century Globalization Project."
Development and Change 29 (1998) 671–96.

Dodd, C. H. *The Interpretation of the Fourth Gospel*. Cambridge: University of Cambridge Press, 1958.

Donahue, John R. *The Gospel in Parable: Metaphor, Narrative, and Theology in the
Synoptic Gospels*. Philadelphia: Fortress, 1988.

Dougherty, Carol. *The Poetics of Colonization: From City to Text in Archaic Greece*. New
York: Oxford University Press, 1993.

Du Quesnay, Ian M. Le M. "Vergils' Fourth Eclogue." Papers of the Liverpool Latin
Seminar 1976. Classical an Medieval Texts, Paper and Monographs 2. Edited by
Francis Cairns. England, Liverpool, 1976.

Dube, Musa W., Andrew M. Mbuvi, and Dora R. Mbuwayesango, eds. *Postcolonial Perspectives in African Biblical Interpretations*. Atlanta: Society of Biblical Literature, 2012.

Dunn, James D. G. *Romans*. Word Biblical Commentary 38A. Dallas: Word, 1988.

Edelman, Diana. "Ethnicity and Early Israel." In *Ethnicity and the Bible*, edited by Mark G. Brett, 25–55. Biblical Interpretation Series 19. Leiden: Brill, 1996.

Edward, Anthony T. *Hesiod's Ascra*. New York: Oxford University Press, 2000.

Evans, Craig. "Mark's Incipit and the Priene Calendar Inscription: From Jewish Gospel to Greco-Roman Gospel." *Journal of Greco-Roman Christianity and Judaism* 1 (2000) 67–81.

Fager, Jeffrey A. *Land Tenure and the Biblical Jubilee: Uncovering Hebrew Ethics through the Sociology of Knowledge*. Journal for the Study of the Old Testament Supplement Series 155. Sheffield: Sheffield Academic, 1993.

Fanon, Frantz. *Black Skin, White Masks*. Translated by Charles Lam Markmann. New York: Grove, 1967.

———. *Wretched of the Earth*. Translated by Constance Farrington. New York: Grove, 1963.

Feldman, Asher. *The Parables and Similes of the Rabbis: Agricultural and Pastoral*. New York: Cambridge University Press, 1927.

Fiensy, David A. *The Social History of Palestine in the Herodian Period: The Land Is Mine*. SBEC 20. Lewiston, NY: Mellen, 1991.

Finkelstein, Israel. "Ethnicity and Origin of the Iron I Settlers in the Highland of Canaan: Can the Real-Israel Stand Up." *Biblical Archaeologist* 59 (1996) 198–212.

Finkelstein, Israel, and Neil Asher Silberman. *The Bible Unearthed: Archaeology's New Vision of Ancient Israel and the Origin of its Sacred Texts*. New York: Free Press, 2001.

Finnegan, Ruth. *Oral Literature in Africa*. New York: Oxford University Press, 1970.

Firmage, Edwin. "Zoology (Fauna)." In *ABD* 6 (1992) 1110–67.

Foerster, Werner. "κτίζω, κτίσις, κτίσμα, κτίστης." In *TDNT* 3 (1965) 1000–1035.

Foster, Elizabeth A. *Faith in Empire: Religion, Politics, and Colonial Rule in French Senegal, 1880–1940*. Stanford, CA: Stanford University Press, 2013.

Foucault, Michel. "Of Other Spaces." In *Rethinking Architecture: A Reader in Cultural Theory*, edited by Neil Leach, 329–57. New York: Routledge, 1997.

Frankfort, Henri A., John A. Wilson, Thorkild Jacobsen, and William A. Irwin. *The Intellectual Adventure of Ancient Man: Essay on Speculative Thought in the Ancient Near East*. Chicago: University of Chicago Press, 1946.

Fretheim, Terence E. "The Book of Genesis: Introduction, Commentary, and Reflections." In *The New Interpreter's Bible: A Commentary in Twelve Volumes*, edited by Leander E. Keck, 1:320–674. Nashville: Abingdon, 1994.

Freyne, Seán. "Urban–Rural Relations in First-Century Galilee: Some Suggestions from the Literary Sources." In *Galilee in the Late Second Temple and Mishnaic Periods Volume 1: Life, Culture, and Society*, edited by David A. Fiensy and James Riley Strange, 75–91. Minneapolis: Fortress, 2014.

———. "Urban–Rural Relations in First-Century Galilee." In *Texts and Contexts: Biblical Texts in Their Textual and Situational Contexts: Essays in Honor of Lars Hartman*, edited by Tord Fornberg and David Hellholm, 597–622. Oslo: Scandinavian University Press, 1995.

Frick, Franck S. "Palestine, Climate of." In *ABD* 5 (1992) 120–26.

Frœlicher, Capitaine. *Trois Colonisateurs: Bugeaud, Fiadherbe, Gallieni*. Paris: Charles-Lavauzelle, 1904.

Furnish, Victor P. *The Theology of the First Letter to the Corinthians*. New Testament Theology. Cambridge: Cambridge University Press, 1999.

Gabriel, Mabel M. *Livia's Garden Room at Prima Porta*. New York: New York University Press, 1955.

Gadjigo, Sambe. *Ousmane Sembène: The Making of a Militant Artist*. Translated by Moustapha Diop. Bloomington: Indiana University Press, 2010.

Garrett, Susan R. "Sociology of Early Christianity." In *ABD* 6 (1992) 89–99.

Getui, Mary, Knut Holter and Victor Zinkuratire, eds. *Interpreting the Old Testament in Africa: Papers from the International Symposium on Africa and the Old Testament in Nairobi, October 1999*. Bible and Theology in Africa 2. New York: Lang, 2001.

Girard, Jean. *Genèse du pouvoir charismatique en basse Casamance (Sénégal)*. Dakar SN: IFAN, 1969.

Goldie, Jane. *Harrap's Shorter Dictionnaire: Anglais-Français/Français-Anglais*. Paris: Harrap, 1993.

Golka, Friedemann W. *The Leopard's Spots: Biblical and African Wisdom in Proverbs*. Edinburgh: T. & T. Clark, 1993.

Gordis, David M. "Ecology." In *ETZ HAYIM Torah Commentary*, 1369–72. New York: Jewish Publication Society, 2001.

Gottleib, Isaac B. "Ḥoni-Ha-Me' Aggel." In *The Oxford Dictionary of Jewish Religion*, edited by R. I. Zwi Werblowsky and Geoffrey Wigoder, 335–36. New York: Oxford University Press, 1997.

Gottwald, Norman K. *The Tribes of Yahweh: A Sociology of the Religion of Liberated Israel, 1250–1050 BCE*. Sheffield: Sheffield Academic Press, 1979/1999.

Graham, A. J. *Colony and Mother City in Ancient Greece*. Manchester: Manchester University Press, 1964.

Graham, Daniel W. "Matter." In *A Companion to Science, Technology, and Medicine in Ancient Greece and Rome*, edited by Georgia L. Irby, 29–42. Blackwell Companions to the Ancient World. Ancient History. Malden, MA: Wiley, 2016.

Green, Miranda. *Animals in Celtic Life and Myth*. New York: Routledge, 1992.

Gregory, Andrew D. "The Creation and the Destruction of the World." In *A Companion to Science, Technology, and Medicine in Ancient Greece and Rome*, edited by Georgia L. Irby, 13–28. Blackwell Companions to the Ancient World. Ancient History. Malden, MA: Wiley, 2016.

Grimsrud, Ted. "Healing Justice: The Prophet Amos and a 'New' Theology of Justice." In *Peace and Justice Shall Embrace: Power and Theopolitics in the Bible*, edited by Ted Grimsrud and Loren L. Johns, 64–85. Telford, PA: Pandora, 1999.

Guelick, Robert A. *Mark 1–8:26*. Word Biblical Commentary 34A. Dallas: Word, 1989.

Gunda, Masiiwa Ragies, and Joachim Kügler, eds. *The Bible and Politics in Africa*. Bible in Africa Studies 7. Bamberg: University of Bamberg Press, 2012.

Gunkel, Hermann. *The Legends of Genesis: The Biblical Saga and History*. Translated by W. H. Carruth. New York: Schocken, 1964.

Habel, Norman C. *The Land Is Mine: Six Biblical Ideologies*. Overtures to Biblical Theology. Minneapolis: Fortress, 1993.

Habel, Norman C., and Vicky Balabanski, eds. *The Earth Story in the New Testament*. Earth Bible 5. Sheffield: Sheffield Academic, 2002.

Habel, Norman C. and Shirley Wurst, eds. *The Earth Story in Genesis*. Earth Bible 2. Sheffield: Sheffield Academic, 2000.

Haenchen, Ernst. *John: A Commentary on the Gospel of John.* Edited by Robert W. Funk and Ulrich Busse. Translated by Robert W. Funk. Hermeneia. Minneapolis: Fortress, 1984.

Hanson, K. C., and Douglas E. Oakman. *Palestine in the Time of Jesus: Social Structures and Social Conflicts.* 2nd ed. Minneapolis: Fortress, 2008.

Harley, John Brian. "Maps, Knowledge, and Power." In *The Iconography of Landscape,* edited by D. Cosgrove and S. Daniels, 277–312. Cambridge: University of Cambridge Press, 1988.

Harrelson, Walter. *From Fertility Cult to Worship.* Missoula, MT: Scholars, 1969.

Hartswick, Kim J. *The Gardens of Sallust: A Changing Landscape.* Austin: University of Texas Press, 2004.

Hasel, Gerhard F., and Michael G. Hasel. "The Unique Cosmology of Genesis 1 against Ancient Near Eastern and Egyptians Parallels." In *The Genesis Creation Account and Its Reverberations in the Old Testament,* edited by Gerald E. Klingbell, 9–29. Berrien Springs, MI: Andrews University Press, 2015.

Hatch, Edwin and Henry A. Redpath. *A Concordance to the Septuagint and the Other Greek Versions of the Old Testament (Including the Apocryphal Books).* Grand Rapids: Baker, 1998.

Heeren, A. H. L. *Historical Researches into the Politics, Intercourse, and Trade of the Carthagians, Ethiopians, and Egyptians.* Oxford: Talboys, 1832.

Hegel, Georg W. F. *Philosophy of History.* Translated by J. Sibree. New York: Prometheus Books, 1991.

Herzog, William. *Parables as Subversive Speech: Jesus as Pedagogue of the Oppressed.* Louisville: Westminster John Knox, 1994.

Hessel, Dieter T. and Larry Rasmussen, eds. *Earth Habitat: Eco-Injustice and the Church's Response.* Minneapolis: Fortress, 2001.

Hessel, Dieter T. and Rosemary Radford Ruether, et al. *Christianity and Ecology: Seeking the Well-Being of Earth and Humans.* Religion for the Word and Ecology. Cambridge: Harvard University Press, 2000.

Hesseling, Gerti. "La terre, à qui est-elle: Les pratiques foncières en Basse-Casamance?" In *Comprendre la Casamance: Chronique d'une intégration contrasté,* edited by François-George Barbier-Wiesser, 243–62. Paris: Karthala, 1994.

Hiebert, Robert J. V. *Genesis.* In *A New English Translation of the Septuagint: A New Translation of the Greek into Contemporary English—An Essential Resource for Biblical Studies.* Edited by Albert Pietersma and Benjamin G. Wright. Oxford: Oxford University Press, 2007.

Holter, Knut. *Yahweh in Africa: Essays on Africa and the Old Testament.* Bible and Theology in Africa 1. New York: Lang, 2000.

———. *Old Testament Research for Africa: A Critical Analysis and Annotated Bibliography of African Old Testament Dissertations, 1967–2000.* Bible and Theology in Africa 3. New York: Lang, 2002.

hooks, bell. *Yearning: Race, Gender, and Cultural Politics.* Boston: South End, 1990.

Hornblower, Simon. "Hellenism, Hellenization." In *The Oxford Classical Dictionary,* edited by Simon Hornblower and Anthony Spawforth, 677–79. 3rd ed. New York: Oxford University Press, 1999.

Hornblower, Simon, and Anthony Spawforth, eds. *The Oxford Classical Dictionary.* 3rd ed. Oxford: Oxford University Press, 1999.

———. *The Oxford Classical Dictionary.* 4th ed. Oxford: Oxford University Press, 2012.

Horrell, David G., Cherryl Hunt, and Christopher Southgate. *Ecological Hermeneutics: Biblical, Historical and Theological Perspectives.* London: T. & T. Clark, 2010.

———. *Greening Paul: Rereading the Apostle in a Time of Ecological Crisis.* Waco, TX: Baylor University Press, 2010.

Horsley, Richard A. *Covenant Economics: A Biblical Vision of Justice for All.* Louisville: Westminster John Knox, 2009.

———. *Jesus and Empire: The Kingdom of God and the New World Disorder.* Minneapolis: Fortress, 2003.

Horton, Robin. "African Conversion." *Africa* 41/2 (1971) 85–108.

———. "On the Rationality of African Conversion: Part 1." *Africa* 45/3 (1975) 219–20.

Houston, Walter. "Justice and Violence in the Priestly Utopia." In *The Bible and Justice: Ancient Texts, Modern Challenges,* edited by Matthew J. M. Coomber, 93–106. London: Equinox, 2011.

Hughes, Christopher. "Art and Exegesis." In *A Companion to Medieval Art: Romanesque and Gothic in Modern Europe,* edited by Conrad Rudolph, 173–92. New York: Blackwell, 2006.

Hultgren, Arland J. *The Parables of Jesus: A Commentary.* Grand Rapids: Eerdmans, 2000.

Jacob, Irene, and Walter Jacob. "Flora." In *ABD* 2 (1992) 804–17.

Jewett, Robert. *Romans.* Hermeneia. Minneapolis: Fortress, 2007.

Jones, Prudence, and Nigel Pennick. *A History of Pagan Europe.* New York: Routledge, 1995.

Journet-Diallo, Odile. *Les Créances de la terre Chroniques du pays Jamaat* (Joola de Guinée-Bissau). CEPHE 134. Turnhout: Brepols, 2007.

Julliard, Andre. "Droit du sol en Guinee-Bissau: Dieu, la terre et les hommes chez les Diola-Ajamat." In *Comprendre la Casamance: Chronique d'une intégration contrasté,* edited by François-George Barbier-Wiesser, 142–47. Paris: Karthala, 1994.

Kahl, Brigitte. "Fratricide and Ecocide: Rereading Genesis 2–4." In *Earth Habitat: Eco-Injustice and the Church's Response,* 53–68. Minneapolis: Fortress, 1989.

———. *Galatians Re-imagined: Reading with the Eyes of the Vanquished.* Paul in Critical Contexts. Minneapolis: Fortress, 2010.

Kane, Cheikh Hamidou. *Ambiguous Adventure.* Translated by Katherine Wood. New York: Walker, 1963.

Kearns, Emily. "Animals, Attitudes to." In *Oxford Classical Dictionary.* 4th ed. Edited by Simon Hornblower and Anthony Spawforth. New York: Oxford University Press, 2012.

———. "Erechtheus." In *Oxford Classical Dictionary.* 4th ed. Edited by Simon Hornblower and Anthony Spawforth, 554–55. New York: Oxford University Press, 2012.

Keel, Othmar, and Silvia Schroer. *Creation: Biblical Theologies in the Context of Ancient Near East.* Translated by Peter T. Daniels. Winona, Lake, IN: Eisenbrauns, 2015.

Keel, Othmar, and Christoph Uehlinger. *Gods, Goddesses, and Images of God in Ancient Israel.* Translated by Thomas H. Trapp. Minneapolis: Fortress, 1992.

Keener, Craig R. *The Gospel of John: A Commentary.* 2 vols. Peabody, MA: Hendrickson, 2003.

———. *Miracles: The Credibility of the New Testament Accounts.* 2 vols. Grand Rapids: Eerdmans, 2011.

Kellum, Barbara A. "The Construction of Landscape in Augustan Rome: The Garden Room at the Villa ad Gallinas." *Art Bulletin* 76/2 (1994) 211–24.

Kelly, Robin D. G. "Introduction: A Poetics of Anticolonialism." In *Discourse on Colonialism*, 7–28. New York: Monthly Review Press, 2000.

Ki-Zerbo, Francoise. *Les Sources du droit chez les Diola du Sénégal: Logiques de transmission des richesses et des status chez les Diola du Oulouf* (Casamance, Sénégal). Paris: Karthala, 1997.

Klynne, Allan. "The Laurel Grove of the Caesars: Looking In and Looking Out." In *Roman Villas around the Urbs: Interaction with Landscape and Environment.* Proceedings of a conference held at the Swedish Institute in Rome, edited by B. Santillo Frizell and A. Klynne, 1–9. Projects and Seminars 2. Rome: Swedish Institute in Rome, 2005.

Koester, Craig R. *Revelation.* Yale Anchor Bible 38A. New Haven: Yale University Press, 2014.

Kohlenberger, John R. III, Edward W. Goodrick, and James A. Swanson. *The Exhaustive Concordance to the Greek New Testament.* Grand Rapids: Zondervan, 1995.

Kohlenberger, John R. III, and James A. Swanson. *The Hebrew English Concordance to the Old Testament with the New International Version.* Grand Rapids: Zondervan, 1998.

LaDuke, Winona. "In Time of Sacred Places." In *Spiritual Ecology: The Cry of the Earth*, edited by Llewellyn Vaughan-Lee, 85–100. Point Reyes, CA: Golden Sufi Center Publishing, 2013.

Lang, Bernhard. *The Hebrew God: Portrait of an Ancient Deity.* New Haven: Yale University Press, 2002.

Lefebvre, Jean. *The Production of Space.* Translated by Donald Nicholson-Smith. Malden, MA: Blackwell, 1974/1991.

Lemel, Harold. "A Land Tenure Profile for Tunisia." *Land Tenure Center: An Institute for Research and Education on Social Structure, Rural Institutions.* Madison, WI: Land Tenure Center, 1985.

Liddell, Henry George, and Robert Scott. *Greek-English Lexicon with a Revised Supplement.* Rev. ed. Oxford: Clarendon, 1996.

Linares, Olga. *Power, Prayer and Production: The Jola of Casamance, Sénégal.* Cambridge Studies in Social and Cultural Anthropology 82. Cambridge: Cambridge University Press, 1992.

Ling, Roger. *Roman Painting.* New York: Cambridge University Press, 1991.

Lopez, Davina C. *Apostle to the Conquered: Reimagining Paul's Mission.* Paul in Critical Contexts. Minneapolis: Fortress, 2008.

Machingura, Francis. *The Messianic Feeding of the Masses An Analysis of John 6 in the Context of Messianic Leadership in Post-Colonial Zimbabwe.* Edited by Joachim Kügler, Lovemore Togarasei, Masiiwa R. Gunda, and Eric Souga Onomo. Bamberg: University of Bamberg Press 2012.

Magesa, Laurenti. *African Religion: The Moral Traditions of Abundant Life.* Maryknoll, NY: Orbis, 1997.

Malina, Bruce J. *New Testament World: Insights from Cultural Anthropology.* 3rd ed. Louisville: Westminster John Knox, 2001.

Malina, Bruce J., and John J. Pilch. *Social-Science Commentary on the Letters of Paul.* Minneapolis: Fortress, 2006.

Malina, Bruce J., and Richard L. Rohrbaugh. *Social-Science Commentary on the Synoptic Gospels.* 2nd ed. Minneapolis: Fortress, 2003.

Manga, Mohamed Lamine. *La Casamance dans l'histoire contemporaine du Sénégal.* Paris: L'Harmattan, 2012.

Manga, Pierre. *La sœur du Bouc: contes diolas du Sénégal.* Paris : L' Harmattan, 2018.

Mark, Peter. *A Cultural, Economic, and Religious History of the Base Casamance since 1500.* Stuttgart: Steiner, 1985.

———. "Fetishers, 'Marybukes' and the Christian Norm: European Images of Senegambians and Their Religions, 1550–1760." *African Studies Review* 23/2 (1980) 91–99.

———. "Urban Migration, Cash Cropping, and Calamity: The Spread of Islam among the Diola of Boulouf (Senegal) 1900–1940." *African Studies Review* 21/2 (1972) 1–14.

———. *The Wild Bull and the Sacred Forest: Form, Meaning and Change in Senegambian Initiation Masks.* New York: Cambridge University Press, 1992.

Martyn, J. Louis. "Epilogue: An Essay in Pauline Meta-Ethics." In *Divine and Human Agency in Paul and His Cultural Environment.* Journal for the Study of the New Testament Supplements 173. Edited by John M. G. Barclay and Simon J. Cathercole, 174–83. New York: T. & T. Clark, 2006.

———. *Galatians: A New Translation with Introduction and Commentary.* Anchor Bible 33A. New York: Doubleday, 1997.

Marut, Jean-Claud. *Le conflit de la Casamance: Ce qui dissent les armes.* Paris: Karthala, 2010.

Mazon, Paul. "Introduction" In *Hésiode: Théogonie, les travaux et les jours le bouclier.* Budé. Edited and Translated by Paul Mazon, vii–xxx. Paris: Les Belles Letters, 2014.

Mazrui, Ali A. "Negritude, the Talmudic Tradition and the Intellectual Performance of Blacks and Jews." In *Hommage à Léopold Sédar Senghor: Homme de Culture,* 300–325. Paris: Présence Africaine, 1976.

Mbiti, John S. *African Religions and Philosophy.* 2nd ed. Oxford: Heinemann Educational, 1969.

McCoskey, Denise Eileen. *Race: Antiquity & Its Legacy.* Ancients and Moderns Series. New York: Oxford University Press, 2012.

Méguelle, Philippe. *Chefferie colonial et égalitarisme diola: Les difficultés de la politique indigène de la France en Base-Casamance* (Sénégal), 1828–1923. Paris: L'Harmattan, 2012.

Meier, John P. *A Marginal Jew: Rethinking the Historical Jesus.* Vol. 5, *Probing the Authenticity of the Parables.* Yale Anchor Bible Reference Library. New Haven: Yale University Press, 2016.

Mercier, Louis-Sébastien. *Memoirs of the Year Two Thousand Five Hundred.* Vol. 2. Translated by W. Hooper. London: Paternoster-Row, 1772.

Mertínez-Alemán, Ana M. "Critical Discourse Analysis in Higher Education Policy Research." In *Critical Approaches to the Study of Higher Education: A Practical Introduction,* 7–43. Baltimore: John Hopkins University Press, 2015.

Michelet, Jules. *Autobiographie: Introduction à L'histoire Universelle.* Paris: Larousse, 1930.

Milgrom, Jacob. *Leviticus: A Book of Ritual and Ethics.* Continental Commentary. Minneapolis: Fortress, 2004.

Mlenga, Joyce. *Dual Religiosity in Northern Malawi: Ngonde Christians and African Traditional Religion.* Luwinga, Mzuzu, Malawi: Mzuni, 2016.

Mofokeng, Takatso. "Black Christians, the Bible and Liberation." *Journal of Black Theology in South Africa* 2 (1988) 34–42.

Moltmann, Jürgen. *God in Creation: A New Theology of Creation and the Spirit of God.* Translated by Margaret Kohl. New York: Harper & Row, 1985.

Moore, Stephen D., and Fernando Segovia, eds. *Postcolonial Biblical Criticism: Interdisciplinary Interactions.* Bible and Postcolonialism. London: T. & T. Clark, 2005.

Morton, Patricia A. *Hybrid Modernities: Architecture and Representation at the 1931 Colonial Exposition, Paris.* Cambridge, MA: MIT Press, 2000.

Mphahlele, Ezekiel. *The African Image.* London: Faber & Faber, 1974.

Muilenburg, James. *The Way of Israel: Biblical Faith and Ethics.* Religious Perspectives 5. New York: Harper & Brothers, Publishers, 1961.

Mwandayi, Canisius. *Death and After-life Rituals in the Eyes of the Shona: Dialogue with Shona Customs in the Quest for Authentic Inculturation*: Bible in Africa Studies 6. Edited by Bamberg: University of Bamberg Press, 2011.

Myers, Ched. *The Biblical Vision of Sabbath Economics.* Washington, DC: Tell the Word, 2002.

Nelson, Stephanie A. *God and Land: The Metaphysics of Farming in Hesiod and Vergil.* Translated by David Gene. New York: Oxford University Press, 2000.

Neusner, Jacob. *The Babylonian Talmud: A Translation and Commentary.* Vol. 7. Peabody, MA: Hendrickson, 2005.

Ngalasso, Mwatha Musanji. "Je suis Venu vous dire. . . Anatomie d'un discours Néocolonial en langue de caoutchouc." In *L'Afrique répond à Sarkozy: Contre le discours de Dakar,* 299–340. Paris: Rey, 2008.

Niang, Aliou Cissé. *Faith and Freedom in Senegal and Galatia: The Apostle Paul, Colonists and Sending Gods.* New York: Brill Academic, 2009.

———. "Postcolonial Biblical Theology in Geographical Settings: The Case of Senegal." In *Reconstructing Old Testament Theology: After the Collapse of History,* edited by Leo G. Perdue, 319–29. Minneapolis: Fortress, 2005.

———. "Seeing and Hearing Jesus Christ Crucified in Gal 3:1 under Watchful Imperial Eyes." In *Text, Image, and Christians in the Graeco-Roman World: A Festschrift in Honor of David Lee Balch,* edited by Aliou Cissé Niang and Carolyn Osiek, 160–82. Princeton Theological Monograph Series 176. Eugene, OR: Pickwick Publications, 2012.

———. "Space and Human Agency in the Making of the Story of Gershom through a Senegalese Christian Lens." *Journal of Biblical Literature* 134 (2015) 882–89.

Niekerk, Attie van. "The Loss of Land and the Earth Mother: African Mythology and the Issue of Land in South Africa." In *Creation Stories in Dialogue: The Bible, Science, and Folk Traditions,* edited by R. Alan Culpepper and Jan G. Van der Watt, 195–251. Biblical Interpretation Series 139. Leiden: Brill Academic, 2013.

Nollé, Johannes. "Boars, Bears, and Bugs: Farming in Asia Minor and the Protection of Men, Animals, and Crops." In *Patterns in the Economy of Roman Asia Minor,* edited by Stephen Mitchell and Constantina Katsari, 53–82. Oakville, CT: Classical Press of Wales, 2005.

Oakman, Douglas E. "Debate: Was the Galilean Economy Oppressive or Prosperous? Late Second Temple Galilee: Socio-Archaeology and Dimensions of Exploitation in First-Century Palestine." In *Galilee in the Late Second Temple and Mishnaic Periods*. Vol. 1, *Life, Culture, and Society*, edited by David A. Fiensy and James Riley Strange, 346–56. Minneapolis: Fortress, 2014.

———. "Elite Control of Food Production in Galilee and Non-Elite Food Security." Paper delivered at the Annual Meeting of Society of Biblical Literature in Denver, 2018.

———. *Jesus and the Economic Questions of His Day*. SBEC 8. Lewiston, NY: Mellen, 1986.

P'Bitek, Okot. *Decolonizing African Religions: A Short History of African Religion in Western Scholarship*. New York: Diasporic Africa Press, 2011.

Palmeri, Paolo. *Living with the Diola of Mof Evvì: The Account of an Anthropological Research in Senegal*. Collana di Antropologia 24. Padova: CLEUP, 2009.

———. *Retour dans un village Diola de Casamance: chronique d'une recherche anthropologique au Sénégal*. Paris: L'Harmattan, 1995.

Pastor, Jack. *Land and Economy in Ancient Palestine*. New York: Routledge, 1997.

Pélissier, Paul. *Les paysans du Sénégal: Les civilisations agraires du Cayor a la Casamance*. Saint-Yrieix: Imprimerie Fabrègue, 1966.

Perdue, Leo G. *Wisdom & Creation: The Theology of Wisdom Literature*. Nashville, TN: Abingdon Press, 1994.

———. *Wisdom Literature: A Theological History*. Louisville: Westminster John Knox, 2007.

Perdue, Leo G., and Warren Carter. *Israel and Empire: A Postcolonial History of Israel and Early Judaism*. Edited by Coleman A. Baker. London: Bloomsbury, 2015.

Péter, Georges. *L'Effort Français au Sénégal*. LEFAR. Toulouse: Boisseau, 1933.

Portères, Roland E. *Aménagement de l'économie agricole et rurale au Sénégal Fascicule II and III*. Gouvernement Général de L'Afrique Occidentale Française. Dakar, 1952.

Powers, David S. "Orientalism, Colonialism, and Legal History: The Attack on Muslim Family Endowments in Algeria and India." *Comparative Studies in Society and History* 31 (1989) 535–71.

Price, S. R. F. "Rituals and Power." In *Paul and Empire: Religion and Power in Roman Imperial Society*, edited by Richard A. Horsley, 47–71. Harrisburg, PA: Trinity, 1997.

———. *Rituals and Power: The Roman Imperial Cult in Asia Minor*. Cambridge: Cambridge University Press, 1984.

Pritchard, James B., ed. *Ancient Near Eastern Texts: Relating to the Old Testament*. 3rd ed. Princeton: Princeton University Press, 1969.

Purcell, Nicholas. "Augustus." In *The Oxford Classical Dictionary*, edited by Simon Hornblower and Anthony Spawforth, 216–17. 3rd ed. New York: Oxford University Press, 1999.

Rabaka, Reiland. *Forms of Fanonism: Frantz Fanon's Critical Theory and the Dialectics of Decolonization*. New York: Lexington, 2010.

———. *The Negritude Movement: W. E. B. Du Bois, Leon Damas, Aimé Césaire, Léopold Sédar Senghor, Frantz Fanon, and the Evolution of an Insurgent Idea*. Critical Africana Studies. New York: Lexington, 2015.

Ruether, Rosemary Radford. *Gaia & God: An Ecofeminist Theology of Earth Healing*. New York: HarperCollins, 1992.

Ragaz, Leonhard. *Die Bibel, Eine Deutung*. Vol. 1, *Die Urgeschichte*. Zurich: Diana, 1990.

————. *A History of Israelite Religion in the Old Testament.* Vol. 2, *From the Exile to the Maccabees.* Translated by John Bowden. Old Testament Library. Louisville: Westminster John Knox, 1994.

Räisänen, Heikki, Elisabeth Schüssler Fiorenza, R. S. Sugirtharajah, Krister Stendahl, and James Barr. *Reading the Bible in the Global Village: Helsinki.* Global Perspectives on Biblical Scholarship 1. Atlanta: Society of Biblical Literature, 2000.

Reed, Jonathan L. *Archaeology and the Galilean Jesus: A Re-Examining of the Evidence.* Harrisburg, PA: Trinity, 2000.

Reeder, Jane Clark. *The Villa of Livia AD GALLINAS ALBAS: A Study in the Augustan Villa and Garden.* Providence: Brown University Press, 2001

Rengstorf, Karl Heinrich. *The Complete Concordance to Flavius Josephus: Supplemented by Namenwörterbuch zu Flavius Josephus by Abraham Schalit.* Study Edition. Volume 1: A–K. Boston: Brill Academic, 2002.

————. *The Complete Concordance to Flavius Josephus: Supplemented by Namen- wörterbuch zu Flavius Josephus by Abraham Schalit.* Study Edition. Vol. 2: Λ-Ω. Boston: Brill Academic Press, 2002.

Roche, Christian, *Histoire de la Casamance: Conquête et résistance: 1850–1920.* Paris: Karthala, 1985.

Rohrbaugh, Richard L. *The New Testament in Cross-Cultural Perspectives.* Matrix: The Bible in Mediterranean Context 1. Eugene, OR: Cascade Books, 2007.

Rossini, Orietta. *Ara Pacis.* Milan: Comune di Roma, 2006/2007.

Russell, Stephen C. "Space, Land, Territory, and the Study of the Bible." *Brill Online* 1/4 (2016) 1–64.

Safrai, Zeʾev. "Agriculture and Farming." In *The Oxford Handbook of Daily Life in Roman Palestine,* edited by Catherine Hezer, 246–63. New York: Oxford University Press, 2010.

————. *The Economy of Roman Palestine.* New York: Routledge, 1994.

Said, Edward W. *Culture of Imperialism.* New York: Knopf, 1993.

————. *Orientalism.* New York: Vintage, 1979.

————. "Orientalism Reconsidered." *Race & Class: A Journal for Black and Third World Liberation* 27 (1985) 1–15.

————. *The World, the Text and the Critic.* Cambridge: Harvard University Press, 1983.

Sala-Molins, Louis. *Le Code Noir ou le calvaire de canaan.* Paris: Presses Universitaires de France, 2002.

Samb, Djibril. *L'interprétation des rêves dans la région Sénégambienne: Suivi de la clef des songes de la Sénégambie, de L'Égypte pharaonique et de la tradition islamique.* Dakar: Les Nouvelles Éditions Africaines du Sénégal, 1998.

Sarna, Nahum. *Genesis.* JPS Torah Commentary. Philadelphia: Jewish Publication Society, 1989.

Sartre, Jean-Paul. "Orphée noir. " In *Anthologie de la nouvelle poésie nègre et malgache de langue française,* IX–XLIV. Paris: Presses Universitaires Française, 1948.

Sauvy, Alfred. "Document: Trois Mondes, Une Planète." *Vingtième Siècle: Revue d'histoire* 12 (Oct.–Dec., 1986) 81–83.

Schnelle, Udo. *Theology of the New Testament.* Translated by M. Eugene Boring. Grand Rapids: Baker Academic, 2007.

Scott, Bernard Brandon. *Hear Then the Parable: A Commentary on the Parables of Jesus.* Minneapolis: Fortress, 1989.

Scott, James C. "Protest and Profanation: Agrarian Revolt and the Little Tradition. Part I." *Theory and Society* 4 (1977) 1–38.

———. "Protest and Profanation: Agrarian Revolt and the Little Tradition. Part II." *Theory and Society* 4 (1977) 211–46.

Segovia, Fernando. "Cultural Studies and Contemporary Biblical Criticism as a Mode of Discourse." In *Reading from this Place*. Vol. 2, *Social Location and Biblical Interpretation in Global Perspective*, edited by , 1–17. Minneapolis: Fortress, 1996.

———. "Mapping the Postcolonial Optic." In *Postcolonial Biblical Criticism: Interdisciplinary Interactions*, edited by Stephen D. Moore and Fernando Segovia, 23–78. New York: T. & T. Clark, 2005.

Sembène, Ousmane. *The Last of the Empire: A Senegalese Novel*. Translated by Adrian Adams. London: Heinemann, 1981.

Senghor, Léopold Sédar. "Chants d'ombre." In *Œuvre Poétiques*. Paris: Seuil, 1964.

———. "Constructive Elements of a Civilization of African Negro Inspiration." *Présence Africaine*," 24–5 (1959) 277.

———. "Elegy of the Circumcised." In *The Collected Poetry*. Translated with introduction by Melvin Dixon. Charlottesville: University of Virginia Press, 1991.

———. *Léopold Sédar Senghor et Présence Africaine*. Dakar: Présence Africaine, 1996.

———. *Liberté 1: Négritude et humanisme*. Paris: Seuil, 1964.

———. *Liberté 3: Négritude et civilisation de l'universel*. Paris: Seuil, 1977.

———. *On African Socialism*. Translated by Mercer Cook. New York: Praeger, 1964.

———. "Postface: Comme les Lamantins vont boire à la source." In *Œuvre Poétiques*. Paris: Seuil, 1964.

———. "Prière de Paix." In *Léopold Sédar Senghor: The Collected Poetry*. Translated with introduction by Melvin Dixon. Charlottesville: University of Virginia, 1991.

———. "Problematic de la Négritude." *Présence Africaine* 78/2 (1971) 3–26.

———. "The Spirit of Civilisation, or the Laws of African Negro Culture." *Présence Africaine: The 1st International Conference of Negro Writers and Artists* (19th–22nd Sept. 1956) 51–64.

———. "What Is Negritude?" *Atlas* (1962) 54–55.

Slaveva-Griffin, Svetla. "Nature and the Divine." In *A Companion to Science, Technology, and Medicine in Ancient Greece and Rome*, edited by Georgia L. Irby, 60–75. Malden, MA: Wiley, 2016.

Sleeman, Matthew. *Geography and the Ascension Narrative in Acts*. Society of New Testament Studies Monograph Series 146. Cambridge: Cambridge University Press, 2009.

Smith, Andrew. "The Reception of On the Cosmos in Ancient and Pagan Philosophy." In *Cosmic Order and Divine Power: Pseudo-Aristotle, On the Cosmos*, edited by Johan C. Thom, 121–31. Sapere 23. Tübingen: Mohr/Siebeck, 2014.

Smith-Christopher, Daniel. *A Biblical Theology of Exile*. Overtures to Biblical Theology. Minneapolis: Fortress, 2002.

———. "Ezekiel on Fanon's Couch: Postcolonial Dialogue with David Halperin's *Seeking Ezekiel*." In *Peace and Justice Shall Embrace: Power and Theopolitics in the Bible: Essays in Honor of Millard Lind*, edited by Ted Grimsrud and Loren L. Johns, 108–44. Telford, PA: Pandora, 1999.

Snodgrass, Klyne R. *Stories with Intent: A Comprehensive Guide to the Parables of Jesus*. Grand Rapids: Eerdmans, 2008.

Soja, Edward. *Thirdspace: Journeys to Los Angeles and Other Real-and-Imagined Places*. Malden, MA: Blackwell, 1996.

Somé, Malidoma Patrice. *The Healing Wisdom of Africa: Finding Life Purpose through Nature, Ritual, and Community*. New York: Penguin Putnam, 1998.

Soyinka, Wole. *Myth, Literature and the African World*. Cambridge: Cambridge University Press, 1976.

———. "Senghor: Lessons in Power." *Research in African Literature* 33 (2002) 1–2.

Spivak, Gayatri C. "Can the Subaltern Speak?" In *The Post-Colonial Studies Reader*, edited by Bill Ashcroft, Gareth Griffiths, and Helen Tiffin, 24–28. New York: Routledge, 1995.

———. *The Post-Colonial Critic: Interviews, Strategies, Dialogues*. Edited by S. Harasym. New York: Routledge, 1990.

———. "Subaltern Studies: Deconstructing Historiography." In *Selected Subaltern Studies*, edited by R. Guha and G. C. Spivak, 3–32. New York: Oxford University Press, 1988.

———. "Strategy, Identity, Writing." In *The Post-Colonial Critic: Interviews, Strategies, Dialogue*, edited by Sarah Harasym, 35–49. New York: Routledge, 1990.

Stamm, Johann, Ludwig Köhler, and Walter Baumgartner. *The Hebrew and Aramaic Lexicon of the Old Testament*. 5 vols. Translated by M. E. J. Richardson. Edited by Mervyn Edwin and John Richardson. Leiden: Brill, 1994.

Stegemann, Ekkehard W., and Wolfgang Stegemann. *The Jesus Movement: A Social History of Its First Century*. Translated by O. C. Dean Jr. Minneapolis: Fortress, 1995.

Stegemann, Wolfgang, Gerd Theissen, and Bruce J. Malina, eds. *The Social Setting of Jesus and the Gospels*. Minneapolis: Fortress, 2002.

Strange, James F. "Nazareth." In *Galilee in the Late Second Temple and Mishnaic Periods*. Vol. 2, *Life, Culture, and Society*, edited by David A. Fiensy and James Riley Strange, 167–80. Minneapolis: Fortress, 2014.

Strecker, Georg. *Theology of the New Testament*. Translated by M. Eugene Boring. Louisville: Westminster John Knox, 2000.

Stuart, Douglas. "Curse." In *ABD* 1 (1992) 1218–19.

Sugirtharajah, R. S. "From Orientalist to Post-Colonial: Notes on Reading Practices." *Asian Journal of Theology* 10 (1996) 20–27.

———. *Postcolonial Criticism and Biblical Interpretation*. New York: Oxford University Press, 2002.

Sundkler, Bengt, and Christopher Steed. *A History of the Church in Africa*. Studia Missionalia Upsaliensia 74. Cambridge: Cambridge University Press, 2000.

Talbert, Charles H. *Romans*. Smyth & Helwys Bible Commentary. Macon, GA: Smyth & Helwys, 2002.

Taringa, Taisekwa Nisbert. *Towards an African-Christian Environmental Ethic*. Bamberg: University of Bamberg Press, 2014.

———. "How Environmental is African Traditional Religion?" *Exchange* 35 (2006) 191–214.

Tcherikover, Victor. *Hellenistic Civilization and the Jews*. Translated by S. Applebaum. New York: Atheneum, 1970.

Thom, Johan C. "The Cosmotheology of *De Mundo*." In *Cosmic Order and Divine Power: Pseudo-Aristotle, On the Cosmos*, edited by Johan C. Thom, 107–20. Tübingen: Mohr/Siebeck, 2014.

Thomas, Louis-Vincent. *Les Diola: Essai d'analyse fonctionnelle sur une population de Basse-Casamance*. Vols. 1 and 2 Dakar: Protat FrPres, Mâcon, 1959.

————. *Et le Lièvre Vint . . . Récits populaires diola.* Dakar: Les Novelles édition africaines, 1982.

————. *Les sages dépossédés: univers magiques d'Afrique noire.* Paris: Laffont, 1977.

————. *La terre africaine et ses religions: tradition et changements.* SHS. Paris: Larousse, 1975.

Thomas, Louis-Vincent, and René Luneau. *Les religions d'Afrique noire: textes et traditions sacrés.* Le Trésor Spirituel de L'humanité. Paris: Fayard, 1969.

Thompson, Marianne Meye. *John: A Commentary.* New Testament Library. Louisville: Westminster John Knox Press, 2016.

Togarasei, Lovemore. *The Bible in Context: Essay Collection.* Bible in Africa Studies 1. Bamberg: University of Bamberg Press, 2009.

Toliver-Diallo, Wilmetta Jesvalynn. *Aline Sitoé Diatta: Addressing Historical Silences through Senegal Culture.* Ann Arbor: UMI, 1999.

Toner, J. P. *Roman Disasters.* Malden, MA: Polity, 2013.

Tonstad, Sigve K. *The Letter to the Romans: Paul the Ecologist.* Earth Bible Commentary Series 7. Sheffield: Sheffield Phoenix, 2016.

Toynbee, J. M. C. *Animals in Roman Life & Art.* London: Pen & Sword, 2013.

Trible, Phillis. "The Dilemma of Dominion." In *Faith and Feminism: Ecumenical Essays*, edited by B. Diane Lipsett and Phyllis Trible, 17–39. Louisville: Westminster John Knox, 2014.

————. *God and the Rhetoric of Sexuality.* Overtures to Biblical Theology. Philadelphia: Fortress, 1978.

Tzuetkova-Glaser, Anna. "The Concepts of *Ousia* and *Dunamis* in *De Mundo* and Their Parallels in Hellenisitic-Jewish and Christian Texts." In *Cosmic Order and Divine Power: Pseudo-Aristotle, On the Cosmos*, edited by Johan C. Thom, 133–52. Sapere. Tübingen: Mohr/Siebeck, 2014.

Udoh, Fabian E. "Taxation and Other Sources of Government Income in the Galilee of Herod and Antipas." In *Galilee in the Late Second Temple and Mishnaic Periods.* Vol. 1, *Life, Culture, and Society*, edited by David A. Fiensy and James Riley Strange, 366–87. Minneapolis: Fortress, 2014.

————. *To Caesar What Is Caesar's: Tribute, Taxes, and Imperial Administration in Early Roman Palestine 63 B.C.E.—70 C.E.* Brown Judaic Studies 343. Providence: Brown University Press, 2005.

Ukpong, Justin et al. *Reading the Bible in the Global Village: Cape Town.* Global Perspectives on Biblical Scholarship 3. Atlanta: Society of Biblical Literature, 2002.

Uzukwu, Elochukwu Eugene. *God, Spirit and Human Wholeness.* Eugene, OR: Pickwick Publications, 2012.

Vaillant, Janet. *Black, French, and African: A Life of Léopold Sédar Senghor.* Cambridge: Harvard University Press, 1990.

Van Seters, John. *The Prologue to History: The Yahwist as Historian in Genesis.* Louisville: Westminster John Knox, 1992.

Vengeyi, Obvious. *Aluta Continua Biblical Hermeneutics for Liberation: Interpreting Biblical Texts on Slavery for Liberation of Zimbabwean Underclasses.* Bible in Africa Studies 10. Bamberg: University of Bamberg Press, 2013.

Versnel, Hendrik S. "Sin." In *The Oxford Classical Dictionary*, edited by Simon Hornblower and Anthony Spawforth, 1410–11. 3rd ed. New York: Oxford University Press, 1999.

Waldman, Marilyn Robinson, and Robert Baum. "Innovation as Renovation: 'The Prophet' as an Agent of Change." In *Innovations in Religious Traditions: Essays in the Interpretation of Religious Change*, edited by Michael A. Williams, 241–84. Religion and Society 31. Berlin: Mouton de Gruyter, 1992.

Wallace-Hadrill, Andrew. "The Golden Age and Sin in Augustan Ideology." *Past and Present* 95 (1982) 19–36.

Watson, Francis. "Strategies of Recovery and Resistance: Hermeneutical Reflections of Genesis 1–3 and Its Pauline Reception." *Journal for the Study of the New Testament* 45 (1992) 79–103.

Weinfeld, Moshe. *Social Justice in Ancient Israel and in the Ancient Near East.* Minneapolis: Fortress, 1995.

Wengst, Klaus. *Pax Romana and the Peace of Jesus Christ.* Translated by John Bowden. London: SCM, 1987.

Wenham, Gordon. *Genesis 1–15.* Word Biblical Commentary 1. Edited by David A. Hubbard and Glenn W. Barker. Waco, TX: Word, 1987.

West, Gerald O. "From a Reconstruction and Development Programme (RDP) of the Economy to the RDP of the Soul: Public Realm Biblical Appropriation in Postcolonial South Africa." In *The Bible and Justice: Ancient Texts, Modern Challenges*, edited by Matthew J. M. Coomber, 122–44. London: Equinox, 2011.

West, Gerald O., and Musa W. Dube, eds. *The Bible in Africa: Transactions, Trajectories and Trends.* Boston: Brill, 2000.

Westermann, Claus. *Roots of Wisdom: The Oldest Proverbs of Israel and Other Peoples.* Translated by J. Daryl Charles. Louisville: Westminster John Knox, 1995.

———. *Genesis 1–11: A Commentary.* Translated by John J. Scullion. Continental Commentaries. Minneapolis: Augsburg, 1984.

Westermann, Dietrich. *Africa and Christianity.* Duff Missionary Lectures 1935. 1937. Reprint, New York: AMS, 1977.

White, Lynn. "The Historical Roots of our Ecological Crisis." *Science* 155 (1967) 1203–7.

Wilson, Robert R. *Prophecy and Society in Ancient Israel.* Philadelphia: Fortress, 1980.

Witmer, Amanda. *Jesus, the Galilean Exorcist: His Exorcisms in Social and Political Context.* Library of the Historical Jesus Studies 10. New York: Bloomsbury, 2012.

Woolf, Greg. *Becoming Roman: The Origins of Provincial Civilization in Gaul.* Cambridge: Cambridge University Press, 1998.

———. "Beyond Romans and Natives." *World Archaeology* 28/3 (1997) 339–50.

———. *Rome: An Empire's Story.* New York: Oxford University Press, 2012.

———. "Roman Peace." In *War and Society in the Roman World*, edited by John Rich and Graham Shipley, 171–94. New York: Routledge, 1993.

Yasur-Landau, Assaf. *The Philistine Aegean Migration at the End of the Late Bronze Age.* New York: Cambridge University Press, 2010.

Zaibet, Lokman T. and Elizabeth G. Dunn. "Land Tenure, Farm Size, and Rural Market Participation in Developing Countries: The Case of the Tunisian Olive Sector." *Economic Development and Cultural Change* 46 (1998) 831–48.

Zanker, Paul. *Roman Art.* Translated by Henry Heitmann-Gordon. Los Angeles: J. Paul Getty Museum, 2010.

———. *The Power of Images in the Age of Augustus.* Translated by Alan Shapiro. Ann Arbor: University of Michigan Press, 1988.

Index of Ancient Documents

Index of Ancient Sources

Index of Modern Authors